HOW TO MAKE
A BETTER SCHOOL

Finlay McQuade
Educational Consultant

David W. Champagne
University of Pittsburgh

Allyn and Bacon
Boston • London • Toronto • Sydney • Tokyo • Singapore

Copyright © 1995 by Allyn and Bacon
A Division of Paramount Publishing
160 Gould Street
Needham Heights, Massachusetts 02194

Library of Congress Cataloging-in-Publication Data

McQuade, Finlay.
    How to make a better school/Finlay McQuade, David W. Champagne.
        p.   cm.
    Includes bibliographical references and indexes.
    ISBN 0-205-14120-X
    1. School management and organization—United States.   2. School
supervision—United States.   3. Educational change—United States.
    I. Champagne, David W.   II. Title.
    LB2805.M262   1995
    371.2′00973—dc20   94-2066
                                                                                                    CIP

Printed in the United States of America

10   9   8   7   6   5   4   3   2   1   98   97   96   95   94

Contents

Introduction

This book is about the process of improving one school, any school. We have tried to make it a useful book for a broad audience, recognizing that many people in many roles contribute to the improvement of a single school. Any one person with a vision can become a person of influence.

Excellent books have already been written about the problems of American education, and much can be done at the national, state, and district levels to address these problems. We write about the process of improving a single school because we work in schools one at a time, and this experience leads us to the conclusion that each school is unique. We are aware of widespread ills in education, but we are not aware of one all-encompassing cause or one solution. Each school must develop its own procedures for self-examination and self-help. Larger and more powerful organizations are at work developing theories, models, and products that will have enormous impact on education in general, but each school must become a sophisticated consumer of general remedies. Besides, there is more to health than medicine. There is such a thing as a healthful lifestyle. This book offers a healthful lifestyle for schools.

Where specific examples seem helpful to our explanation of the process of school improvement, we include them. Most of these examples are drawn from observations in actual schools, and some combine practices we have found in several schools. Some are hypothetical, intended to clarify an argument rather than to cite an actual case. We hope that readers will find these examples useful and applicable in schools that they know, but we have not set out to prescribe the content of an education. We make no attempt to tell teachers what or how they should teach or students how they should study. Our purpose is prescriptive, but what we recommend is a series of procedures for improving the academic program of any school, not a specific curriculum or teaching method. It will soon become clear, in fact, that one of our themes is local control of curriculum and instruction, so that each school meets the needs of its own students.

But what about content? What should be taught? How should it be taught? We urge educators to ask these questions courageously, determined to follow the answers into action. State-of-the-art educational methods—what is known about diagnosing student needs, designing and evaluating programs, and managing effective schools—are sufficiently well developed that schools can teach successfully just about anything we want students to learn.

We can teach students to read, to compute, to solve problems, to care about others, to set goals, to persevere, to make their way in the world, to find their way around the world, to navigate the universe! If students in a school are not now learning what the school has promised to teach, then the school must change. It is no use waiting for other students to show up. Students and their parents must not permit schools to continue to do what they have always done—or permit teachers, principals, superintendents, and professors of education to continue to do what they have always done—simply because they have always done it. We must be clear about the goals of education, the short-term and the long-term goals, and implement programs that work. As we do whatever has to be done, schools for our children and grandchildren might become very different from the schools that we attended.

At an elementary school in Philadelphia, to make sure that all the students have clean clothes, the principal does at least one load of wash a day. In Pittsburgh, leaders in the business community are collaborating with the schools to develop "sabbatical" programs for drop-outs. As the former students learn that education has value in the workplace, they are motivated to try again in the schools. One of the worst middle schools in Boston became one of the best by getting teachers and parents together to face and solve educational problems. Together, they decided to extend the length of the school day and to bring the students to school on Saturday mornings. Every student in this school is teamed up with an adult pen pal in business or government, a program that includes the mayor of the city and the superintendent of schools. At a rural high school in Massachusetts, ecology students study land that has been purchased for development and help developers present ecologically sound proposals to the zoning board. In Minneapolis, one school has "learning centers" in locations where students can best learn from experience. They go to school in the theater district, or the business district, or the agricultural campus of the University of Minnesota.

We urge readers to let your imagination loose as you read the chapters of this book. We believe that the procedures we describe will help you realize your vision of a better school.

How to Make a Better School

1

MAKING THE
SCHOOL COHERENT

WHAT IS COHERENCE?

Bells shatter concentration in a school every forty-five minutes, more or less. One bell tells students to pack up and move somewhere else; another bell tells them when they're supposed to have arrived. In this way, students bounce from math to English to physical education to history to a special assembly on world hunger to computer keyboarding. When students have any say in what they will do for short periods of time, they squeeze in a quick lunch, meet with a teacher about a missing homework assignment, or cram in an extra ten minutes of study before a test, all the while maneuvering to meet their best friends and avoid their worst enemies, who will embarrass or bully them. For homework, they have a few math problems, a few pages of history, some vocabulary words in a foreign language, a writing assignment in English about *Catcher in the Rye,* and at least one long-term project that can be postponed for an hour of TV. Something similar occurs the next day: a new chapter in math, ten more years of history, and maybe a field trip to an atomic power station along with students from another science class who have finished the atomic power chapter already and seem to ask all the intelligent questions.

When Theodore Sizer (1984) visited American high schools and followed students from class to class, he found that incoherence was an outstanding characteristic of the experience. He found what he described as an academic supermarket, where students "pick things up," with little demand and no incentive for synthesis.

Horizontal Coherence

When what is learned in one class is related to what is learned in another, students should also learn about the relationship. Mathematics is used constantly as a tool for scientific investigation, yet students seem to forget what they have learned in math classes when they enter science classes. Consequently, science teachers tend to lower their expectations to simple calculations that all the students can do without hours of additional instruction. Because coherence is not a priority, science classes often bring together students who are "math" years apart. Some might have finished two years of algebra, while others in the same science class might be struggling through their first year. If science in the curriculum were more closely linked with mathematics, students at all levels would discover practical applications for the mathematics they practice in math classes but otherwise might never use. The mathematics curriculum would also address concepts and procedures that are fundamental to scientific investigations but are generally omitted in the sequence of "pure" mathematics. Many students leave high school knowing next to nothing about statistical significance, for example, yet they start learning about the "scientific method" in elementary school.

There are endless opportunities to help students connect what they learn in one subject with what they learn in other subjects. The difficulties that discourage horizontal coherence are not in the subjects themselves. Even when the overlap between two subjects is obvious and everyone, including the students and teachers, agrees that connecting the disciplines is a good idea, it might not happen. American history and American literature in the eleventh grade is as close as we come to a national curriculum, yet relatively few schools require these two courses to be closely related. Fortunately, resistance to horizontal coherence is eroding. Interdisciplinary study is considered a necessary feature of new middle schools (Carnegie Council on Adolescent Development 1989), and professional organizations now support the efforts of educators interested in making a change (e.g., Jacobs 1989; Vars 1987). When the curriculum is organized coherently, what is taught in one subject supports and complements what is taught in other subjects.

Students learn that learning is patterned, connected, and applicable outside the classroom, that it does not come in tightly knotted, brown paper parcels, on schedule, in forty-five minute periods between the bells.

Vertical Coherence

The experience of learning from year to year should also be coherent, so that students can apply what they learned in eighth-grade math to problems they meet in tenth-grade science. The high school chemistry course is one that suffers notably from this type of incoherence. High school science teachers struggle to teach "Chemistry" in one year, and students struggle to learn the math and the concepts through concentrated lectures and highly contrived but relatively few practical experiences in the lab. Yet chemistry can begin in nursery school and be a part of every science course throughout school. Chemistry in high school need not be a single, one-year course, but an explanation, consolidation, and extension of much that has been learned before. Vertical coherence is not a new idea, of course, and there is, in fact, quite a lot of chemistry in a typical elementary and middle school curriculum. If teachers are unaware of what has gone before, however, they cannot help their students organize and integrate this growing body of knowledge. In mathematics and foreign languages, on the other hand, there are fairly obvious appearances of year-to-year coherence, yet after years of study in these subjects, many students lack a sense of the "wholeness" of their knowledge. Students in algebra classes will be stumped because they have "forgotten their fractions," for example, and students in the third or even the fourth year of a foreign language will be unable to combine their understanding of the rules of case, tense, and gender into meaningful sentences.

Students have to know something to learn something. Prior knowledge is a prerequisite crucial to new knowledge (Hirsch 1987; Resnick 1987). If students have insufficient knowledge when they begin to read, they will not comprehend the text in front of them. If they have insufficient knowledge when they listen in class, they will not understand the teacher's explanation. The expectation is that knowledge is compounded year after year in school. Unfortunately, ignorance is also compounded. We can help students make progress by making sure they have sufficient prior knowledge each time they undertake to learn something new. Although we recognize the need for entry-level skills at each level of the curriculum, we often neglect the need for entry-level knowledge. If the language arts curriculum planned to provide students with the prior knowledge needed to understand successive reading selections, for example, more students might enjoy the experience of reading. In middle and high schools, we should choose literature that the students can read and understand instead of literature that they should read and cannot understand.

Transfer

A third type of coherence entails the transfer of learning and thinking skills. The brainstorming that stimulates creativity in English can stimulate creativity in physics. The method of scientific inquiry learned in biology can lead to discoveries in history. The circles and boxes and arrows used in computer science to organize procedures can organize procedures in other subjects, too. Tactics of learning and thinking, however, are not readily transferred from one subject to another. They are not tools in the sense that calculators and databases are tools, allowing a student to punch in facts and figures from various subjects with equal ease. To transfer complex processes of thought, students must receive explicit instruction and favorable opportunities to build understanding in each content area.

Surely there are no graduates of American schools who have not been told how to read actively. Active readers employ different strategies for different reading purposes. They read and reread, they take notes, or they skim. In order to comprehend a text, they preview the pages, paying particular attention to headings, topic sentences, and illustrations; they wonder what they will learn before they begin to read, and while reading they wonder what they will learn next; they make predictions based on what they have learned thus far, and they check their predictions by reading further in the same text or by reading other, related texts. It is generally agreed that students would learn more if they read this way in every subject. Once they know how, do they read this way in any subject? Experience suggests that they do not. Bereiter (1984) describes an educational psychology class in which the teacher asked her students to read a long and difficult article and to learn as much as possible from it. They were given only ten minutes in which to do this. Almost all the students began reading at the first word and continued reading sequentially until the ten minutes were up. Later, they all said that they had known of different reading strategies that would have been more useful, but they did not think of using these strategies at the time. The transfer of skills from one domain to another requires the express effort of teachers who make transfer a goal, individually and in concert with one another.

Mission

There is yet another way in which a school can be coherent. Schools often claim to be teaching students how to be good citizens or how to manage in an ever-changing world or how to think creatively: Yet the baseball coach and the history teacher might be teaching distinctly different and perhaps contradictory concepts of citizenship; the world defined by the school might seem to the student to be forever *un*changing; an—often the case in any institution—truly creative thinkers might find themselves in trouble. Schools are given or take on missions of high and abstract purpose that are hard to accomplish and hard to evaluate. If a school takes its mission seriously, the entire institution and all its resources will be organized to accomplish that overriding purpose. Standardized tests and winning seasons will have meaning only if they contribute to the mission.

We were discussing mission with all the administrators of a fairly large independent school situated on three campuses, elementary, middle, and high school. They wanted to develop procedures for evaluating the entire school. The school's statement of mission was long and complex, with at least a dozen distinct elements. We described the difficulties of evaluating a program that undertook to do so much and asked if there was anything in the mission that they considered to be of paramount importance. They discussed this for some time without agreeing, whereupon we asked each administrator to list what he or she considered to be the top three priorities inherent in the school's mission. One topic appeared in all their lists: respect for others. We asked where in the school we would find respect for others being taught. The administrators could not refer us to any particular program or teacher, but they hoped that every teacher was teaching students to have respect for others. We asked what sort of respect for others they expected a graduate of the school to display. It was a question they had never before addressed. They had never discussed, much less decided, what would cause them to think they had been successful in achieving their most cherished educational goal.

Schools are given highly specialized buildings, sophisticated equipment, hundreds of tons of books, and a workforce of highly trained professionals. It takes at least twelve years to educate each student and costs something in the region of $50,000 to $100,000 per student. To do the job well, everyone in a school should know what the mission is. Every person and every resource should be dedicated to the mission.

WHY HAVE COHERENCE?

Try to learn something incoherent. Try to remember a set of random numbers or a series of nonsense syllables. Incoherence does not make sense, which is what students often point out when they say, "This doesn't make sense!" True, not everything in life is coherent—not everything does make sense—and therefore students must also learn to deal with incoherence. But much of what students have to learn in school is supposed to be coherent. Bodies of knowledge like economics, physics, history, or linguistics become organized as generation after generation of scholars learn from their predecessors, add their own discoveries, and reorganize what they know. Cognitive science tells us that individual learning is also a process of discovery and reorganization (Resnick and Klopfer 1989). Students should be gathering information, comparing what they have learned with what they already know, organizing, gathering more information, reorganizing—and in this way constructing their own bodies of knowledge. Historians make generalizations about the past and are able to cite abundant details to illustrate and validate their generalizations. Scientists can recover information they have forgotten because they know the periodic table of elements or the common properties of waves. Math teachers who speak of the beauty of mathematics are more likely to share their sense of beauty if they can explain to their students what division of fractions has in common with division of whole numbers. The perception of coherence facilitates understanding—in many cases *is* understanding. It simply makes sense to strive for coherence wherever and whenever coherence serves the educational purpose of the school.

There are other, institutional and logistical reasons to have a coherent school. Studies of excellent schools and businesses have shown that the most successful institutions are coherent institutions (Squires, Huitt, and Segars 1984; Peters and Waterman 1982). If you ask a member of one of these institutions what the institution is all about, you are likely to receive in response a definite statement of the institution's mission and outstanding features. Ask another member the same question, and you are likely to receive a similar response. Successful schools and businesses are organized around a few clearly articulated principles, which everyone understands and strives to realize through personal effort. Coherence is a bond; it fosters teamwork.

There is a tendency for schools, like all institutions, to decay—to become incoherent. New students, teachers, parents, and administrators bring new ideas and new expectations. New problems appear, are seen from new points of view, and require new solutions. Change is inevitable, but success is not. Thoughtless change can lead to a loss of effectiveness as easily as blind adherence to the ways of the past. Simply adding new units or courses to the curriculum without ensuring their coherence in the whole scheme of a student's education results in confusion. If new teachers in the school teach what they taught at other schools, without considering the past experiences and future needs of their current students, student achievement will suffer. As the school changes, basic principles that have brought success in the past should remain, or, alternatively, yield to new principles that unite and direct the efforts of a changing community. But basic principles are not basic unless they are manifest in goals and objectives, tests to measure student achievement, criteria for evaluating teachers, speeches delivered on Parents Day, and all the daily activities of teachers and students. The coherence of the curriculum provides the basis for choosing texts and other materials, for determining whether or not field trips are worth the disruption of regular classes, for adding courses, and for designing inservice for teachers. Coherence is essential to teamwork, management, and self-preservation as well as to understanding.

HOW IS COHERENCE ACHIEVED?

One person cannot make a school coherent. The entire community of the school must first accept the value of coherence and be prepared to contribute to it. Few will object in theory that what is learned in sixth grade should be related to what is learned in eighth, or that what is learned about *A Tale of Two Cities* in English class should be related to what is learned about the French Revolution in history. The curriculum at present, however, might be a warren of remotely connected courses and programs, some of which have been added to the curriculum as a result of impassioned advocacy. Students, teachers, parents, or administrators might object to any significant restructuring of territory they have helped to shape or have adopted through usage as their own. It is important, then, that coherence first be considered as a problem of coordination: Are the various cells and divisions of the school working together to optimize the education of the students?

Once asked to address the topic of coordination, teachers will usually leap at the chance to work together, and significant steps toward coherence can be made simply by permitting them to do so. Problems of personality and point of view will arise, of course, and will inhibit teamwork on some fronts while compatible colleagues forge ahead on others. Administrators have to be prepared, therefore, to examine the nature of conflicts that develop around issues of coordination. Since all the teachers agree that library skills are needed across the curriculum, why are some teachers arguing so strenuously with the librarian who is trying to coordinate library assignments? The answer to this question might be the librarian's way of interacting with teachers or with students, and the solution to the problem might require administrative intervention designed to help the librarian learn a more effective style. The efforts of teachers and administrators working toward coherence must be supervised.

Management is central to coherence. Empowered teachers generate new ideas continually, but teachers cannot teach classes and manage the school simultaneously. Teachers working together have to meet together. When do they meet? Scheduling teacher time in addition to student time is a managerial challenge. Teams of teachers plan initiatives. Who sets the deadlines, garners the resources, persuades the opposition, and takes the flak? When time and resources needed for one initiative jeopardize the success of another, who resolves the conflict? In independent schools, where teacher empowerment is a tradition, curriculum is no more coherent than it is in public schools. Individual teachers and teams of teachers tend to go their own way, adding bits and pieces to the house that Jack built. Coherence has to be facilitated. People authorized and expected to do the facilitating are principals, deans, directors, headmasters, department chairs, team leaders, and curriculum coordinators.

But people in managerial positions have to do more than facilitate in order to achieve coherence. They have to see the need and take every chance to foster cooperation at all levels. If a superintendent knows that the principals of neighborhood schools are not planning a coherent transition for students moving from elementary to middle to high school, then the superintendent must bring the principals together to work on coherence. The head of an independent school might have to ask the division heads to do the same thing. Principals and division heads have to bring department heads together. Department heads need not wait until teachers in the department beg for a more coherent curriculum. Academic leaders have to extend the *expectation* that the educational experience of students be coherent.

Most schools have a Curriculum Council or some such group of teachers and administrators who have some responsiblity for managing the school's curriculum. Often this council consists of department heads, team leaders, or grade-level representatives. If the school has a curriculum coordinator, this person probably chairs the Curriculum Council. Developing and maintaining the coherence of the curriculum should become this group's major occupation.

Involving academic leaders does not in itself produce coherence; coherence requires a plan. The sooner the planning begins, the better, but schools always have a full agenda just being a school, and a major planning effort requires special incentive. An impending evaluation by the school's accrediting agency; a major change in administrative hierarchy; a changing population of students; competition from another school; dissatisfied students, parents, or teachers; pressure from the superintendent or the Board—incentives to start improving the school are many and varied. A sensitive and energetic leader will take advantage of all the available incentives, but an emerging vision of coherence will become the most powerful incentive of all.

Coherence of Goals and Objectives

At the center of the plan there should be a clear understanding of what the school is meant to teach. This central purpose, philosophy, or mission of the school should be written and circulated throughout the school community. Everyone must know it and subscribe to it. It is the preamble to the constitution. Such statements are historical documents for some schools; other schools have managed without them. Some statements are written or modified by incumbent administrators, some by action of the Board, some by consensus of everyone involved. If a school does not now have a statement of mission, it is our recommendation that the entire community of students, parents, teachers, and selected consultants be involved in creating one. A plebiscite of stakeholders is not needed to make final decisions, but everyone should have a chance to contribute initially through surveys, questionnaires, and interviews. The mission is expected to endure. In striving to fulfill its mission, the school builds its identity and reputation. Any subsequent change of mission (if the school has been organized to fulfill its mission) will be a major change, and major changes are not undertaken lightly or often.

Analysis of the mission yields a set of goals for the school (see Fig. 1-1). These goals are more specific and may change more often than the mission, because actions based on enduring values will change, even if the values remain constant. It may be part of a school's mission, for example, to prepare students for the workforce of the immediate geographical area. Thus, in a given part of the country, preparation for work in agriculture might once have been a principal goal of the school, then work in industry, then work in human services. Now graduates entering the local workforce might join multinational corporations and live in different parts of the world for periods of time throughout their careers.

Let's imagine that the mission of a hypothetical school contains the following two statements:

From the Mission

Liberty School provides thorough preparation for those students who wish to go to college. . . . Students learn to value their education at Liberty because it provides them with increasing understanding of their lives and their ever-expanding environment.

There would surely be more to the mission than this, further defining Liberty's purpose and uniqueness. We have selected these two statements because of their generic qualities. Yet these two statements, which might form a part of the mission of thousands of schools, can help shape and focus a curriculum.

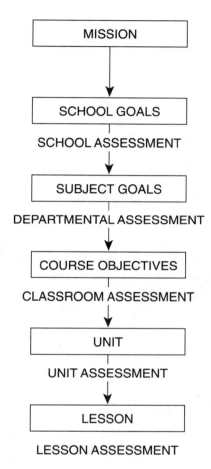

FIGURE 1-1 Goals and Objectives Derived from the Mission

First they are translated into goals that are slightly more specific and probably more responsive to change. At Liberty, for our present purposes, these goals might include:

From the School Goals

1. *Students will acquire the knowledge, skills, and spirit of inquiry required for success in college.*
2. *They will learn to use their knowledge and skills when solving*

practical and philosophical problems they face as individuals and as responsible members of a democratic society.

Liberty School is making a commitment to a certain type of education. Teachers will strive to teach not only knowledge and skills, but also a spirit of inquiry, and students will learn to apply their knowledge and skills to real-life problems. Further, the students will learn to value their education.

It is the job of educational leaders at Liberty to see that these and all the other goals of the school are realized. In classrooms, teachers use tests and other forms of assessment to discover how successfully students have learned what they were supposed to learn. Principals, heads of school, and academic deans must develop forms of assessment to discover how successfully students in general have achieved the goals of the school. Assessing achievement of school goals might be novel and challenging at first, but assessment is a powerful incentive to higher achievement (see Chapter 6). Assessment of student achievement and program evaluation (see Chapter 2) are fundamental to school improvement. Without too much trouble, Liberty School can find out how its graduates fare in college. Assessing the students' problem-solving abilities might appear to be more difficult. However, this can be done by setting problem-solving criteria and testing or interviewing samples of the student population to discover how many of the students meet the criteria.

Responsibility for achieving the school goals is shared equally by all the divisions and departments in the school. Each division or department, therefore, must also have goals, and these goals must clearly lead to student achievement of school goals. For example:

From Goals for Learning in Science

1. *Science students will be able to explain and give examples that illustrate basic concepts and principles generally accepted by the scientific community.*
2. *Science students will learn to apply these concepts and principles when solving problems in all science courses in the Liberty School curriculum.*
3. *Science students will learn to write essays in which they show how*

knowledge of the concepts and principles of science helps to clarify, ameliorate, or solve problems in contemporary society.

From Goals for Learning in Social Science

1. *All students will be able to describe from memory, orally and in writing, significant events and trends in the political, economic, and cultural history of the United States.*
2. *All students will learn to think, read, and write critically on historical topics:*

   a. *to sustain a discussion by making assertions, asking questions, and defending their opinions*
   b. *to formulate a thesis in an essay and demonstrate the validity of the thesis with historical evidence*
   c. *to examine primary sources, extract data, and use the data as evidence in an argument*

3. *All students will learn to demonstrate, using historical evidence, the similarities and differences between events and issues in the past and events and issues they consider to be significant in the present.*

These are not the only goals in science and social science. They are selected to illustrate how two threads of Liberty School's mission are woven into the curriculum. Knowledge and skills required for college are applied to problems—not textbook problems only, but problems that confront the students in their lives outside school. All departments or branches at Liberty School set similar goals, which state in clear English, as free of educational jargon as possible, what students will learn to do. Goals for learning do not describe the methods that teachers employ or the opportunities that teachers provide. Because goals for learning describe the desired behavior of the students, they lay the groundwork for focused teaching and, in due course, curriculum evaluation.

School leaders devise means to assess student achievement of school goals. Similarly, division and department leaders devise means to assess the goals of each division and department. Because teachers also assess student achievement in the classroom, the school needs a comprehensive strategy for coordinating assessment at all three levels.

A school that has a written mission, school goals derived from the mission, subject goals derived from the school goals, and a strategy for assessing student achievement has the beginning of a coherent curriculum. Curriculum committees within the school can examine this documentation and ask such questions as these:

In English classes, is there any difference between reading for college preparation and reading for relevance to the lives of the students?

Would the study of local history help students learn to value the usefulness of the historical method?

If students are to use math for solving practical problems, shouldn't science classes include math that the students are learning in math classes, and math classes include problems that students are solving in science classes?

Achieving the mission is not easy. It requires a coordinated team effort, exerted continuously. The coherence of the emerging curriculum will be evident as it develops. The documents produced become a text to help students see the interconnectedness of their daily experiences in school.

Mission and goals are more than words on paper; organization for coherence presses on. It is the responsibility of school leaders and all the teachers to see that goals for learning are realized. How does a biology course, for example, contribute to the science goals listed earlier? These goals require science courses to teach sound scientific information, problem solving in the lab, and the relevance of biology to individual and social problems. Objectives for introductory biology at Liberty include:

From Biology Objectives

1.   *Students will learn the necessary lab skills for each exercise so that they can follow and fulfill written directions independently.*
2.   *Through a variety of exercises in the biology lab, they will:*

    a.   *illustrate well-known biological principles*
    b.   *solve problems without preconceived results*
    c.   *solve problems that students themselves have posed*

3.   *They will employ critical thinking and their knowledge of biology to formulate and defend their own ethical positions on topics of current social significance.*

The biology teachers at Liberty set objectives for the courses they teach. The whole process of development evolves from the mission of Liberty School to produce a curriculum appropriate for the students at Liberty School. The curriculum must have the input of teachers who know the students and who know their own strengths and limitations as teachers. They will make use of curricular materials developed by experts elsewhere, and they might call in local experts to help them shape their courses, but they know their own needs best and they know their students. If the biology teachers do not understand the concept of a coherent curriculum and have not been consulted in the process of setting school goals and science goals, then the courses they create might not contribute significantly to these higher-level goals or to the school's mission. Some teachers asked to write objectives for their courses might copy the objectives out of each chapter of their textbook, thinking that these best state what they teach and what they should teach. Perhaps Liberty School has a young biology teacher with no previous curriculum-writing experience. Perhaps the administration would just as soon ask curriculum experts to create the curriculum in biology. Under these circumstances it is especially important to include teachers in the process of curriculum development. Then they can meet and learn from consultants in science education, biologists at local colleges, and biology teachers at other schools. Administrators who do not have faith in their teachers must remember that teachers who are kept in the dark cannot deliver a superior course, no matter who designs it. The process of curriculum development, of making the school coherent, is a process of professional development. Indeed, new curriculum is almost inevitably going to take teachers into new territory, and inservice opportunities to learn about new methods and materials will inevitably arise. When teachers implement a curriculum they have helped to write, they understand it and want to make it work.

The curriculum that students experience in their twelve or more years of school is made from thousands of component parts, both large and small, that schools buy from hundreds of manufacturers and dealers. A curriculum is not delivered like a new automobile, fully assembled and ready to go. A school's curriculum includes textbooks, manuals, films, kits, cassettes, manipulatives, games, field trips, software, exercises, tests, and subcontracted mini-courses, some of which come with an itinerant teacher. If the central office selects and supplies major parts of the curriculum for several schools in a district, teachers in each school must still assemble the parts and add hundreds of smaller parts that they choose for themselves. Teachers must be a part of the process of achieving coherence if it is all to "make sense" to the students in any one school. There is no reason to expect that an introductory biology text written by a professor at a university in Illinois will match neatly with an advanced text written by a committee and edited by a professor in Florida. And neither textbook will follow up and reinforce the highly motivating series of field trips the Liberty Middle School has arranged with the Liberty City Zoo. Liberty teachers have to do that themselves. And the principle of teacher involvement, naturally, holds true for every subject in the curriculum.

As things now stand, public school teachers are usually given a curriculum, including texts and other materials, that defines their course objectives. Teacher's guides include suggested activities and recommended methods of instruction. Independent school teachers, on the other hand, are sometimes given only the title of the course—sometimes not even that—and expected to decide on everything else. Neither of these extremes is ideal. Teachers should participate in the design of their courses, but they should also be expected to collaborate with colleagues and other experts, both in education and in their respective disciplines.

Teachers who have participated in developing objectives for their courses then develop the day-by-day objectives for each unit of each course and each lesson of each unit. The idealistic goals of the school are easily trivialized in the classroom unless teachers and students believe in them. It is in the daily interactions between students and teachers that school goals and subject goals are realized. If teachers are successful, the goals are realized in what the students do, what they practice, what they study for on tests. Hence, a unit from an English course might require the students to:

Objectives for English Unit

1. *Write a personal essay describing a moral dilemma that they experienced and how it was solved. Readers of the essay should be able to infer the author's present evaluation of the solution by the tone of the essay, even though the evaluation may not be stated explicitly.*
2. *The essays will be read and discussed in peer groups. Classmates will discuss the author's evaluation and speculate about other ways in which the dilemma might have been solved.*

3. *Authors will revise the essays using what they have learned from the discussions.*

4. *Essays will be graded on the quality of the writing and how well they communicate the growth of moral reasoning since the original decision was made.*

Similarly, a unit in an earth science course at Liberty, still working out the two themes of college preparation and understanding of one's own life and environment, might consist of:

Objectives for Earth Science Unit

1. *Each student will choose a TV or radio station and keep a notebook record of weather forecasts for two weeks.*
2. *Each student will learn to read the instruments in the school's weather station and keep accurate records of weather conditions.*
3. *Students will compare the weather forecasts with the weather experienced and write a report that they will send to the TV or radio station whose forecasts they have studied.*
4. *In a unit test, students will be expected to explain how each instrument in the weather station works, what it measures, and how the variable is significant in weather forecasting.*

As teachers collaborate, they modify the courses they have been teaching to bring them into the larger patterns of a coherent curriculum. In a school where teachers believe in coherence, there will not be much tolerance of colleagues who stubbornly defend established territory in conflict with the school's mission. It is much easier to cooperate, and to expect cooperation, when everyone is doing it.

Fulfilling the Goals and Objectives

The school cannot come to a halt while new plans are laid. Students show up every day. They have to be taught every day. Teachers throw their energies into the status quo, making it work as best they can. They might find it hard to visualize success beyond present levels of achievement. Goal setting must be optimistic, however. Goals do not describe the status quo; they aim beyond it. They are not mundane. Educational goals are the hopes held by a community for its children.

If new goals are created, change must occur. If tarnished old goals that once seemed impossible to achieve are dusted off and found to be relevant, change must occur. Teachers who have contributed to the formation of new goals will usually be eager to make the necessary changes, but they might not know how. Goals are problems to be solved, and solving them might seem to be impossible. Addressing the problems, making plans, trying something different—all require imagination, leadership, and high morale. Goal setting is not an idle exercise; it has consequences. Teachers need time for meetings, time for planning, time for professional development, and time for teaching their classes. If teachers are to be committed to the task of school improvement, the Board and administration must also be committed. The whole endeavor must be supported with adequate funds and feasible schedules.

The creation of a coherent school has to be seen as an evolutionary process that has first to be set in motion. Not everything will be done at once. Some changes have to wait until students have learned prerequisite skills or developed more favorable attitudes. Students at risk of dropping out of school because their courses seem remote from their interests do not necessarily rejoice when introduced to Shakespeare or calculus. First things first. And first things have to work before second things even begin. Some changes will require teacher retraining, and some will require additional specialists. Some teachers will start to do things that teachers in the school have not done before. They might become counselors as well as teachers. They might make closer alliances and confer with parents. They might expand their classrooms into the community and become entrepreneurs, or publishers, or research scientists. At the very least, they might have to learn more about statistics to teach social studies or more about paleontology to teach about dinosaurs. In other occupations and professions, workers often lose their jobs because of changes in technology or the marketplace. Education has been slow to change, and although teachers are laid off in times of economic crisis, relatively few in the profession have faced the option of major retraining to avoid unemployment. Probably because schools have resisted change for so long, they are now under pressure to change rapidly. Teachers and administrators must realize that the solution to some of the problems of education is not school as they have known it in the past.

The process that underlies change is the process of curriculum development. It has to be coordinated, so that idiosyncratic teachers join the team and reluctant teachers try something different. As it progresses, and more and more of the curriculum is directed toward coherent objectives, revision slows down to keep pace with evaluation. Are the objectives reached, the goals achieved? Where they are not, curriculum and instruction are examined, modified, tried in the classroom, and re-evaluated. As school and community change, as new insights evolve, goals and objectives also change.

In time, coherence seeps into all areas of the school. Tests are revised. What do they measure, how do the results affect decisions, how do these decisions contribute to the mission of the school? How are teachers evaluated? Are evaluative criteria consistent with the objectives that teachers and their students are expected to reach? How are students recognized and rewarded? Are grades assigned on the basis of all the objectives of the course or only a few? Are extracurricular activities advancing the mission? How are they evaluated? How is the school regarded in the community? Are parents and prospective parents aware of the exciting things going on here?

SUMMARY

In a coherent school, there are four forms of coherence:

1. *Horizontal coherence:* What students learn in one class supports and reinforces what they learn in other classes.
2. *Vertical coherence:* The knowledge and skills that students learn are useful and relevant as they continue to learn.
3. *Transfer:* Knowledge and skills learned in class are useful and relevant in other situations.
4. *Mission:* Everything that students learn in school contributes to fulfillment of the school's mission.

The missions that schools undertake are fulfilled through careful coordination and allocation of all resources. A coherent school is organized to fulfill its mission. Coherent schools offer students a coherent educational experience leading to knowledge and understanding, which are also coherent.

A coherent school is created through teamwork. Educational leaders coordinate the teamwork and make cooperation possible. Coherence emanates from the school's mission. The mission is translated into school goals, which, when achieved, represent fulfillment of the mission. Similarly, there are goals for every subject, which, when achieved, represent achievement of school goals. Teachers translate the subject goals into specific learning objectives for every course and every unit in the curriculum. Student achievement of goals and objectives is assessed at three levels: the classroom, the department, and the school.

As the process of development continues, every procedure and program is drawn into the coherence of the school: assessment of student achievement, professional development of teachers, teacher evaluation, policies and practices for hiring new teachers, extracurricular activities, expectations of staff. Maintaining this coherence as the school evolves, allowing it to change in response to changing circumstances, is the responsibility of academic leaders.

REFERENCES

Bereiter, C. (1984). "How to Keep Thinking Skills from Going the Way of All Frills." *Educational Leadership* 42:1, 75–77.

Carnegie Council on Adolescent Development. (1989). *Turning Points: Preparing American Youth for the 21st Century.* New York: The Carnegie Corporation.

Hirsch, E. D., Jr. (1987). *Cultural Literacy: What Every American Needs to Know.* Boston: Houghton Mifflin.

Jacobs, H. H. (Ed.). (1989). *Interdisciplinary Curriculum: Design and Implementation.* Alexandria, Va.: Association for Supervision and Curriculum Development.

Peters, T. J., and R. H. Waterman. (1982). *In Search of Excellence: Lessons from America's Best-Run Companies.* New York: Harper & Row.

Resnick, L. B. (1987). *Education and Learning to Think.* Washington, D.C.: National Academy Press.

Resnick, L. B., and L. E. Klopfer (Eds.). (1989). *Toward the Thinking Curriculum: Current Cognitive Research.* Alexandria, Va.: Association for Supervision and Curriculum Development.

Sizer, T. R. (1984). *Horace's Compromise: The Dilemma of the American High School.* Boston: Houghton Mifflin.

Squires, D. A., W. G. Huitt, and J. K. Segars. (1984). *Effective Schools and Classrooms: A Research-Based Perspective.* Alexandria, Va.: Association for Supervision and Curriculum Development.

Vars, G. F. (1987). *Interdisciplinary Teaching in the Middle Grades.* Columbus, Ohio: National Middle Schools Association.

2

EVALUATING THE CURRICULUM

USEFUL EVALUATION

Although the chapters in this book are not arranged chronologically like a set of instructions, we decided to put this chapter on curriculum evaluation near the beginning of the book and before the chapter on curriculum development. If that seems strange, think about it for a moment. We are writing about school improvement. Every school that has opened its doors to students already has a curriculum. Any attempt to improve the curriculum is, de facto, an evaluation. Curriculum evaluation is not an appendix to curriculum development. Evaluation precedes development. When evaluation reveals a problem, development attempts to solve the problem. Conversely, when a curriculum seems to be working well, no more than fine tuning will be necessary.

The concept "curriculum" is indistinct at its edges. It blurs imperceptibly into "instruction," "administration," "buildings and grounds," and all the other components of schools. Some principals see the public address system as an opportunity to teach the entire school, for example. Heads of independent schools—most of whom would rather address students in an assembly than use a public address system—are even more likely to think of themselves as teachers on a grand scale. Daily announcements or assemblies, then, become a part of the "curriculum." The daily schedule, which profoundly affects student learning, might also be included in "curriculum." If extracurricular activities are conceived as leadership training, arts education, or physical education, then student government, glee club, and athletics are all embraced by the curriculum concept. If our discussion of curriculum evaluation seems to be all-inclusive, it is because our definition of curriculum is equally inclusive.

Curriculum evaluation cannot be clinically pure and totally objective. There is no absolute standard to which we can hold up incontrovertible facts and conclude that a given curriculum is excellent, or mediocre, or hopeless. Evaluation is conducted by people who are sometimes biased, sometimes indifferent, sometimes insensitive. It can be quick or slow—and "quick" does not necessarily mean "slipshod," just as "slow" does not necessarily mean "thorough." No evaluation reveals all the facts, only those facts that someone has chosen to look at. The Association for Supervision and Curriculum Development ingeniously asked six evaluation experts to describe how they would go about evaluating a humanities curriculum at Radnor Middle School in Pennsylvania. Their six different proposals are printed in one of the most entertaining and informative books on curriculum evaluation (Brandt 1981). One proposal (Bonnet 1981) advised the principal to conduct her own, preemptive evaluation in order to save the program from independent, disinterested evaluators. Another (Scriven 1981) condemned the program to the scrap heap because its goals, objectives, and general outline were evidence of gross incompetence. While all the proposals contain generally applicable principles of evaluation, anyone looking for the one right method would be disappointed. The field of curriculum evaluation is wide open. Since there are so few rules, we argue, any attempt to evaluate an educational program might as well be useful.

Useful evaluation provides the information needed for decision making. Decision makers ask the questions. Evaluators seek the answers. If no one asks any questions, the data that a school collects routinely—teetering stacks of standardized test scores, for example—will gather dust. Then, when someone does ask a question, the superabundance of readily available data is likely to be irrelevant.

GOALS, OBJECTIVES, ASSESSMENT

The two most important questions that decision makers should ask are "What are the students supposed to be learning?" and "Are they learning what they're supposed to be learning?" No one seeking answers to these two questions should have far to look if the school's curriculum has been organized as we recommend. The first is answered by goals and objectives (see Chapters 1 and 3). The second is answered by assessment (see Chapter 6). It would be nice if all the people who have developed and now use the curriculum—curriculum specialists, teachers, and students—were in agreement about its goals and objectives, but widespread clarity of purpose is not yet commonplace. Surprisingly, schools can muddle along without it. Even when goals are clearly stated, however, assessment tends to be haphazard. Standardized tests measure a limited kind of achievement that is undeniably related to academic success but is nevertheless peripheral to many of the goals schools usually set for themselves and their students. Assessment of more valued forms of achievement is left to the uncoordinated efforts of teachers, whose standards, even in a single school, are enormously varied. Evaluators, on the other hand, have been emphatic when asking the two fundamental questions. As a result, most educators are familiar with the idea that clear objectives and careful assessment are needed "for the purpose of evaluation." Some school districts, therefore, are adding evaluation experts to curriculum development teams (Beswick 1990).

An expert can help a curriculum team anticipate "down-the-road" evaluation. But there are experts, and then there are other experts. Most educators have accepted the principle of "measurable" objectives. Some, however, are convinced that "measurable" means "trivial." When we urge teachers to cling to their highest aspirations and aim for their loftiest goals, we are sometimes scolded, "But you can't measure love for learning," or "You can't measure *real* understanding." Anxious because they cannot quantify their most valued goals, cautious educators will reduce the love for learning to something they can count and something that students will almost surely achieve, something like "Each student will deliver one oral report on one self-selected book per term." A different expert, however, might help a development committee envision the circumstances in which students really do love to learn. As athletes know, envisioning is a step toward success. It is also a step toward evaluation. As Ralph Tyler put it in *Basic Principles of Curriculum and Instruction* (1949), "The only way that we can tell whether students have acquired given types of behavior is to give them an opportunity to show this behavior." Evaluation can be as simple as that. Given the opportunity, students do what we have tried to teach them to do—or they do something else.

If they do something else frequently and publicly, careful evaluation might be superfluous. Students whose needs are adequately met do not cut as many classes as they attend, do not bring weapons to school, do not threaten teachers. When problems are obvious, it is time to do something about them. Nevertheless, an estimate of the severity of a problem might help to attract the resources needed to solve it—or to reduce the hysteria caused by one or two exceptional incidents. How many students cut classes? How many classes are cut? How many students bring weapons to school? How many teachers have been threatened—and with what, exactly? Even as a school deals with its problems, evaluation is a helpful guide. Has the community service program reduced absenteeism? Have metal detectors reduced the frequency of physical assaults? Has the integration of vocational and academic education improved teacher-student relations?

School Improvement

If the problems are not obvious, if the school more or less manages from day to day, where does improvement begin? An evaluation might ask students, teachers, parents, and alumni, "What is the most important lesson we should teach our students?" and "How well are we teaching this most important lesson at present?" The School Board in Belleville, Illinois, has ordered its priorities by distributing a list of curricular goals throughout the community and asking for opinions concerning their relative importance (Cipfl 1984). The same district has developed criterion-referenced "exit" tests to provide information about educational outcomes. Teachers examine the results of these tests to estimate the effectiveness of various segments of the program.

Sanders (1988) suggests three methods for single schools embarking on improvement programs. The Problem-Solving Approach begins each year with a preschool stock taking, in which the strengths and weaknesses of the school are identified. Administrators and teachers decide which deficiencies should be addressed in the coming year. They form committees to study these selected problems, with the understanding that the committees will report at mid-year. Objectives for improvement are based on committee reports. Subsequently, each committee formulates and oversees the implementation of a plan for

Power and Purpose Influencing an Evaluation

A. Who has authorized the evaluation (immediate boss)?

B. Who will conduct the evaluation (evaluator)?

C. What is the formal relationship between the immediate boss and the evaluator?

D. Does the immediate boss have authority to improve or terminate the curriculum being evaluated?

E. What does the immediate boss hope to accomplish?

F. What information does the immediate boss need in order to accomplish this?

G. What does the evaluator have to do to get this information?

H. Who else might influence the continuation or effectiveness of the curriculum?

    1.

    2.

    3.

I. What is the relationship between the immediate boss and these other people?

J. Will any decisions made by these other people overrule or obviate decisions made by the immediate boss?

K. How will these other people use the information that the immediate boss has requested and the evaluator will obtain?

L. What other information might these other people need in order to make good decisions?

M. What would have to be done to acquire the information that these other people need?

N. Is the immediate boss willing to expand the evaluation to obtain this additional information?

FIGURE 2-1 An Informal Power Estimate

change, then reports again at the end of the year. Long-term projects are carried over from one year to the next. The Program Review Approach sets up a committee to review one or two programs each year, so that each program will be reviewed once every five years. In anticipation of each review, grade-level and departmental committees prepare a self-evaluation. Recommendations made by the Program

Review Committee become the school's agenda for improvement. The Discrepancy Approach asks the school staff to identify qualities and programs that in their opinion would make the school ideal. The principal sorts these recommendations into categories and makes sure that the composite picture of the ideal school fulfills all legal and accrediting requirements. Administrators and teachers then compare the actual school with the ideal school. Improvement is then a matter of reducing discrepancies between the actual and the ideal.

A Power Estimate

Asking if existing programs achieve their goals is fundamental to evaluation. But other questions follow in quick succession. "Are all the students learning well?" "Are all parts of the curriculum working well?" "How is the curriculum implemented in various classrooms?" "Can all or any of the students achieve at a higher level?" "Is higher achievement worth an increase in effort and cost?" "Are the resources allocated to this program appropriately balanced in the context of all programs?" It soon becomes obvious that different people with different interests ask different questions. Even when evaluation experts help a curriculum committee to design and evaluate a new curriculum, even when the curriculum is shown to accomplish everything it was supposed to accomplish, the superintendent, the school committee, or a group of parents—anyone with power—can change the rules, ask different questions, and get different answers. Evaluation, inevitably, yields to power. Our advice to anyone evaluating an educational program is, before all else, to conduct an informal, confidential power estimate (see Fig. 2-1).

Even if the person authorizing the evaluation (the immediate boss) and the person conducting the evaluation (evaluator) are one and the same, it is still worth exploring these issues of power and purpose. Initial understanding might save an otherwise wasted effort. If the immediate boss and the evaluator are separate people, or separate groups of people, then the power estimate might be a subject for discussion between the two.

After issues of power and decision making have been clarified informally and discreetly by the principal parties involved, the scope of the evaluation can be explored openly and in more detail. The evaluator will probably want to interview other interested parties if the immediate boss is willing to expand the scope of the evaluation to meet their needs. Information that these other people need for good decision making is anticipated by the questions they ask. *Has the curriculum achieved its stated goals? Do students enjoy the process of learning? Is the program more or less effective than other programs competing for the same students? Has the curriculum been implemented as promised in the original proposal? Does the curriculum teach skills that are tested on districtwide tests? Is the program within budget? Is student achievement satisfactory in all classrooms? Is student achievement consistent with the career goals of the students? Is any part of the curriculum ineffective or redundant?*

Since ordinary educators and members of school boards are not always as clear and focused as evaluators would like, the evaluator will probably find it necessary to help everyone, the immediate boss and everyone else involved, arrive at a list of useful, answerable questions, the answers to which will meet their needs.

PLANNING AN EVALUATION

A list of pertinent questions leads to a chart like the one in Figure 2-2. This example concerns the effectiveness of a middle school health program. At a time when the health of teenagers is threatened by various forms of chemical abuse, sexually transmitted diseases, and debilitating dietary problems, the conventional textbook course that conveys knowledge about normal and abnormal body functions is probably insufficient. Evaluation of this middle school health curriculum is more concerned with student understanding and use of knowledge. Since the program is intended to be preventive, it should help students make decisions in unfamiliar situations as well as make daily decisions in familiar situations, like brushing and flossing their teeth. One question asks if students are likely to pay attention to principles of good health when they find themselves in unfamiliar circumstances. We see no way to be certain that any of the students interviewed will actually behave as predicted, yet the opinions of students interviewed in friendship groups seem as good a source of information about their future behavior as any other source we can think of. Another question asks how this school's health program compares with programs in other schools. Unless data from other schools are published, comparative evaluations require cooperation between the participants. An incentive for participation is a chance to share expertise, not only during

Evaluation of Middle School Health Curriculum
Questions to Be Answered by Evaluation

Question	Information	Source	Method
Is the health curriculum taught as intended?	Methods of instruction, resources, etc., compared to guidelines	Teachers, classroom observer	Observer compares practice with recommendations
Are students learning the principles of healthful living?	Student understanding of course content	Students and teachers	Criterion-referenced test
Has the program influenced their health-related behavior?	Changes of behavior as a result of taking the course	Students and parents	Questionnaire completed by students and parents
Are they likely to use the principles in unfamiliar, health-threatening situations?	Prediction of student behavior in unfamiliar health-threatening situations	Students	Interviews of students in friendship groups
Is the content of the program appropriate for our middle school students?	Opinions concerning appropriateness of topics and goals	Students, parents, and health professionals	Topics and goals accompanied by a questionnaire
Is our program as good as the health programs in other middle schools?	Comparison of our program with similar programs in other schools	Assessment of student performance in other programs	Same evaluation administered in selected other schools

FIGURE 2-2 Chart Planning an Evaluation

the evaluation, but afterwards as well, when the results are studied and teachers share the nuts and bolts of successful practice.

The instruments used in an evaluation further define the information to be gathered. Anyone creating a criterion-referenced test to measure student knowledge of health principles must have a list of these principles. Anyone asking students how they will make decisions in unfamiliar situations must have some preconceived notions about health-threatening situations that students are likely to encounter before they become healthy adults. Stakeholders in the evaluation—those whose questions the evaluation sets out to answer—should have a chance to shape the instruments before the instruments are used. Teachers can supply the list of principles taught in the health program. Students, especially older students who have graduated from the program, parents, and health professionals can anticipate the dangers that lie ahead of middle schoolers. Since program improvement is the principal purpose of this type of evaluation, the team charged with the task of analyzing the data and modifying the program should also be consulted. Teachers and consultants on this team will want to know how students in different categories perform on the test or what they say in the interview. They will want to have descriptions of the health programs taught in other participating schools—and so on.

The evaluation may be conducted by one or more people according to need. A plan like the one illustrated in Figure 2-2 will help an evaluator estimate needs based on the number of sources and the difficulty of gathering information. Members of an evaluation team may be full-time or part-time, experienced or inexperienced. Inexperienced, part-time evaluators—teachers and administrators with other responsibilities to take care of every day, for example—cannot be expected to accomplish as much as full-time professionals contracted to do the job. Nevertheless, evaluation is the precursor of improvement, and schools must help teachers and administrators find time in which to do it. Sometimes it is wise, and politically advantageous, to bring in a team of experts, especially when the effort is funded by an outside source, but expert consultation for teachers and administrators doing routine, in-house evaluation will cost less and last longer. This way, the people who must analyze data and make plans for improvement are likely to support the evaluation and see its implications.

Our advice is to plan each evaluation as a discrete project, with a purpose, a timeline, a product, and a decision to be made. When the decision is made, the project is finished. It may be repeated, even repeated at regular intervals, with the same purpose, a similar schedule, and similar data—but each evaluation must lead to a fresh decision. If the same decision is a foregone conclusion, evaluation is a meaningless exercise. This year's evaluation might have the same outcome as last year's, but the decision should be made anew. On one occasion when we were helping a school make a change in its curriculum, we became aware of teacher resistance. When we asked why they resisted, they complained about excessive record keeping. They were still reporting information on forms that were part of a pilot study conducted four years earlier. The decision had been made long ago, but no one had wrapped up the project and ended the data collection.

Once the data are in, much depends upon how they are organized and represented. Evaluation reports rarely contain everything discovered. Knowing the purpose of the evaluation helps evaluators decide what to include in the report, how to represent various types of data, and how to help decision makers identify the relevant issues. Stakeholders in the evaluation will appreciate rough drafts of the data and an opportunity to ask for a modified format. The final report is organized to answer the original questions as accurately, completely, and directly as possible.

A CYCLE OF CURRICULUM EVALUATION AND DEVELOPMENT

It is possible to crank up an evaluation whenever important decisions have to be made. However, a sudden urgency to make a decision may not allow sufficient time to ask the right questions or get the right answers. It is better to anticipate decisions—if possible—well in advance. The usual routine might turn upside down in an instant, but many decisions can be made carefully and calmly on a schedule.

A survey of all the programs currently operating in the school will usually suggest that some are doing very well, some are merely satisfactory, and some are overdue for revision. One program, perhaps, is fairly new. Perhaps it is managed by a dynamic leader who inspires students and other teachers. Parents rave about the program. It is clearly the most successful program in the school. Yet five years from now, it might have to be revised or scrapped. Times change. Events that change whole nations and small communities also change schools. Manufacturing jobs go overseas. Products are made to be replaced rather than repaired. The service industry expands. Corporations open branches all over the world. The suburbs creep into the country. Middle-class parents move to communities with better schools. The values and the lifestyles of students diverge from the values and lifestyles of teachers. World affairs bring different immigrants with different needs. Every five years, at least, even the best educational programs are due for evaluation.

It would be a mistake, however, to undertake a whole-school evaluation every five years. Evaluation leads to improvement, and improvement means change. If the school's problems are severe, radical change across the board might well be the only solution. Otherwise, a cycle of evaluation, change, and steady improvement is preferable. We suggest a five-year cycle, which means that a fifth of the school is evaluated every year. Each program evaluated then has four years in which to make the changes suggested by the evaluation. There are various ways to divide the school into fifths. An elementary school might choose one or more grade levels each year; a secondary school might choose one or more subjects. Programs that are closely related can be put in the same cycle: prekindergarten and kindergarten, for example, or English and history. The best combination of programs designated for simultaneous evaluation and development will be evident to administrators and teachers familiar with the school.

The cycle consists of:

Year One: Self-study, evaluation
Year Two: Revision of curriculum, inservice for teachers
Year Three: Inservice for teachers, pilot implementation,
                    formative evaluation
Year Four: Continued implementation
Year Five: Continued implementation
Year One: Self-study, evaluation

The Curriculum Council is in a good position to oversee this cycle of evaluation and development. A major responsibility of this council is fulfillment of the school's mission. The council monitors goals and outcomes (see Chapter 1). Each goal of each program must advance the school's mission; each assessment of student learning must show progress toward a goal. The council will decide which programs to put in which cycle, how evaluation and development committees will be formed, to whom they will report, and so on. At the beginning of Year One (or sooner), the council, the teachers in each program to be evaluated, the Curriculum Coordinator (or principal or head of the school) must discuss the upcoming evaluation. We cannot even count all the evaluation models that have been described in the professional literature—certainly more than we can list and categorize. Because we connect evaluation with decision making, our advice is to start with the questions that people in the school want answered. There are questions about goals: "What exactly have we been trying to teach?" "What do the students most need to learn?" There are questions about outcomes: "How much of what we tried to teach have the students learned?" "Have they learned anything we did not try to teach?" There are questions about implementation: "Has the curriculum been taught the way it was meant to be taught?" "Has it been given the resources needed for success?" And there are questions about process: "What parts of the curriculum can be improved?" "Are the units and courses connected and in sequence?" Different types of questions require different approaches to evaluation. Sometimes one approach will answer all the questions; sometimes different approaches must be combined in a single evaluation.

Evaluation of Goals

Determining the goals of the current curriculum may or may not be a simple matter. The goals might be clearly conceived and clearly written. Teachers might know and accept these goals and introduce nothing contrary or distracting into their classes. On the other hand, the goals might not be written or, if written, might be interpreted differently by different teachers. The evaluator must find the degree to which there is consensus or disparity about the goals and, if consensus is lacking, discover what goals teachers in the program expect their students to achieve. So much is description.

Then there is prescription. An evaluation of goals must compare the goals to student needs. Various constituencies of the school will have diverse opinions concerning student needs. Evaluators should solicit these opinions. They should also consult subject specialists, experts in child development, future employers, college admissions officers, and other sources in a position to predict what students ought to be able to do in the future. Of all the needs identified, the school may address only those that advance the mission. The goals of each program, therefore, state explicitly what students must learn if the school is to fulfill its mission. If students need to learn more than is stated, or something other than is stated, then new goals and new curriculum are in order. If the mission no longer meets the needs of students who come to the school, then the mission must be questioned.

It is likely that this approach alone will produce major changes in curriculum and instruction. There is no need to evaluate outcomes, implementation, or process if the goals of the curriculum are no longer desired.

Evaluation of Outcomes

Usually, when teachers give tests, all the students are tested and graded. When schools use tests for curriculum evaluation, however, a random sample of students might suffice, 5 percent of a large population but up to 20 percent of smaller populations. Criterion-referenced tests measure how much of the curriculum students have learned or how well they have learned to do certain tasks (Popham 1981, 1988). If the curriculum is unique to the school, the school must create its own criterion-referenced tests. If the curriculum is used elsewhere, however, some suitable tests might already exist. In order to use criterion-referenced tests for curriculum evaluation, a school must know what the students have been taught and how well they are expected to perform. The tests measure performance, but any determination of merit requires the setting of a standard. Criterion-referenced tests need not be paper-and-pencil tests. Students in a health program might be expected to perform CPR correctly while practicing on a dummy, or to choose a balanced meal in the cafeteria. Students in a science program might be expected to formulate a hypothesis and test it, using whatever resources have been made available. As long as tests of performance give students an opportunity to do what they have learned to do, tests for the purpose of evaluation can take advantage of all the methodology developed for assessment of student achievement (Chapter 6).

In English classes in Springfield, Massachusetts, for example, students are asked to read a story and write about the story or about personal experiences in some way related to the story. The assignment includes tasks they have done routinely in class, including small-group discussions about the reading, activities to stimulate ideas for writing, and peer editing of first drafts. Teachers read and grade all the writing produced. In addition, the Director of English collects copies of the first and final drafts written by a random sample of students, 5 percent of all students at a certain grade level. A group of teachers is trained to read and grade this collection of student writing according to four traits: the writer's "presence" in the work, the structure of the writing, the completeness of the work, and improvement achieved through revision of the first draft. In this way, objectives, instruction, assessment, and curriculum evaluation are all closely related.

In contrast, standardized tests compare the performance of individual students and groups of students to other individuals and groups from a great variety of schools throughout the country. Because standardized tests are used in so many different schools, they do not measure achievement of local goals. Most of the standardized tests available to schools are paper-and-pencil, computer-scored tests. They measure student performance of general tasks that have been associated, one way or another, with academic success. Students, teachers, and parents may or may not value this type of performance, although they probably do recognize the importance of the scores to individual students and the school as a whole.

Evaluation of Implementation

In Chapter 3, we make some recommendations concerning the shape and substance of a school's curriculum. Existing curriculum, however, comes in all shapes and sizes. It might contain fully developed classroom scenarios, so that scenes in one classroom look very much like scenes in another classroom, with a different cast of characters. It might be no more than a collection of materials, like a textbook, a teacher's manual, and a set of kits for teaching science. It might be entirely intangible, no more than a commitment to a set of objectives made by teachers who are free otherwise to teach as they please. No matter what the curriculum consists of, evaluation of implementation presumes that some agreement has been made: "In order to teach X, we will do Y."

Evaluation for implementation checks to see if this agreement has been fulfilled. The approach requires two sets of data: data describing the curriculum as agreed and data describing the curriculum as taught. If no agreement has been made, everything evaluators do to arrive at a description of the taught curriculum can still be done. It might well be imperative to have such a description, but a description does not constitute an evaluation. The goals, outcomes, and process of the taught curriculum can all be evaluated, but without an agreement to implement something called "the curriculum," evaluation of implementation is irrelevant.

Why evaluate implementation at all? If the students are learning, does it matter how they learn? Yes, it does matter. If the cause of learning is not understood, much of the time and energy devoted to learning might be wasteful. If, on the other hand, the students are not learning, then something must be changed. But what should be changed? If the curriculum as it was conceived has not been implemented, or has been implemented improperly, it would be wasteful to scrap it, or even to modify it significantly. Before condemning a curriculum it is wise to evaluate its implementation. If, however, the curriculum to be evaluated is fragmented, diffuse, and generally disparaged, or if it has been taught for years by teachers who are very familiar with it, the Curriculum Council would have good reason to choose another type of evaluation.

The data needed to evaluate an implementation will vary, depending upon the curriculum that has been adopted. If the curriculum includes materials, an evaluation should discover when and how the materials are used. If the curriculum includes information that the students must learn, an evaluation should find out how much of this information was taught and how much of it the students actually learned. If the curriculum is specific about objectives, an evaluation should examine methods of assessment and levels of achievement. If the curriculum is not specific about objectives, then the technique of mapping (English 1980) will help to identify objectives that teachers emphasize at various stages of the program.

Other relevant information may include:

- Amount of time given to the curriculum in the schedule of classes
- Amount of time given to various types of activities in the classroom
- Amount of homework assigned
- Availability of equipment
- Suitability of classrooms

- Class size
- Classroom artifacts like handouts, bulletin boards, student writing, etc.
- Opinions of students concerning pace, clarity, sequence, workload, etc.
- A daily log of classroom events

Much of this data gathering will seem like "snooping" unless teachers and students understand and agree that implementation of curriculum is a perfectly proper thing to evaluate. Teachers and students are principal stakeholders in the curriculum. If their concerns are addressed in the process of evaluation, they are more likely to tolerate the intrusions of evaluators.

Consultation with teachers and students will do more than ease diplomatic relations. Their opinions and attitudes are crucial to any implementation. The Concerns Based Adoption Model (CBAM) developed at the Research and Development Center for Teacher Education at the University of Texas (Hall and Hord 1987) emphasizes this personal side of change. The scale in Figure 2-3 describes the behavior of "users of an innovation" at different levels of understanding and commitment. The highest level is "Renewal," when teachers have done as much as they possibly can to implement the curriculum and are looking for ways to improve it.

Evaluation of Process

Curriculum evaluation can identify which parts of the curriculum are working well and which parts ought to be better. Here again, the opinions of teachers and students are indispensable. They are intimately acquainted with the curriculum, and they will identify the strengths and weaknesses discovered through steady use. Because they are thoroughly involved, they will also have suggestions for making the curriculum better. An evaluation should not depend entirely upon opinions, of course, even the opinions of teachers whose expertise is central to the matter. On the other hand, an evaluation cannot gather all the data it is possible to gather. There must be some selection. The opinions of teachers and students will direct attention to critical issues that warrant attention.

Reports of professional associations will also help to identify

VI **RENEWAL:** State in which the user reevaluates the quality of use of the innovation, seeks major modifications of or alternatives to present innovation to achieve increased impact on clients, examines new developments in the field, and explores new goals for self and the system.

V **INTEGRATION:** State in which the user is combining own efforts to use the innovation with related activities of colleagues to achieve a collective impact on clients within their common sphere of influence.

IVB **REFINEMENT:** State in which the user varies the use of the innovation to increase the impact on the clients within immediate sphere of influence. Variations are based on knowledge of both short- and long-term consequences for clients.

IVA **ROUTINE:** Use of the innovation is stabilized. Few if any changes are being made in ongoing use. Little preparation or thought is being given to improving innovation use or its consequences.

III **MECHANICAL USE:** State in which the user focuses most effort on the short-term, day-to-day use of the innovation with little time for reflection. Changes in use are made more to meet user needs than client needs. The user is primarily engaged in stepwise attempt to master the tasks required to use the innovation, often resulting in disjointed and superficial use.

II **PREPARATION:** State in which the user is preparing for first use of the innovation.

I **ORIENTATION:** State in which the user has recently acquired or is acquiring information about the innovation and/or has recently explored or is exploring its value orientation and its demands upon user and user system.

0 **NONUSE:** State in which the user has little or no knowledge of the innovation, no involvement with the innovation, and is doing nothing toward becoming involved.

FIGURE 2-3 Levels of Use

Source: Hall and Hord 1987. Used with permission.

important issues. Evaluation matches features of the curriculum against the recommendations and requirements of curriculum task forces, local and state departments of education, accrediting agencies, research foundations, articles written by authorities in the field, and so on. If members of the evaluation team lack the knowledge to make this type of appraisal, one or more consultants might be asked to visit the school, make recommendations, and help to fill in a background of theory and practice in the field.

If evaluation of process continues for one entire school year, the evaluating team and the teachers in the program (there is likely to be overlap) have an opportunity for productive collaboration. Teachers do not as a rule organize their assessments to provide evaluative information about the program. In a year dedicated to self-evaluation, however, teachers may be asked to work closely with colleagues teaching similar objectives at other levels or teaching other sections of the same course. Identical tests, or identical items on different tests, will yield comparative information that the teachers might not get otherwise. The process of teaching and learning is easier to evaluate throughout the year, when the program is underway, than at the end, when outcomes are usually evaluated. Nevertheless, parts of criterion-referenced tests given at the end of a program can be made to correspond to various stages or components of the curriculum. Three or four items on a paper-and-pencil test at the end of the year might not be enough to reveal a problem with a month-long unit in a year-long course, but criterion-referenced tests do not have to be identical for every student. If five forms of the test are given to a group of students, the three or four items on a single topic become fifteen to twenty items, permitting a more detailed analysis of group achievement. On the other hand, if the test is not a paper-and-pencil test at all, but a "performance" test or "exhibition" (Sizer 1992), it is still possible to isolate and evaluate parts of the whole as they correspond to parts of the curriculum. A series of one-act plays, for example, might be capably directed, imaginatively staged, well attended, but poorly acted. Mathematical investigations conducted by groups of sixth-graders might be mathematically sound, useful, well written, and well illustrated, but might avoid the mathematical models taught in sixth grade.

Cognitive maps used in curriculum development (Chapter 3) are useful also for the purpose of curriculum evaluation. McKeown and Beck (1990) interviewed fifth-graders in order to discover what the students knew about the American Revolution before they had studied the period in their history class and sixth-graders a year later in order to discover what they had retained. The researchers constructed a cognitive map, or "semantic net," as they call it, of the information needed to answer all the questions they would ask in their interviews (see Fig. 2-4). Individual student responses during the interview were scored, so that the difference between the knowledge of the fifth-graders and the sixth-graders could be analyzed quantitatively. The researchers also constucted a map of each student's knowledge. One sixth-grader's knowledge is represented by the map in Figure 2-5. Comparison of the template (Fig. 2-4) and the student map (Fig. 2-5) shows the student's ignorance of "No taxation without representation" and her mistaken belief that the war was fought between Americans and Spanish. The advantage of maps is that they illustrate the ways in which students organize their knowledge. This sixth-grader has exaggerated the importance of Columbus in the development of the United States. She believes that Columbus's discovery of America, which is celebrated on the Fourth of July, enabled settlers to follow, "and they came over and started settling in and started moving over in the east, where they started making the United States." She links these "settlers" to her knowledge of the "13 Colonies" when she says, "They made 13 colonies and they formed like a nation." McKeown and Beck report that this student's view of Columbus was not atypical among the students interviewed.

This particular study draws attention to problems in elementary-level textbooks in American history, but it is evident that such a study would be invaluable for history teachers in any school. Its methodology is well within the capabilities of an evaluation committee, particularly in a school where cognitive maps are used in curriculum development. Moreover, if students were taught to construct their own maps as a means of organizing and representing knowledge (see Chapter 5), student-made maps could be compared to a template, thus eliminating the need for interviews.

When assessment of student achievement reveals a problem, the next step is to find the cause. Students might not enter the program with sufficient prior knowledge. Something crucial might be missing from the curriculum. Classroom tests might have failed to detect the problem when it first occurred. Teachers' expectations of their students might not match standards set for the purpose of curriculum

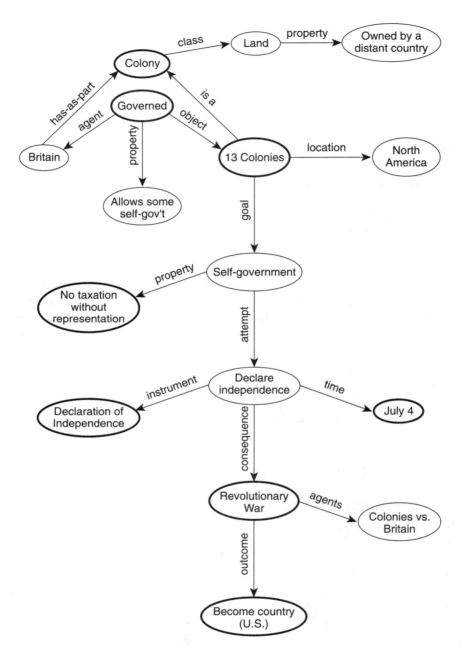

FIGURE 2-4 Semantic Net of Knowledge about the American Revolution

Source: M. G. McKeown and I. L. Beck (1990), "The Assessment and Characterization of Young Learners' Knowledge of a Topic in History," *American Educational Research Journal 27,* 688–726. Copyright © 1990 by the American Educational Research Association. Reprinted by permission of the publisher.

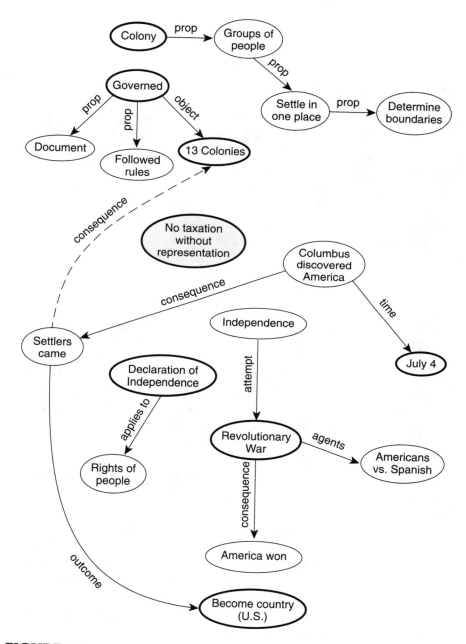

FIGURE 2-5 Semantic Net of a Sixth-Grader's Knowledge about the American Revolution

Source: M. G. McKeown and I. L. Beck (1990), "The Assessment and Characterization of Young Learners' Knowledge of a Topic in History," *American Educational Research Journal 27,* 688726. Copyright © 1990 by the American Educational Research Association. Reprinted by permission of the publisher.

evaluation. Students might have insufficient time to practice an important skill. Their motivation might be low. Evaluation of process, therefore, continues until the cause is understood. Entering students are given a diagnostic test. The written curriculum is compared to the taught curriculum. Evaluators and teachers collaborate to create new tests for classroom use. Teachers examine their tests and grades and compare their standards to the standards used for curriculum evaluation. Students are given more time to practice to see if that makes a difference. They are asked if they know the goals of the program—and asked if they care. If curriculum evaluation can identify the cause of a problem, curriculum development has a chance of solving it.

EVALUATION AND DEVELOPMENT

Rather than waiting until a new curriculum has been implemented, schools are advised to continue the process of evaluation throughout the process of development. Someone on the development team should have the express responsibility for evaluating the new curriculum during development and after implementation. If, for example, an evaluation of goals has prompted an effort to reconstruct the curriculum to achieve new goals, then another evaluation, however brief, should make sure that the new goals pass whatever test the old goals failed. Then, as the new goals are translated into objectives, the development team should anticipate and describe the student behavior that will constitute success of the reconstructed curriculum. Such foresight will facilitate the evaluation of outcomes when the time comes and will help direct the development team toward tangible results.

If student achievement depends upon specific instructional methods, then the methods should be described. Eventually, teachers will implement the curriculum and administrators will supervise them. Even if the teachers and supervisors receive training, they will need a manual to consult as they become independent. Imagine the potential disaster if supervisors, acting in good faith but excusable ignorance, were to pressure teachers into doing the wrong thing. Outcomes would be jeopardized, and morale would suffer. Later, when disappointment sets in, the question would arise, "Was the curriculum implemented as intended?" If no guidelines for implementation were ever recorded, an argument is likely to ensue. Evaluation of the implementation might prove to be impossible at that point. The curriculum that was taught might be modified or scrapped, but the curriculum that was planned might be lost forever.

Almost all schools are subject to mandatory evaluations. State and district requirements are usually supported—and probably enforced—through periodic evaluation. Pennsylvania, for example, requires public schools to address the "Twelve Goals of Quality Education" (see Chapter 6 and note on page 185). To foster achievement of these goals, the Pennsylvania Department of Education (1987) provides a package of tests and questionnaires called the Educational Quality Assessment (EQA). Members of a curriculum development team in a Pennsylvania school will almost certainly be aware of the Twelve Goals. They should also know the contents of the EQA. As development proceeds, they will be in a position to determine the relevance of the EQA to their objectives. If they intend to teach the students behavior that is not specifically assessed by the EQA, then they must develop alternative methods of assessment. Evaluation of state and districtwide goals may be mandatory and may be useful, but it does not obviate a school's need to evaluate its own curriculum. Evaluation leads to improvement, and improvement means higher student achievement of preferred goals. If mandatory evaluation records the change, it may be a happy coincidence.

EVIDENCE OF
SUCCESSFUL EVALUATION

It is not difficult to differentiate between schools that evaluate curriculum regularly and routinely and schools that do not. Traces of curriculum evaluation include the following:

- When discussing the academic program with parents, press, and members of the Board, teachers and administrators will cite evidence of success.
- All the teachers and administrators know how the curriculum is evaluated and what the school is doing to improve.
- The Curriculum Council oversees a cycle of evaluation and development in each division of the school.
- Representatives from each division report the results of self-

evaluation to the council and discuss implications for curriculum development.
- Teachers in the school are not threatened by curriculum evaluation.
- They distinguish between curriculum evaluation and teacher evaluation. They help to design and willingly participate in curriculum evaluation projects.
- Administrators and teachers ask for and receive consultation in the process of curriculum evaluation.
- Decisions are based on information provided by curriculum evaluation. If information is lacking, decision makers make every effort, in any time available, to get the information they need.
- When curriculum development teams meet to begin their work, they refer to evaluation reports produced in the school. Upon completion, they show how their proposed new curriculum solves problems that were found in the old curriculum.

SUMMARY

There are many ways to evaluate curriculum. Useful evaluations provide the information needed for decision making. Before the evaluation begins, therefore, it is important to identify decision makers and anticipate the information they will find useful. An evaluation is then organized around questions that elicit this information. The two most important questions to ask about curriculum are "What are the students supposed to be learning?" and "Are they learning what they're supposed to be learning?" These questions are easily answered if the curriculum has clear goals, clear objectives, and a comprehensive program for assessing student achievement. For this reason, evaluation consultants can be helpful during the process of curriculum development.

Since schools tend to be complex, with various departments, divisions, and courses, it is difficult to evaluate the whole school curriculum all at once. We recommend a five-year cycle of evaluation. In this cycle, one-fifth of the school's programs are evaluated each year. During the following four years of the cycle, teachers and administrators responsible for a program that has been evaluated make appropriate revisions to the program, conduct related inservice for teachers, and implement the revisions. Coordinated evaluation cycles are supervised by the school's Curriculum Council. Administrators and teachers conducting a self-evaluation have to decide which questions to try to answer in the course of an evaluation. Questions might be about the goals, outcomes, implementation, or process. Different types of questions will entail different approaches to evaluation. A single approach might suffice in some evaluations, but others might require a combination of approaches.

Some evaluation can take place during the process of curriculum development. Curriculum developers should try to ensure that goals are appropriate for the students in the program and that the curriculum contains guidelines for teachers who will implement it. Concept maps used for curriculum development may also be used for curriculum evaluation. Development teams should be aware of mandatory evaluations and make sure that the developing curriculum meets all the required standards.

REFERENCES

Beswick, R. (1990). *Evaluating Educational Programs.* (ERIC Document ED324766).

Bonnett, D. G. (1981). "Five Phases of Purposeful Enquiry." In R. S. Brandt (Ed.), *Applied Strategies for Curriculum Evaluation.* Alexandria, Va.: Association for Supervision and Curriculum Development.

Brandt, R. S. (Ed.). (1981). *Applied Strategies for Curriculum Evaluation.* Alexandria, Va.: Association for Supervision and Curriculum Development.

Cipfl, J. L. (1984). "How to Evaluate Your School Instructional Program." Paper presented at the Annual Meeting of the National School Boards Association, Houston, Texas. (ERIC Document ED247647).

English, F. W. (1980). "Curriculum Mapping." *Educational Leadership* 37:7, 558–559.

Hall, G. E., and S. M. Hord. (1987). *Change in Schools: Facilitating the Process.* Albany, N.Y.: State University of New York Press.

McKeown, M. G., and I. L. Beck. (1990). "The Assessment and Characterization of Young Learners' Knowledge of a Topic in History." *American Educational Research Journal 27,* 688–726.

Pennsylvania Department of Education. (1987). *Educational Quality Assessment: Commentary.* Harrisburg, Pa.: Pennsylvania Department of Education.

Popham, W. J. (1981). *Modern Educational Measurement.* Englewood Cliffs, N.J.: Prentice-Hall

Popham, W. J. (1988). *Educational Evaluation* (2nd ed.). Englewood Cliffs, N.J.: Prentice-Hall .

Sanders, J. R. (1988). *Approaching Evaluation in Small Schools.* (ERIC Document ED296816).

Scriven, M. (1981). "The Radnor Evaluation Derby." In R. S. Brandt (Ed.), *Applied Strategies for Curriculum Evaluation.* Alexandria, Va.: Association for Supervision and Curriculum Development.

Sizer, T. R. (1992). *Horace's School: Redesigning the American High School.* Boston: Houghton Mifflin.

Tyler, R. T. (1949). *Basic Principles of Curriculum and Instruction.* Chicago: University of Chicago.

3

DEVELOPING THE CURRICULUM

MISSION

Does the school have a mission? It cannot be all things to all people. Who are its clients? What should it offer that they do not have? If the school has been operating without a mission, the prospect of asking, "What is our fundamental purpose?" might strike fear in the faint-hearted. Dormant conflicts might be revived. Other conflicts might arise. Powerful individuals with vested interests might claim to know what is best for the students. How will these conflicts be resolved? Who will have the final say? To an insecure principal, an embattled committee, or a threatened minority, starting from scratch might seem like a horrible idea.

Nevertheless, we recommend a mission. Anyone embarking on a program of curriculum development must first examine the school's mission. Fulfillment of the mission is the purpose of curriculum, as it is the purpose of everything else about the school. Without a mission, coherent curriculum development is virtually impossible. Change might occur, but *development* means progress toward a goal. If the school does not have a mission, then that is where curriculum development should begin. But what do you do if you are asked to develop curriculum yet lack the authority to produce a mission? Perhaps you are a teacher, a student, or a parent who has been appointed to a curriculum committee. We suggest that you ask the members of the committee if they are aware of the school's mission. If they seem confused, or uncertain, try to interest the principal in the problem.

Maybe you can get the principal and the committee to read this and other books on the subject—*Managing the Nonprofit Organization* by Peter Drucker (1990), for example, or the excellent newsletters published by Independent School Management (1991). Some powerful individual or group has to be persuaded to start the process of formulating, adopting, and dedicating the school to a mission.

No matter who starts the process, any group formed to produce a new mission should represent all the stakeholders in the school (National Association of Secondary School Principals 1987; Stone 1987; Nebgen 1991). If everyone is asked to contribute, and all contributions are respected, the mood is likely to be cooperative. If, however, someone comes to the first meeting with a mission already written and asks the group to approve it, then preconceived fears of dissension might be justified. The right mission for the school will evolve. It will broaden the common ground instead of deepening the differences. It will bind the work group into a team. Discussion should address the following questions:

1. Who are the school's most eligible clients? Consider families and communities as possible clients as well as students. A redefined mission might expand or reduce the current clientele.
2. What are the strengths of the school? Its mission might lie in doing better what it now does best.
3. What are the school's major problems? Identifying these problems might clarify the school's mission. Solving them might become the mission.
4. Imagine the most desirable outcomes the school can possibly achieve. What should graduating students be able to do? What high hopes might they fulfill?

Out of information and insights produced by these discussions, the school's mission will be distilled. A summary report of the proceedings will serve as a first draft—too wordy and indistinct for a finished statement, but containing the essential ingredients of a mission: students, resources, and desired outcomes. The report should be distributed to all members of the group so they can carry the discussion into their various constituencies, both formally—at a meeting of the parents association, for example—and informally, among respected colleagues and friends. This provides a period of time for reflection and ordering of priorities.

Mission is more than purpose and requires more than consensus. Drucker (1990) lists three "musts" of a mission: opportunities, competence, and commitment.

Opportunities

There are opportunities in education to accomplish wonderful things. However, an opportunity at one school might be a *fait accompli* at another. At a certain elementary school, it might be wonderful if all the children learned to read at grade level. At another elementary school, where all the children read at grade level or above, that might not seem like a wonderful accomplishment. At a certain middle school, it might be wonderful if all the students leaving at the end of eighth grade were eager to continue their education in high school. At another middle school, all the eighth-graders might have their sights set on college. At a certain high school, it might be wonderful if all the graduates were able to speak a second language. At another high school, bilingualism might be a fact of life. Each school has an opportunity to do something wonderful, and considering the diversity of schools and communities, each opportunity is unique.

Commitment

Identification of a worthy goal is not sufficient to produce a mission. A mission must be wholeheartedly endorsed by everyone, or almost everyone, involved. To achieve it, everyone must make an effort; otherwise the mission serves only a portion of the school. It must also be enduring, but "enduring" does not necessarily mean "long-term." An enduring goal might soon be achieved, but once achieved, it is worth achieving again and again. A business committed to serving the needs of its customers can serve the needs of today's customers, tomorrow's customers, and customers in the next century.

Competence

A mission inspires the finest efforts of everyone who accepts it, but it should not be impossible. It might *seem* impossible to some people, but not for very long. It is the job of leadership to convince skeptics that the mission *will* be accomplished, and the best way to do that is to show results. The mission is achieved not through luck and hope, but competence and effort. The right mission is one the school can achieve. If it becomes too easy to achieve, however, it has outlived its purpose as a mission, because it does not inspire excellence.

Mission statements vary in length and tone. Some do double duty as slogans. Savannah Country Day School prints its mission statement, "To search for the excellence in each of us," on all its publications. Other missions are sober lists of outcomes. If the mission is not easily grasped in a single thought, further distillation might enhance its impact upon the school. The official mission of the Gow School in South Wales, New York, is a paragraph long:

> *The mission of The Gow School is to prepare dyslexic young men for college and the future by helping them to understand and address their special learning needs, to fulfill their academic, physical, artistic, social, spiritual and emotional potential, to develop ethical standards of behavior, to assume responsibility for their own actions with integrity and consideration of the needs of others, to meet the demands of an ever-changing environment, and to become leaders who make a difference in the world.*

Inherent in this mission are two fundamental goals, to help dyslexic students achieve academic success and to prepare them for positions of leadership. The headmaster and faculty summarize the mission in this abbreviated form, which then becomes the mission.

A new mission might effect a transformation. The transformation of Sears, Roebuck and Company from a struggling mail-order firm to a huge retailing corporation is attributable, Drucker (1990) claims, to its mission of service to the American farmer. The restructuring of schools in Winona, Minnesota, including everything from site-based management to a new communications network in the community, has been directed by its mission of success for *all* students (Sambs and Schenkat 1990). But even when change is gradual, a clear sense of mission ensures purpose, progress, and direction. To the faculty at Savannah Country Day School, the concept of individual strengths and weaknesses was not new. Nevertheless, adoption of the mission "to search for the excellence in each of us," has added impetus to their efforts to build a pedagogy based on individual achievement.

The transformation of the Johnson City Schools, New York, is well documented (Spady 1984; Vickery 1985, 1987, 1988, 1990). Their mission is defined by five exit behaviors (Vickery 1990). Johnson City graduates are expected:

1. To have high self-esteem as learners and as persons
2. To function at high cognitive levels, not just at the level of standardized tests
3. To be good problem solvers, communicators, decision makers, competent in group processes, and accountable for their own behavior
4. To be self-directed learners
5. To show concern for others

These general outcomes are further defined by clear goals for every program. Student achievement is assessed in relation to program goals and to the breadth of the mission. By every measure, standardized tests and various means of assessing "significant" outcomes, the Johnson City Schools have accomplished a remarkable turnaround.

A sense of mission is powerful, but not magical. It inspires effort, but it is not accomplished without followthrough. In Chapter 1, we have shown how the mission permeates a school through goals and objectives. Just writing the goals and objectives takes effort, never mind the effort of achieving them. They are not a record of the past; they lure us expectantly into the future. Some intelligent, conscientious educators will argue that the school as it now exists is perfectly satisfactory. Others, just as intelligent and conscientious, will advocate change. If the mission is new and the purpose of goal setting is improvement, there must be change.

How does an academic leader infuse the school with the confidence and imagination to change? He or she might find support in the greater educational community. The recommendations of national associations like the National Council of Teachers of English, the American Council of Teachers of Foreign Languages, the National Council of Teachers of Mathematics, the National Council for the Social Studies, the National Science Teachers Association, and others have much in common. Although educational journals are enlivened by debate, there is remarkable consensus around general principles. Change in education is a national agenda.

LESS IS MORE

The typical curriculum in American schools is jammed with courses, subjects, topics, principles, concepts, and cases to which students are "exposed" for short periods of time. Opportunities to study anything in depth are rare. Although diverse topics might be related by principles, or process, or context, students hardly ever study the interrelatedness. In mathematics they learn a complex procedure just well enough to repeat it during a test, and then they are taught another procedure, and another, and another, year after year. Students who cannot keep up are called "slow" learners, and those who learn quickly are moved into "accelerated" classes. History courses "cover" huge amounts of factual material in chronological order, even when the curriculum purports to teach critical thinking. Students learning a second language spend hours memorizing long lists of words and phrases governed by every case and tense and rule, but speak the language for only a few seconds a day. Even in advanced classes, we observe students speaking English when they have real information to convey, like why they are late for class, or why they must leave early, and using their second language only to answer questions about information contained in the textbook. It would be optimistic to say that the flight from topic to topic results in superficial learning. Gardner (1991) summarizes a wealth of evidence to show that college students are ignorant of fundamental principles in subjects they have studied for years. Adults, including those who have had a "good" education, are likely to base their conclusions about the social and natural world on naive theories formed in childhood rather than scientific theories and rules of reasoning that were taught—but not learned—in school.

Professional associations in all disciplines advise teachers to "cover" less so that students will learn more. In *Curriculum and Evaluation Standards for School Mathematics,* the National Council of Teachers of Mathematics (1989) lists topics for decreased attention in the curriculum. In grades K–4, for example, students might spend less time on "complex paper-and-pencil computations," but more time on the "meaning of fractions and decimals," the "use of calculators," and "everyday problems." The National Council for the Social Studies (1989) lists twenty-four criteria (see Fig. 3-1) for evaluating curriculum. None of these even hints that the best curriculum covers the most material. If all twenty-four were achieved in a social studies

Scope-and-Sequence Criteria

A social studies scope and sequence should:

1. state the purpose and rationale of the program;
2. be internally consistent with its stated purposes and rationale;
3. designate content at every grade level, K–12;
4. recognize that learning is cumulative;
5. reflect a balance of local, national, and global content;
6. reflect a balance of past, present, and future content;
7. provide for students' understanding of the structure and function of social, economic, and political institutions;
8. emphasize concepts and generalizations from history and the social sciences;
9. promote the integration of skills and knowledge;
10. promote the integration of content across subject areas;
11. promote the use of a variety of teaching methods and instructional materials;
12. foster active learning and social interaction;
13. reflect a clear commitment to democratic beliefs and values;
14. reflect a global perspective;
15. foster the knowledge and appreciation of cultural heritage;
16. foster the knowledge and appreciation of diversity;
17. foster the building of self-esteem;
18. be consistent with current research pertaining to how children learn;
19. be consistent with current scholarship in the disciplines;
20. incorporate thinking skills and interpersonal skills at all levels;
21. stress the identification, understanding, and solution of local, national, and global problems;
22. provide many opportunities for students to learn and practice the basic skills of participation from observation to advocacy;
23. promote the transfer of knowledge and skills to life;
24. have the potential to challenge and excite students.

FIGURE 3-1 Criteria for Evaluating Social Studies Curriculum

Source: National Council for the Social Studies 1989. Reprinted by permission.

curriculum, it would never occur to students that history is "a total skim," as one student described his European history course. "We covered 2,000 years. Every week we were assigned to cover a 30-page chapter" (Newmann 1988). The American Council on the Teaching of Foreign Languages (1986) has published guidelines for assessing the proficiency of students using a second language. Speakers at the novice level in French are described as "unable to make one's needs known and communicate essential information in a simple survival situation." Students at an advanced level, however, "can talk in a general way about topics of current public interest . . . can give autobiographical information . . . can make a point forcefully and communicate needs and thoughts in a situation with a complication (e.g., calling a mechanic for help with a stalled car, explaining suspicious-looking possessions to a customs official)." Students learning to use an unfamiliar language for such purposes need to spend more time using it than is usually provided in foreign language classes. In science, English, and the arts, the message is similar: more time for exploration, reflection, and tasks that have purpose and meaning in themselves.

Practicing the Discipline

None of the academic disciplines is only a body of knowledge. Each is also a practice. Mathematicians, physicists, historians, geographers, writers, anthropologists, actors—all "do" something. Even amateur connoisseurs "do" something. People who read do things that non-readers do not. People who go to art museums do things that non-museum-goers do not. People who love the culture of Europe, Africa, China, or pre-Columbian America do things to satisfy their love of culture that non-culture-lovers do not. Bilingual travelers do things that monolingual travelers cannot do. As students learn the various academic disciplines, they should become more able as well as more knowledgeable. If they are not learning to practice the discipline, they are not really learning the discipline at all. They are learning something else, a scholastic version of the real thing: "school math," "school history," "school science," and so on.

When learning is practical, it has context. Textbook problems are generic and sanitized. Problems in context are specific and messy. The contrast is captured marvelously in the first chapter of *All Creatures Great and Small*, by James Herriott (1972). He describes a difficult calving in a cold and mucky barn in the Yorkshire dales. He is stripped to the waist, his arm deep inside the cow, pushing mightily against her contractions, trying with the tips of his fingers to slide a cord around the calf, which is stuck sideways in the uterus. His feet slip in the muck. Aching and miserable, he remembers the illustration of calving in his college textbook. The vet is wearing a white coat, looking "as if he had just had a good dinner and thought he might do a bit of calving for dessert."

A "cost of the carpet" problem in a textbook asks the students to multiply the area of the carpet by the unit cost of the carpet. If the problem is tricky, the students will have to convert square feet to square yards. A practical problem, in contrast, asks students to write a proposal for carpeting the classroom. The room is not one rectangle, but several rectangles. Unit conversions produce awkward fractions. The width of a roll of carpet is less than the width of the room. The completed carpet will have seams. Ideally, the seams are located in areas of least traffic. The customer, of course, pays for any carpet that is cut from the roll. Some carpets are inexpensive and wear quickly. Some are expensive and resist wear. Some colors are attractive but show dirt. Others are dull but disguise dirt. Some excite the interest of the students. Others are unremarkable. Then there is the question of the pad! Practically speaking, the result of a calculation is rarely the answer to a problem.

Generic, decontextualized learning has a purpose. Obviously, it would take a long time to teach students to calculate by teaching them to carpet rooms. An education that consists only of decontextualized learning, however, fails to teach students that learning is useful (see Chapter 5). At present, school learning is almost entirely decontextualized—although we realize that many exceptional teachers in exceptional schools have allowed reality to enter their classes. Typically, students are given literature to read because it helps them understand other literature, not because it helps them understand the world they live in. They are asked to write about character and symbol and dramatic climax, not about love and greed and hope. They learn that history is "other people's facts" (Holt 1990) and other people's theories, not facts and theories they can claim as their own. They study science using standard chemicals, frictionless pulleys, and pure strains of fruit flies.

The dean of studies in a boarding school told us about a boy who wanted to quit chemistry. "It has nothing to do with anything anybody cares about," the boy said. He did not want to go to college, anyway.

He wanted to open a branch of his father's business, selling oil and gas in rural New Hampshire. The dean knew that helping the boy was not simply a matter of signing a "drop-add" permission slip. He agreed to visit the class, talk with the chemistry teacher, and then to talk with the boy again. The next day, he found the chemistry class studying gas laws. It had never occurred to the student, or to the teacher, that gas laws had anything to do with the business of selling oil and gas in New Hampshire. The next weekend, the boy's chemistry assignment was to go home for a long talk with his father, about chemistry, the gas laws, and the business. On Monday, he told the rest of the class about his discoveries. It proved to be a turning point for the student—and for the teacher.

A topic arising frequently in discussions of change in schools is standardized tests. How will the change affect test scores? What about College Boards? There is some feeling that practical, applied skills are appropriate for vocational education, but not for students who will go to college. The College Board does not take that position. The College Board has made it clear in its "Thinking Series" of publications that the practice of a discipline is central to learning.

Dennie Palmer Wolf says in the introduction to *Reading Reconsidered* (1988):

> Part of what a field offers students is a characteristic *way of thinking.* Just as there is an experimental method for physicists and the rigors of fieldwork for anthropologists, there is a way of thinking about texts that is centrally (if not exclusively) literary. Not to teach students these habits of mind would be to cheat them just as surely as if we kept them away from books written before 1900 and burned all poetry.

Tom Holt says in *Thinking Historically* (1990): "The professional historian is trained to build a historical narrative from traces and leavings by applying disciplined intuition and analysis. I would argue that high school students could and should do the same."

Silver, Kilpatrick, and Schlesinger say in *Thinking Through Mathematics* (1990):

> If students are to develop the power to use mathematics productively once they leave school, they need opportunities to use it

productively while they are there. More attention needs to be focused on the thinking that students are doing about the mathematics they are learning. . . . "To understand what they learn, [students] must enact for themselves verbs that permeate mathematics curriculum: 'examine,' 'represent,' 'transform,' 'solve,' 'apply,' 'prove,' 'communicate.' This happens most readily when students work in groups, engage in discussion, make presentations, and in other ways take charge of their own learning." (Mathematical Sciences Education Board 1989)

Bette Hirsch says in *Languages of Thought* (1989):

Teachers and researchers are developing and debating a revised view of language learning that is rapidly extending older approaches. It is a view that alerts us to the communicative aspects of language. It is also a point of view that underscores the resources students bring to language learning, and thus suggests novel approaches to teaching based on authentic tasks. . . . Proficiency-oriented and ESL teachers are interested in teaching language use, as well as knowledge of a language. They argue that communication is the heart of language. Much of what they stress underscores getting a message across, or getting the gist of someone else's message. In this light, grammar and vocabulary—the usual "stars" of language teaching—become tools for speaking, listening, and writing, rather than ends in themselves. (di Pietro 1981; Molinsky and Bliss 1988; Omaggio 1986)

National standardized tests and national trends in education have a "chicken-and-egg" relationship. College Board Achievement Tests are based on typical high school courses. The knowledge they presume is taken from textbooks widely used in high school classes. Theoretically speaking, the curriculum comes first, and then the tests. Practically speaking, the reverse is true. Now that the tests exist, high school courses are based on the tests. Many schools are reluctant to change the curriculum for fear of lower test scores.

We do not wish to minimize the dilemma, yet we have confidence it will be resolved before long. A great wave of educational reform is underway. Confidence in standardized tests is eroding. Those who advocate "teaching for the test" do not seem to be passionately attached to the test or the curriculum that prepares students to take it. They are simply yielding to the force of circumstances. As circumstances change, pressures change. New goals, new curricula, new methods of instruction demand new methods of assessment (see Chapter 6). The widely supported New Standards Project, a joint endeavor of The Learning Research and Development Center (University of Pittsburgh, Pa.) and the National Center on Education and the Economy (Rochester, N.Y.), has begun to field-test performance assessment in mathematics and language arts, a significant step toward the development of a new system of national examinations (Resnick and Resnick 1992; O'Neil 1993).

INTERDISCIPLINARY CONNECTIONS

A scientist writing a paper for presentation at a conference is concerned about the clarity of the writing. An art historian considering the authenticity of a painting thought to be a Rembrandt uses information gained through chemical analysis of the paint. A Jewish psychologist treating an Irish immigrant is helped by knowledge of Catholicism. A mathematician uses a computer to examine the fractal formation of cauliflowers. An American historian studying the Vietnam War reads documents written in French. A chemical engineer trying to make better paper for artists learns the technique of etching. The practice of any discipline is informed by other disciplines because all the disciplines are ways of understanding the world around us, which is not divided into subjects like a school. If students are taught to practice the disciplines, the problems they encounter will force them to integrate knowledge and skills that they have learned in different classes. They will also use organizational skills, interpersonal skills, moral principles, and common sense that they have learned in various settings outside school. Inevitably, also, they will discover where they are ignorant, and they will feel the need to go on learning.

Curriculum is interdisciplinary by degrees and may be enhanced by decisions about the organization of the school. Vars (1987) lists three ways to organize time, teachers, and students for interdisciplinary study: block-time and self-contained classes, interdisciplinary teams, and total staff approach.

Block-Time and Self-Contained Classes

The block-time, self-contained mode imposes few changes on conventional schools. Teachers of each subject are encouraged to develop projects that require students to integrate knowledge and procedures learned in other classes. While studying the Civil War in a history class, for example, students might read the work of Walt Whitman, Stephen Crane, and Ambrose Bierce. They might also relate the physics of projectiles and the chemistry of gunpowder to strategy in Civil War battles. This sort of integration is common in elementary schools, because the same teacher teaches history and English and science—and a lot besides. In middle and high schools, an English teacher and science teacher might be invited as "guest teachers" in the history class. Alternatively, the English curriculum might be arranged to include the literature of the Civil War while U.S. history classes are studying the same period. Extensive integration of the disciplines is virtually impossible within this model, because the student group from one history class will be separated and mixed with other students in other classes. Only a few of these other students will be studying the Civil War at the same time. Some will not be taking a history course at all. To further frustrate integration, teachers of other subjects might decline invitations to connect their disciplines with the Civil War because the connections are not central to the educational objectives of their separate courses.

Interdisciplinary Teams

With the interdisciplinary team approach, the same group of four or five teachers teaches the same one hundred (or so) students. The team is free to pursue interdisciplinary studies because no other students or teachers are involved. If members of the team agree, they can change the daily schedule, combine classes, team teach, or go on a field trip. Even if the team sticks to block-time scheduling and self-contained classrooms, the interdisciplinary possibilities are enhanced. Teachers may develop a thoroughly integrated curriculum around general topics like "global warming." A webbing diagram is a helpful device for conceptualizing and planning integrated units. (National Association for Core Curriculum 1981). The general topic is placed in the center of the web, and various activities, approaches, and assignments that consitute a study of the topic are listed around the outside. Then each teacher on the team selects activities to include in the unit, making sure that all the activities are consistent with the goals and objectives of the curriculum in each subject. The completed diagram (see Fig. 3-2) shows the general topic, the subjects of the curriculum, and activities matched with each subject.

Total Staff Approach

With the total staff approach, the whole school takes a few days to study a single topic. Students in an elementary school, for example, make and fly kites; calculate the dimensions, angles, and areas of kites; read about the history of kites; learn about the aerodynamics of kites; decorate kites; and write about the experience of flying a kite. For one week an independent school, K–12, devotes every class at every level to some aspect of the Renaissance, culminating in a Renaissance Fair, with costumes, booths, music, games, and a parade.

Inner- and Interconnectedness

Although many schools have developed interdisciplinary curricula in these various forms, most students most of the time learn about each discipline separately. We do not recommend a complete reversal of this state of affairs. Each discipline has developed a body of knowledge and a mode of inquiry with logical and empirical innerconnectedness. Students learning science learn to make connections between their experience of objects falling to earth, their observations of the sun and the moon, and theories about the curvature of space. Students learning grammar learn to connect the use of nouns with the use of gerunds and to modify gerunds the way they modify nouns when speaking and writing. Knowledge of the *inter*-connectedness of the disciplines need not threaten the *inner*-connectedness of each discipline. Teachers working in interdisciplinary settings must be careful to maintain the coherence within each discipline.

Teachers planning interdisciplinary units must be sure that activities chosen for inclusion really do advance the goals and objectives of each subject. They might experience some pressure to include activities that suit the theme but may not advance the students' mastery of knowledge and skills that are central to each subject. To include the

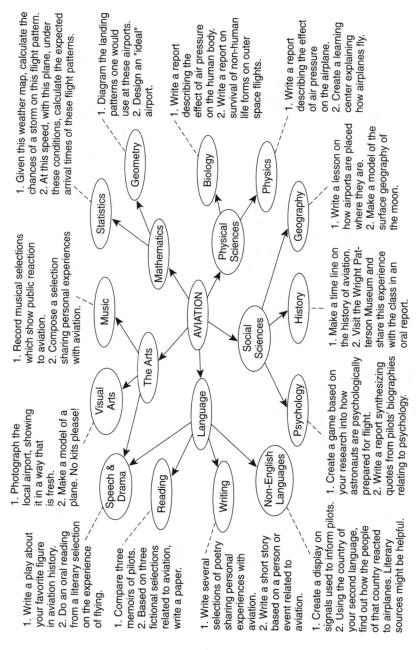

FIGURE 3-2 Webbing Diagram for Unit on Aviation

Source: Cited in Vars 1987; THE CORE TEACHER, Vol. 31, No. 2 (Spring, 1981), p. 5. Reprinted with permission of the National Association for Core Curriculum, Kent State University, Kent, OH 44242-0001.

effects of air pressure on airplanes in a physics course (see Fig. 3-2) seems reasonable, but only if students learn to relate knowledge of air pressure to other concepts and principles they have been learning in physics. Similarly, the art teacher would have to think twice before deciding that a field trip to take pictures at the airport was an appropriate activity in visual arts, and the language arts teacher would have to think twice before asking students to write poems about experiences with aviation. If the geography teacher plans a lesson on "how airports are placed where they are," the lesson should include good geography. However, an understanding of all the factors influencing the location of airports might in itself require an interdisciplinary unit that bursts the seams of a unit on aviation.

The webbing diagram illustrates the possibilities and some of the dangers of an interdisciplinary curriculum. Typically, schools are organized by subject. Even in self-contained classrooms it is not unusual to teach one subject at a time, although many of the elementary teachers we observe help the students make connections between the subjects. In middle schools and high schools, faculty are organized into departments by subject, and students are less likely to make connections between the subjects. Some schools, however, particularly the new middle schools, have begun to organize faculty into teams of teachers who teach the same children, regardless of subject. This practice helps divide large middle schools into smaller, self-contained units that strengthen interpersonal relations among students and teachers (Carnegie Council on Adolescent Development 1989). These interdisciplinary teams also help teachers emphasize the interconnectedness of the disciplines. They meet regularly as a team to discuss children they all teach, and during these meetings they plan interdisciplinary "units" like the "Aviation Unit" (Fig. 3.2). They no longer function as a "department" with all the other teachers of the same subject. This mode of organization seems to emphasize *inter*-disciplinary coherence rather than *inner*-disciplinary coherence. Innerdisciplinary coherence is supported by the teacher's association with other teachers of the same subject, who have taught the children in the past and will teach them in the future. Unless there are safeguards in planning and management of the curriculum, organization by teams instead of departments might disrupt the long-term, gradual accumulation of knowledge and skills.

There is tension between the need to advance student learning in each discipline and the need to integrate the disciplines. We believe that integration occurs when student practitioners tackle complex, real-life problems. Each school must face the need for interdisciplinary learning and make some choices about how to make it happen.

DEEP UNDERSTANDING AND HIGH-ORDER THINKING

"Grasp" is often used as a metaphor for learning. There is nothing wrong with the word itself; "to grasp" means "to hold" or "to take hold of eagerly or greedily." Yet there is something tenuous about "grasp," something desperate. Much of the learning in school is motivated by fear of failure and desire for the social rewards that come with success. Much less is motivated by intrinsic interest in the subject or a strong desire to master the skills of the discipline. Students take notes, develop good work habits, spend hours on homework, attend extra-help sessions, make flash cards, and quiz one another when they review for a test. After the test has been graded, they read the teacher's comments, count the points, and double-check the teacher's arithmetic. How many go back to the test, identify what they did not know, and try to relearn it? Few parents would expect this behavior of a child. It is enough that students had at least a "grasp" of what they were taught.

In *The Unschooled Mind* (1991), Howard Gardner reviews much of the research that has led cognitive science to a new understanding of understanding. Gardner develops a model that explains why understanding is more profound and less easily achieved than knowledge. Understanding is a composite of knowledge, skill, and intuition. Knowledge is acquired and organized in symbolic form, usually language. Students accumulate much of their knowledge through listening and reading. Knowledge is organized into mental models, which interconnect and form the structure of a discipline. Skills, in contrast, are procedures used by experts as they manipulate more tangible material and solve specific problems. Intuition seems to be a sensorimotor way of knowing that begins in early childhood and persists throughout life, often independent of knowledge.

Gardner describes the school experience of lectures, discussions, note cards, and tests as an accumulation of knowledge in symbolic form. The value of this type of learning is that it is relatively quick and inexpensive. Students can read and write and talk about the structure of government without running for office or writing a bill or taking a case to court. They can learn about optics with limited experience of lenses and lasers and sources of light, just enough to permit symbolic representation of the concepts. Students can learn in large groups. Assessment is easy—a matter of counting the number of correct answers on a test, or, at most, grading short essays. Skills are harder to teach than knowledge. It takes a long time to acquire skills, and they depend upon context. To teach skills, the school needs materials, equipment, facilities. Students have to go to places other than the classroom—not just occasionally, as they go on a field trip, but constantly, as a nurse goes to the hospital or a farmer to the barn. Teaching intuition presents even greater problems, because students have the world figured out intuitively before they enter kindergarten. If the wisdom of the ages that they learn in school is to make a difference in how they live their lives, it must meet and modify their deep-seated, personal intuition. Understanding cannot be confined to the classroom. It must do business in the world outside.

In *Education and Learning to Think,* Lauren Resnick (1987) looks at cognitive research from another point of view. Gardner describes "deeper" understanding. Resnick describes "higher"-order thinking:

- Higher-order thinking is *nonalgorithmic.* That is, the path of action is not fully specified in advance.
- Higher-order thinking tends to be *complex.* The total path is not "visible" (mentally speaking) from any single vantage point.
- Higher-order thinking often yields *multiple solutions,* each with costs and benefits, rather than unique solutions.
- Higher-order thinking involves the application of *multiple criteria,* which sometimes conflict with one another.
- Higher-order thinking involves *uncertainty.* Not everything that bears on the task is known.
- Higher-order thinking involves *self-regulation* of the process. We do not recognize higher-order thinking in an individual when someone else "calls the plays" at every step.
- Higher-order thinking involves *imposing meaning,* finding structure in apparent disorder.
- Higher-order thinking is *effortful.* There is considerable mental

work involved in the kinds of elaborations and judgments required.

It is evident that if students are to learn to think at this level, they
will have to do more than pack in huge quantities of knowledge in
symbolic form. No one suggests that it is easy to accumulate, organize,
and remember knowledge, or that knowledge is trivial in the grand
scheme of education. On the contrary, cognitive scientists emphasize
the centrality of knowledge in expert behavior (Glaser 1984). Simply
put, knowledge is not enough. Once we accept this limitation and begin
to develop curriculum to teach students to *do* something *with* their
knowledge, we must move away from educational practices that
seemed right for knowledge but are wrong for understanding and
wrong for the higher levels of thought. The coercive paraphernalia of
quizzes, points, and semester averages that so often replace assessment
is not likely to produce self-regulated learners who set their own goals,
monitor their own progress, and appraise their own strategies. Teaching students to write answers to other people's questions is not usually
the best way to teach them to practice a discipline. Whole-class instruction and uniform assignments based on the reading of textbooks will
not have much effect upon the intuition of each individual student in
a class of twenty or more.

Learning to ride a bicycle is emblematic of education that lasts a
lifetime. Once you can do it, you can always do it. Some school learning
has this quality of endurance. Those who learn how to read and write,
add and subtract, construct an argument, let x equal the unknown,
divide white light into its spectrum, draw a likeness, or sing four-part
harmony enjoy a level of understanding that lasts a lifetime. It is
inconceivable that *everything* learned will be learned forever, but it is
quite conceivable and realistic to expect that *more* of what we teach in
school will endure. Anyone developing curriculum today must decide
which high-priority lessons will be learned at the deepest levels of
understanding. Then, when it is finally agreed that "coverage" and
"grasping" are not the goals of education, the curriculum developer
must deconstruct the familiar arrangement of classrooms, teachers,
textbooks, tests, and homework and reconstruct another concept of
school that may contain the familiar elements, but only if they contribute to deeper understanding and higher-order thinking.

GOALS

Goals are the medium of change. The mission is bedrock. It changes infrequently, and when it changes, the results are cataclysmic. Goals are more like topsoil. This patch or that patch can be improved without major disruption. As teachers and curriculum specialists write and revise the goals of educational programs, they keep the school up to date.

The task of writing program goals is led by department heads or other academic leaders. Teachers in elementary schools might be organized into teams, with a leader who has shown particular strength and interest in the teaching of a particular subject. When ready, each department or team presents its goals to the Curriculum Council.

The council represents diverse interests in the school. In some schools, the Curriculum Council is a committee of department heads. In others, representatives are chosen by various groups who have a say in curriculum—administration, students, parents, and Board, as well as faculty. A Curriculum Council is a board of "academic trustees." The council makes schoolwide academic decisions and fosters communication. Its existence urges administrators to anticipate those circumstances that are likely to affect classes and to seek advice from the council *before* making administrative decisions. Likewise, any department considering a change in curriculum or instructional policy is urged to bring a proposal to the council for discussion. If the change influences curriculum and instruction in other departments or divisions of the school, it should be approved and monitored by the council. The person who chairs the Curriculum Council will be influential. Ideally, he or she will be a respected and capable academic leader, a teacher, department head, or curriculum coordinator.

A well-prepared Curriculum Council will have guidelines and criteria for academic goals and objectives. When department heads and team leaders present newly created goals to the council, they must be prepared to show that these goals follow the guidelines and meet the criteria. We recommend at least the following:

1.   The goals address the needs of the students.
2.   They predict what students are likely to learn.

3. They embody the school's mission.
4. They contribute to a coherent educational experience for students taking courses in several subjects.
5. They are consistent with expertise in a discipline.
6. They are consistent with educational research and the recommendations of professional associations.

There will, of course, be differences of opinion. The needs of students, the implications of research, the merit of recommendations are all subject to debate. Nevertheless, differences must be recognized and resolved—or at least accommodated—in order to stake out larger areas of common ground. The council may ask a department to revise its goals—to share the responsibility for achieving a part of the mission, perhaps, or to set higher standards of achievement. As academic trustees, the members of the Curriculum Council must be "obsessed with quality," in the words of W. Edwards Deming (Rhodes 1990a, 1990b).

Department heads and team leaders, unfortunately, are not always chosen because they can write curriculum, or even because they are capable leaders who can help teachers work as a team. Many department heads are chosen simply because they are senior teachers. If the curriculum is to develop in such a way that it serves the clients identified in the mission, the efforts of teachers and department heads have to be supported with expert leadership. A curriculum coord- inator on the staff should be able to give that support. Most often, support takes the form of listening in meetings, reading drafts, trying to understand the wishes of teachers. Sometimes a facilitator has to help teachers listen to other teachers, students, parents, or admin- istrators, because all have points of view and genuine interests to be served. A facilitator takes notes at meetings and from them creates rough drafts of the goals, objectives, or materials that groups are asked to create. These are returned for review and revision. The curriculum coordinator might have a secretary, who becomes a secretary for teachers writing curriculum. Administrative clout helps. Teachers in some schools cannot make photocopies without permission. Scheduled meeting times, comfortable conference rooms, coffee and cookies, a folder containing handouts, notebook, pen—there are many ways, large and small, to support teachers working on curriculum. The curriculum coordinator helps each team formulate goals, present them to the council, and act on the council's requests for revision.

COURSES AND OTHER PROGRAMS

The departments or teams who write the goals for each subject are in the best position to sketch out the courses and other programs that will enable students to achieve the goals.

The result may be a sequence starting with simple tasks like counting and progressing to more complex tasks like multiplication and division—but educational programs are not required to follow such a sequence. Some tasks may be learned in any order, and students are still able to integrate them. Some complex tasks are so thoroughly integrated that they resist division into parts. It is not useful, for example, to teach students to write by first teaching parts of speech, then simple sentences, then complex sentences, then paragraphs, then whole compositions. Young children are able and eager to write stories and poems long before they are able to recognize and name the parts of speech, and they use perfectly good sentences before they know what a sentence is. Creating sequential curriculum where sequence is not appropriate is one way to frustrate the students' eagerness to learn. When planning courses that lead to educational goals, teachers have to analyze the nature and capabilities of the students as well as the nature of the goals.

Above all, as curriculum develops it must follow the dictates of learning, not the conventions of school. If conversing with native speakers is the best way to learn to speak a second language, then students learning to speak that language should converse with native speakers. If community service raises the self-esteem and aspirations of at-risk students, then community service should become a part of the curriculum for at-risk students. If enjoyment of reading is an educational goal, then the curriculum should include reading that the students enjoy. The best ways to achieve the goals of education are not always obvious, but when they are, it only makes sense to follow them. Occasionally the path is blocked. The school might not have the funds; the city might not have the resources. Schools can be forgiven for not attempting the impossible. Doing everything possible, however, might entail a different schedule, a different type of test, a different role for teachers, a different contract. We are inclined to say that curriculum development *must* challenge the conventional way of doing things in schools. We are not persuaded that teaching one subject for a period of forty-five minutes to a group of twenty to thirty students in a classroom is the best way to teach everything. It may not be the best way to teach anything.

Small groups of teachers working on curriculum tend to become isolated as they develop a common understanding distinct from other teachers and other groups. They specialize, focus on a problem, read about it, study the research, adopt a common point of view, and become advocates. While group identity, ownership, and pride are highly desirable, everyone concerned with the quality of the whole school must be alert to the dangers of fragmentation. Preliminary reports to the Curriculum Council—outlines, sketches, and speculations presented for discussion—help the faculty to see the whole as they work on the parts. If learning a second language really is easier for students who know the grammar of their first language, then English teachers have a role in teaching Anglophones a second language. If mathematics teachers want their students to use algebra, science teachers can help. When children write haiku in English classes, they might understand the concept of economy in Japanese drawings. It is not sufficient that English teachers say, "We don't teach grammar." Or that science teachers say, "We have no time for algebra in science." Or that art teachers say, "We do pumpkins in October." The council and the curriculum coordinator must encourage interdisciplinary thinking. The time to make the connections and to get teachers to cross boundaries is in the early stages of curriculum development, when plans are in flux and group identity is pliable.

Individual teachers and interdisciplinary teams take pieces of the whole and pursue them in greater detail. We talk of "courses and other programs" because the concept of school as a series of "courses" may exclude useful alternatives. These might include apprenticeships, investigations, retreats, independent projects, exhibitions, and so-called "extracurricular" activities as well as teaching and learning in conventional classrooms.

Curriculum development as done by teachers is different from curriculum development as done by specialists who work for publishers and learning centers. Curriculum specialists do not teach five classes a day. Nor do they know their customers by name. They learn the wishes and whims of a huge audience through market analysis and demographics. They write, evaluate, revise, and package texts, workbooks, teachers' guides, and supplementary materials. Their resources far exceed those available to teachers working in schools. Teachers cannot duplicate the design and detail of published curriculum and should not try. The curriculum they type and photocopy is the context in which glitzier published materials are used. If teams of teachers do their job well, students will make connections between one set of published materials and another set, from textbook to lab manual, from documentary film to interactive video disk, from one teacher's materials to another teacher's materials, from last year's materials to this year's materials.

Much has been written about the process of selecting educational materials (e.g., Farr and Tulley 1985; Bailey 1988; Tyson and Woodward 1989). Compared to the huge number of hours that students will spend poring over textbooks that are published in sets and span years of schoolwork, teachers spend very little time choosing materials. Perhaps selection committees make hasty decisions because these are the only decisions they are asked to make. Teachers who have hammered out goals for each subject they teach, who have planned a sequence of objectives from year to year, who chart the progress of their students, who develop original materials to blend with published materials, who assess student achievement of all the learning objectives—these teachers will be very picky before they let published materials into their classrooms. They will know that any curriculum, purchased or homemade, has to be consistent with the goals of the school, the objectives of the course, the capabilities of the students, and the methods used in the classroom. Well-informed teachers cut and paste an effective curriculum using parts of published materials, modifying and supplementing other parts, filling in and making do as their budget allows.

Teachers working together in a single school will enjoy more freedom from bureaucratic constraints than teams working for a large district. The Pittsburgh Public Schools, for example, appoints a "Panel of Experts" to review each proposal for new curriculum. Curriculum writers—selected according to guidelines—report to the panel midway through the process of development and submit their final product to the panel. If the product does not meet "Action Plan Standards," it goes back to the writers for revision and resubmission. In contrast, a teacher developing a new course in an independent school needs only the department head's approval—and maybe not even that. Because resources are diffuse when divided among individual schools and concentrated when spent on centralized projects, the districtwide curriculum will probably be thicker and, from a theoretical point of view, "better" than the school-specific curriculum. But the best curriculum cannot affect student achievement if it is not used. And its benefits do not materialize if it is used by teachers who do not understand it, do not believe in it, and do not adapt it appropriately for specific groups of students. Districtwide curriculum, then, must be supported by districtwide inservice. This is especially true of "state-of-the-art" curriculum developed by experts, who, by definition, have knowledge and abilities that teachers have not had a chance to acquire. Centralization tends to leave classroom teachers on the periphery. As schools become more independent through site-based management, more of the funds and more of the expertise available to the central office must be channeled directly to teams of teachers working in the context of a single school. If teachers grow along with the curriculum they develop, they do not have to be brought up to speed through subsequent inservice.

The Curriculum Council and the curriculum coordinator counter the isolationist tendencies of teachers. They bring teachers from different subjects together when teams are formed, and they bring teams together for cross-fertilization. Teams write the objectives for each course, locate and evaluate student materials, consult with experts, identify and try out promising techniques, devise appropriate methods of assessment, and, it is hoped, enjoy the camaraderie and the satisfaction of shared problem solving.

SCOPE-AND-SEQUENCE CHART AND COURSE DESCRIPTIONS

After mission and goals come a scope-and-sequence chart, a complete set of course or program descriptions, and guidelines to explain the options available to individual students (see Fig. 3-3).

Curriculum at this organizational level serves several purposes. It requires teachers to collaborate and to make important decisions. It connects methods, materials, and assessments to educational goals. It brings coherence and purpose to each student's experience of school. And it communicates the school's priorities. Because these organizational documents are available to everyone interested in the school, they should meet high standards of clarity, style, and appearance. Although teachers need not be burdened with the design and editing of school publications, they should know how the products of their labor will be laid out, printed, and distributed before they hand them over to administrators and editors.

Anything too elaborate invariably results in waste. Curriculum

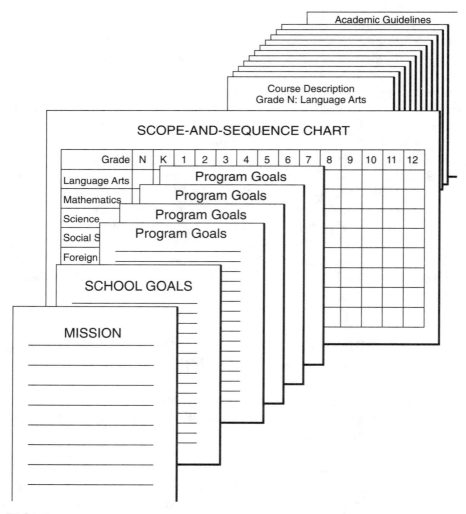

FIGURE 3-3 Documents for Managing the Curriculum

controlled by teachers evolves rapidly—so rapidly, in fact, that the Curriculum Council and curriculum coordinator will be hard pressed to manage the process of change. Printed documents are soon out of date. Some plans work, others do not, and all can be improved upon implementation. Although the curriculum is printed and made available to the community, it should be reviewed, revised, and reprinted every year. If its components are too detailed, if it is not reviewed continually and revised continually, then neglected stacks of paper accumulate on bottom shelves of backroom cupboards. Disjunctive change replaces curriculum management. Programs develop separately, evaluation becomes sporadic, teachers do their own thing, and the school becomes incoherent. If, on the other hand, the documents used for managing the curriculum are general and brief, they are easily revised. As innovations come before the Curriculum Council and the curriculum is changed, the curriculum coordinator keeps a record of the changes. Once a year, the documents are brought up to date.

The scope-and-sequence chart is an index to the course descriptions. It extracts the topics of course objectives and shows the sequence in which students encounter those topics as they progress through school. A whole-school scope-and-sequence chart has limited use, however. It is relatively easy to represent the content of courses in a sequence of topics, but not so easy to represent attitudes, dispositions, and skills. Course content differs from grade to grade. Science, for example, is often divided into courses like Earth Science, Life Science, Physics, Chemistry, and so on. These courses are further divided into topics of study like Oceans, Ecology, Plants, Animals, Energy, Matter. Each science course has different topics. Words used to describe attitudes and dispositions, on the other hand, are much the same at all grade levels. A scope-and-sequence chart for science might list "Curiosity" and "Lab Skills" at every grade level. Because scope-and-sequence charts emphasize sequence, unchanging goals like "Curiosity" in science or "Enjoyment of Reading" in language arts are often omitted. Nevertheless, while a scope-and-sequence chart cannot tell the whole story, it can function as an index.

An inquiring reader will find much of interest in the school's scope-and-sequence chart. When do students start a second language? When do they start algebra? Is there a core curriculum for all students? Are college-level courses available to seniors? Will students learn about their own ethnic culture? Are the sciences separated or integrated? Is there any evidence of interdisciplinary coordination?

Anyone interested in more detail should be able to turn to a set of course descriptions and find the same topics in the same sequence as those listed on the scope-and-sequence chart. If the scope-and-sequence chart is organized by subject and grade, course descriptions should be organized according to the same system. If "Fourth-Grade Science" on the scope-and-sequence chart includes "Earth Science," "Weather," and "Climate," then "Earth Science," "Weather," and "Climate" will appear in the course description of "Fourth-Grade Science." If the scope-and-sequence chart shows that "Tenth-Grade English" consists of "Creative Writing," "Literary Analysis," and "Argument," then the course description for "Tenth-Grade English" will explain the whats, whys, and wherefores of these same three topics. This degree of clarity might seem too obvious to belabor. Nevertheless, when we visit schools and ask to see the curriculum, invariably we are given stapled stacks of paper, some thin, some thick, some crisp and white, some dusty and yellow, with no apparent organizing principle. Someone might say, "Let me know if anything is missing." If anything were missing, how would we know?

The course or program descriptions may be brief. Since it is convenient to have each course or program on a separate sheet, we favor a two-page limit, front and back of a single sheet. We recommend four sections in each description: Objectives, Materials, Methods, and Means of Assessment, recognizing that schools might add other information to meet other needs. Because we are interested in curriculum management, we would want to scan the objectives of all courses in a single subject to see if a student who has taken a sequence of courses would achieve the goals for the department or subject. We would compare the objectives and means of assessment of each course to see that they correspond. We would check to see that the methods a teacher describes are appropriate for the specified objectives. Course descriptions have many uses. Students and their advisors refer to them when selecting courses of study. Teachers perusing them learn how the courses that they teach are related to other courses their students have taken, are taking, or will take. Parents learn about the courses in which their children are enrolled. Above all, they enable the school to monitor and manage a coherent curriculum.

The documents we have described so far—mission, school goals, department or subject goals, scope-and-sequence chart, and course descriptions—might seem cumbersome to readers in certain independent schools, where the "official" curriculum is a list of course titles published in the school catalogue. To readers familiar with public schools, the degree of coherence we recommend might seem novel, but the bulk of the documents will seem slight in comparison to actual practice. To all readers, we say: Documentation of the school's curriculum, like everything else, should contribute to the school's mission. The documents must be developed in sufficient detail to ensure quality, coherence, and unity of purpose, but not in so much detail that revision is discouraged. Continual evaluation produces continual change, and teachers must have the freedom to tinker with their courses, as long as the tinkering serves the mission of the school. We cannot sympathize with the compulsive curriculum coordinator who protests: "Don't mess up my nice neat scope-and-sequence chart!" Word processing and desktop publishing make revision easy.

THE TEACHER'S CURRICULUM

There is another layer to the curriculum that does not go on display— although it is not kept secret, either. This is the level at which teacher and student interact daily in the classroom. At this level it does not matter that the lesson plans, materials, and handouts in one classroom are different from those in another classroom. Different classes, different teachers, different students, different materials—uniformity would be quite inappropriate. Some teachers write everything down on paper, everything that they will do and everything their students will do. Other teachers work effectively from outlines. Some teachers create and write their own activities, lab manuals, worksheets, everything needed for whole units of instruction. Other teachers use only pub- lished materials, cementing them together with lessons they form in their heads and can change in an instant. State regulations for curriculum differ, as do district regulations. In independent schools, where few regulations apply, we find as much, but no more variety.

Regardless of regulations, what is sound practice? What should all teachers have in their possession as they start to teach a new course? To ensure that all courses are well designed and that teachers have all the necessary resources, the Curriculum Council should provide teachers and curriculum writers with a set of guidelines for developing the "Teacher's Curriculum." The council might reasonably expect all new programs to meet certain specifications. These will differ from school to school, since the relative degree of freedom and accountability afforded to teachers is a salient characteristic of school culture. The list of specifications suggested in Figure 3-4 might be revised to suit the needs of a specific school.

A Place to Begin

It is a comforting fiction to think of curriculum as a well-worn route from point A to point B. No two students go through a course by the

---

Guidelines for New Programs

Each proposal should contain:

1. A description of students for whom the program is intended
2. Educational needs met by the program
3. A rationale explaining educational philosophy, special facilities or resources required, and any unique or unusual features of the program
4. The number of teachers required, their proposed duties, and necessary qualifications
5. Comparison with alternative programs and reasons for selecting the proposed program
6. Objectives of the program
7. A summary of the program explaining organization, sequence, and relationship of units
8. Objectives, materials, activities, and assessment for each phase or unit of instruction
9. Methods for recording, measuring, and reporting student achievement
10. Means of assessing student achievement of the program objectives.

FIGURE 3-4   Specifications for Programs Submitted to the Curriculum Council for Approval

same route, or end up in the same place, or arrive at their destinations at the same time. Nevertheless, an educational program is supposed to make a difference between what students can do at the beginning and what they can do at the end. Some measure of their individual capabilities at the beginning is essential, but often neglected. A curriculum intended for students with a disposition to learn will be quite wrong for students who have little interest in learning. One that assumes a wealth of prior knowledge will be wrong for students who lack the necessary background. A well-designed curriculum, therefore, will include a description of the students for whom it is intended. Such a description will serve three ends. It will encourage the authors to identify and meet the needs of those students they have targeted as clients. It will help teachers using the curriculum decide whether or not it is right for the students who appear in their classrooms (see following section on "Adoption"). And it will help teachers fill in the background for students who are not quite ready to begin.

An End

Objectives are the end of the curriculum. Even if the objectives of a program set high expectations for most students, they are minimal insofar as they are expectations for all students. No one can ever know, or predict, everything that students will learn in an educational program—and some of what they learn might be undesirable as well as unintended. Nevertheless, students have a huge capacity for learning, and unintended outcomes can be just as important and just as valuable as intended outcomes. Flexible teachers are alert to the unexpected and adjust their grading policies to reward students who learn something other than the planned objectives. Objectives are a general destination, but every student learns something personal along the way. Of course, some students go further than others. Some achieve at levels far beyond the objectives of the course. The curriculum used by teachers should state the "official" objectives, yet recognize and encourage unintended outcomes of both types: personal enrichment and stunning achievement.

A Design That Connects the Beginning and the End

Between the first day of instruction and the last, something is learned, but not all at once. All the components of the course add up, bit by bit,

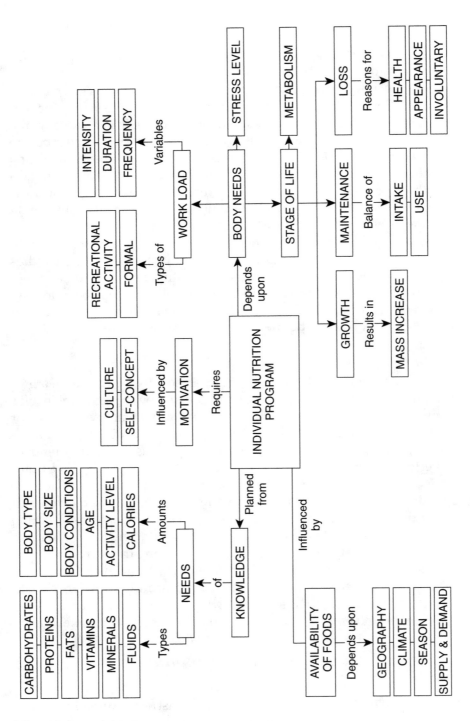

FIGURE 3-5 Example of Cognitive Map for Unit on Nutrition

to the final objectives. The curriculum helps the teacher and the students organize and consolidate countless bits and pieces of learning. Curriculum developers sometimes use a cognitive map, also called a "concept map" and a "semantic net" (see Fig. 3-5 for an example) to plan a coherent sequence of lessons (Cliburn 1986; Posner and Rudnitsky 1986). Cognitive maps show how concepts are related to one another. The content of one unit or an entire course can be represented in the form of concept maps.

Anyone constructing such a map to plan a unit or a course is confronted with choices and must decide which concepts are central and which are peripheral, which relationships are essential and which, if any, might be omitted. The first step is to list all the concepts within a given body of knowledge. Each concept is summarized in a word or phrase on an index card or "stickum" note. These cards or "stickums" are arranged so that interrelationships among the concepts are suggested by proximity and symmetry. Words or phrases written on lines drawn between the concepts further clarify the relationships. Almost certainly, especially if several people collaborate, alternatives will arise. The map will undergo much revision as some concepts are omitted, others are added, and the layout is rearranged. As sections of the map are assigned to lessons or units in an emerging curriculum, further revision almost certainly will occur.

This stage of development, when the cognitive map and units of instruction are almost complete but not finished, is a good time for consultation with subject specialists. Curriculum developers need a chance to explain the map and the sequence of units and to ask if their arrangement is consistent with what is known and recommended in the discipline. In its final form the map will help teachers see the coherence of the course. As they adapt the curriculum to the needs of various groups, the map will help teachers preserve an essential core. If several teachers in the same school are using a curriculum, a cognitive map will help them discuss the course content and permissible variations. Cognitive maps, needless to say, are also teaching devices that help students as much as they help teachers and curriculum developers (Cliburn 1986; White and Gunstone 1992; see also Chapters 2 and 5).

Objectives for each unit of a course are derived by analyzing the course objectives, remembering that some objectives are achieved through an accumulation of subtasks and others through repetition of the whole. Each unit, therefore, might include some combination of knowledge (a section of the cognitive map), one or more subtasks, and one or more of the indivisible whole tasks. Affective objectives tend to be organic and indivisible rather than divisible and sequential. If students at the end of the course are to value what they have learned, they must value what they are learning along the way. If they are expected to go on learning voluntarily after the course has ended, they must learn voluntarily as the course progresses.

A student who attains all the objectives of all the units will attain the objectives of the course. The curriculum should provide teachers with a description of each unit, including materials that have been provided, recommended supplementary materials, and modes of instruction suggested by the unit objectives. Some programs might not be conceived in units. Skills courses, for example, might be conceived as a series of projects in which students practice the integrated skills and procedures of an art or discipline. The teacher's curriculum for these programs should describe the skills that students must learn in order to achieve the final objectives. If the teacher is expected to coach students while they practice and perform, then the curriculum should explain the teacher's role, with examples and illustrations pertinent to specific skills.

The Means of Assessment

No matter how the curriculum is organized, it should describe the means of assessing student achievement. If the curriculum is a series of units, there will be some form of assessment at the end of each unit. This assessment is formative. When students do not perform as well as expected, teachers must make some adjustment in the way they have been teaching, and students must make a complementary adjustment in the way they have been learning. A well-constructed curriculum will help teachers recognize satisfactory performance and formulate alternative strategies if needed. In the end there is a summative assessment. Teachers must assess student achievement of all the objectives of the program. If a program purports to raise self-esteem, the teacher should know how self-esteem is assessed. If it purports to teach the scientific method, the teacher must know how the scientific method is assessed. The teacher's repertoire of instruments, however, might not include the best means of assessment for every objective, especially if the program is new. Curriculum writers, therefore, have an obligation to solve these problems of assessment in advance and to help the teacher develop satisfactory procedures.

A Dialogue with the Teacher

A teacher does what a teacher can to serve the needs of the students. If they fail to understand, the teacher backs up, regroups, and tries again. If the students cannot make leaps of understanding, the teacher puts down stepping-stones to help them along. If they lack interest, the teacher looks for a way to kindle interest. If they surge ahead, the teacher improvises another challenge. Ideally, the teacher's adaptations and additions, large or small, are in sync with all the other components of the curriculum. A well-constructed curriculum speaks to the teacher, explains how the curriculum has been constructed, and invites the teacher to adapt it to the needs of the students. This rationale is the authors' dialogue with the teacher. If the curriculum includes a phone number that teachers can call for advice, so much the better.

ADOPTION

An assistant superintendent for curriculum might feel satisfied when an elaborate curriculum including objectives, guidelines for instruction, student materials, supplementary materials, instruments for assessment, all endorsed by a panel of experts, is in the hands of teachers who have been thoroughly "inserviced." The district's finest teachers may have worked on the program. The secrets of their success have been analyzed, refined, and written into the curriculum. Master teachers have teamed with consultants to conduct workshops for all the other teachers. Everything a school district is supposed to do has been done. In all probability, the cutting-edge curriculum will work at least as well as any other curriculum in the district has ever worked. But will it work in every classroom? Will it be evaluated in every classroom? How soon after implementation will it be evaluated? Within the first month? And if in any one classroom it is not working as planned, what then?

Perhaps no one could have predicted that the curriculum would fail in certain classrooms. Perhaps, on the other hand, the people who could have made the prediction were never asked. We know from experience that many schools have populations of students for whom nothing ever seems to work. Was the new curriculum created with these students in mind? At a recent workshop for middle school language arts teachers, we asked, "What is your greatest challenge? Where do you need help?" One teacher replied, "Keeping kids in their seats long enough to read something." Another replied, "Getting the kids to come to class." The materials that these teachers asked their students to read and the methods they used to teach their students to read better were perfectly defensible—just the sort of reading instruction that any informed language arts teacher would recommend for middle school students. But they were not working. And the new wrinkles introduced at the workshop probably would not work, either, since they were intended for students who come to school and sit agreeably in their seats These two teachers and their principals probably could have predicted before the year even began that the reading curriculum would not work in some of their classrooms.

We recommend that "adoption" become a formal stage of curriculum development. In this stage the teachers responsible for implementing a curriculum examine it carefully—even if they themselves are its authors—and appraise its appropriateness for each class they teach. We would require teachers to write a report to their principal, explaining why the curriculum is or is not right for their students. If the teachers favor adoption and the principal endorses their recommendation, the curriculum is adopted. If any teacher does not favor adoption or has reservations about adoption, then the teacher and the principal have a problem to resolve. It might be resolved "in house," or it might challenge the resources of the whole community. Requiring a simple statement that says, "This curriculum is right for the students in this classroom" would make it harder for school administrators and school boards to ignore problems that teachers cannot ignore.

SUMMARY

Curriculum development is guided by the school's mission. If the school does not have a mission, or if the mission is obsolete, then curriculum development begins with the mission. The mission is manifest in goals for every program and objectives for every course in the school. As teachers and administrators revise their goals and objectives, they should learn about relevant research and recommended practices. Current trends in education include reduced content to enable more learning, the practice of the disciplines, interdisciplinary connections, and curriculum aimed at deeper understanding and higher-order thinking. A Curriculum Council oversees and integrates the work of teams developing curriculum in various subjects. The council is chaired by a teacher or curriculum coordinator, whose administrative position and influence support the efforts of teachers. This is the person who has primary responsibility for maintaining and updating the documents of the curriculum: the mission, school goals, program goals, and objectives for every course.

The written curriculum used by teachers is more detailed than the documents used for managing the school's curriculum. The teacher's curriculum will probably contain materials prepared professionally and distributed by publishers. Teachers create the context in which these materials are used, adding activities, assignments, and supplementary materials that give coherence to the course. The teacher's curriculum takes many forms, since every classroom contains a unique group of students with a unique teacher. However, all curricula at the classroom level should have certain features, including a place to begin and a place to end, a design that connects the two, and appropriate methods of assessment. Each curriculum should be adopted specifically for each group of students. We recommend a written "adoption" statement signed by the classroom teacher and the principal. If one or the other cannot in all conscience sign a statement that says the curriculum is appropriate for a group of students, then every effort should be made to develop a curriculum that meets with approval.

REFERENCES

American Council on the Teaching of Foreign Languages. (1986). *ACTFL Proficiency Guidelines*. Hastings-on-Hudson, N.Y.: American Council on the Teaching of Foreign Languages.

Bailey, G. D. (1988). "Guidelines for Improving the Textbook/Material Selection Process." *NASSP Bulletin* 72:506, 87–92.

Carnegie Council on Adolescent Development. (1989). *Turning Points: Preparing American Youth for the 21st Century*. New York: The Carnegie Corporation.

Cliburn, J. W. Jr. (1986). "Using Concept Maps to Sequence Instructional Materials." *Journal of College Science Teaching* 15:4, 377–379.

di Pietro, R. (1981). "Discourse and Real-Life Roles in the ESL Classroom." *TESOL Quarterly* 15:1, 27–33.

Drucker, P. F. (1990). *Managing the Nonprofit Organization: Practices and Principles.* New York: Harper Collins.

Farr, R., and M. A. Tulley. (1985). "Do Adoption Committees Perpetuate Mediocre Textbooks?" *Phi Delta Kappan* 66:7, 467–471.

Gardner, H. (1991). *The Unschooled Mind.* New York: Basic Books.

Glaser, R. (1984). "Education and Thinking: The Role of Knowledge." *American Psychologist* 39:2, 93–104.

Herriot, J. (1972). *All Creatures Great and Small.* New York: St. Martin's Press.

Hirsch, B. (1989). *Languages of Thought.* New York: The College Board.

Holt, T. (1990). *Thinking Historically: Narrative, Imagination, and Understanding.* New York: The College Board.

Independent School Management. (1991). *Ideas and Perspectives* 16:2, 5–7.

Mathematical Sciences Board of Education. (1989). *Everybody Counts: A Report to the Nation on the Future of Mathematics Education.* Washington, D.C.: National Academy Press.

Molinsky, S. J., and B. Bliss. (1988). *Express Ways: English for Communication.* Englewood Cliffs, N.J.: Prentice-Hall.

National Association for Core Curriculum. (1981). *The Core Teacher* 31:2, 5.

National Association of Secondary School Principals. (1987). *Developing a Mission Statement for the Middle Level School.* Reston, Va.: National Association of Secondary School Principals.

National Council for the Social Studies. (1989). "Report of the Ad Hoc Committee on Scope and Sequence." *Social Education* 53:6, 375–376.

National Council of Teachers of Mathematics. (1989). *Curriculum and Evaluation Standards for School Mathematics.* Reston, Va.: National Council of Teachers of Mathematics.

Nebgen, M. (1991). "The Key to Success in Strategic Planning Is Communication." *Educational Leadership.* 48:7, 26–28.

Newmann, F. M. (1988). "Higher-Order Thinking in High School Social Studies: An Analysis of Classrooms." (Report). National Center on Effective Secondary Schools. Madison: University of Wisconsin.

Omaggio, A. (1986). *Teaching Language in Context.* Boston: Heinle and Heinle.

O'Neil, J. (1993). "On the New Standards Project: A Conversation with Lauren Resnick and Warren Simmons." *Educational Leadership* 50:5, 17–21.

Posner, G. J., and A. N. Rudnitsky. (1986). *Course Design* (3rd ed.). New York: Longman.

Resnick, L. B. (1987). *Education and Learning to Think.* Washington, D.C.: National Academy Press.

Resnick, L. B., and D. Resnick. (1992). "Report on New Standards Tasks and

Protocols for Piloting Project 2.1: Alternative Approaches to Assessment in Mathematical Problem Solving." Center for Research on Evaluation, Standards, and Student Testing, Los Angeles; Learning Research and Development Center, University of Pittsburgh, Pa. (ERIC Document ED348380).

Rhodes, L. A. (November 1990a). "Why Quality Is Within Our Grasp . . . If We Reach." *The School Administrator,* 31–34.

Rhodes, L. A. (December 1990b). "Beyond Your Beliefs: Quantum Leaps Toward Quality Schools." *The School Administrator,* 23–26.

Sambs, C. E., and R. Schenkat. (1990). "One District Learns about Restructuring." *Educational Leadership* 47:7, 72–75.

Silver, E. A., J. Kilpatrick, and B. Schlesinger. (1990). *Thinking Through Mathematics.* New York: The College Board.

Spady, W. G. (1984). *Organizing and Delivering Curriculum for Maximum Impact.* (ERIC Document ED249579).

Stone, S. C. (1987). *Strategic Planning for Independent Schools.* Boston: National Association of Independent Schools.

Tyson, H., and A. Woodward. (1989). *Educational Leadership* 47:3, 14–17.

Vars, G. F. (1987). *Interdisciplinary Teaching in the Middle Grades.* Columbus, Ohio: National Middle Schools Association.

Vickery, T. R. (1985). *Excellence in an Outcomes-Driven School District.* (ERIC Document ED293913).

Vickery, T. R. (1987). "Evaluating a Mastery Learning High School." Paper presented at the Annual Meeting of the American Educational Research Association, Washington, D.C. (ERIC Document ED293812).

Vickery, T. R. (1988). "Learning from an Outcomes-Driven School District." *Educational Leadership* 45:5, 52–56.

Vickery, T. R. (1990). "A Workable Model for Total School Improvement." *Educational Leadership* 47:7, 67–70.

White, R., and R. Gunstone. (1992). *Probing Understanding.* New York: Falmer Press.

Wolf, D. P. (1988). *Reading Reconsidered.* New York: The College Board.

4

DEVELOPING THE REST OF THE SCHOOL

EXTRACURRICULAR ACTIVITIES

The use of the word "academics" shows that other important things go on in a school. If a principal at a PTA meeting said, "Academics come first at this school, " most people in the audience would understand what was meant. Few, we suspect, would wonder why the principal had said something so obvious. Academics do not always come first. The priority of classes is challenged almost every day in almost every school. In order to go to an away game and play before dark, the soccer team has to leave early, taking students out of classes. In the last week before the performance, the director of the musical demands extra rehearsal time, and star performers are released from classes virtually on request. An announcement in their mailboxes tells teachers that classes will be cancelled for a special assembly on AIDS. School stops for a Halloween parade and costume competition. Seniors are excused the day before and the day after the prom. Members of the band are pulled out of classes for music lessons. Students going to the Model United Nations miss three days of school. The glee club goes on tour for a week. There are countless examples, even in schools where "academics come first."

Athletics are a fairly constant threat to academic priority. The very sound of the word "academics" in juxtaposition with "athletics" suggests an equality, as if they were two sides of a coin. Everyone says that academics should come first, but a naive observer in a typical high school might think otherwise. Athletes wear parts of their uniforms to class. Banners inside and outside the school pronounce the school's support of its teams. Hype before a championship game warrants a special assembly in the auditorium. Hundreds, maybe thousands, of spectators come to watch the games. Newspapers report the scores. Athletes receive magnificent trophies and accolades at traditional banquets. At the start of almost every class a teacher chats with athletes about sports. In times of hardship, athletic programs are rarely sacrificed to ensure the quality of academic programs, but class size increases and arts programs are cut. Students do not protest when athletic obligations take them out of school. Teachers protest, but the practice continues anyway. The director of athletics holds a powerful position in most high schools. Sometimes, unfortunately, there is no "director of academics" to lead the school to academic triumphs.

The conflict between classes and other activities shows how important these other activities have become. Teachers who hate to release their students from class might characterize extracurricular activities as "playtime," suspecting that students use the activities as an excuse to avoid less desirable alternatives, like "work." No doubt there is some truth to this assertion—it is hard to deny when one sees students pack up their books and leave class with a self-satisfied smirk. Nevertheless, the appeal of idleness cannot account for the satisfaction students find in sports, plays, publications, and clubs. A veteran English teacher who also coached soccer in his first years of teaching told us about a twenty-fifth reunion he attended recently. A little group of middle-aged men, including a recording engineer, the owner of a riding school, a reporter, and a physician, gathered around to tell him how important he had been in their lives, but not as an English teacher—as a soccer coach. We overheard another English teacher in a department meeting telling his incredulous colleagues about a student who had written five drafts of an article before turning it in to the school newspaper. Social studies teachers at a boarding school not known for its academic excellence reported that fifteen students spent an entire weekend in the library, preparing for their first regional meeting of the Model United Nations. No social studies class had ever inspired that sort of effort. Earl Reum, who coordinated student activities in Denver, Colorado, for thirty years, maintains that a full, high-quality activities program is an effective deterrent to drugs and gangs (National Association of

Secondary School Principals 1992). If for no other reason than that they are very important to students, extracurricular activities should be examined carefully.

They are too important in the school to leave to chance. Over a period of years, certain activities might flourish for a while and then languish for lack of interest. One student told us that his club met only once one year, and that was for the yearbook picture. The survival of extracurricular activities depends upon natural selection. While responsiveness to student interest is a virtue of extracurricular activities, unregulated competition for funding and support might actually be discriminatory. Activities have educational purposes. Reum claims that among other things they teach students to be responsible, to follow directions, to present themselves in public, and to present their ideas clearly and articulately—all "employable" skills that will serve them well in the future. But how many students receive these benefits? And how are activities started? What about the students who do not belong to any activity? Do they not deserve the opportunities that extracurricular activities afford? There may be other activities, not presently offered, that are just right for them, but who would know unless someone takes the trouble to understand their needs?

A study of migrant students in Texas (Springstead et al. 1981) showed that in spite of a huge drop-out problem, migrant students tend to like school, like their teachers, and like other students in the school. In general, they think that their schools are fair to Mexican-Americans and fair to migrant students. But few migrant students enjoy academic success, and few participate in extracurricular activities. The ASPIRA Association (1990) reports that 10 percent of all Hispanics drop out of school, a rate that remained stable for the ten years between 1978 and 1988, during which time the drop-out rate of all other students declined from 6.6 to 4.4 percent. Working primarily in Eastern states, ASPIRA attempts to counter the problem by organizing clubs to address the needs of Hispanic students. Most of these clubs are based in schools, although some are based in other community centers. ASPIRA Association's mission is to develop future Hispanic leaders. ASPIRA clubs emphasize the opportunities available to Hispanic students, not their deficiencies. Club members are *Aspirantes*. Clubs offer workshops, seminars, and discussion groups to develop academic and leadership skills. In addition, they provide individual counseling, family counseling, and college counseling. An internship program enables members to work in government and business under the guidance of mentors. Counselors helping launch a new club teach the members how to set group goals, hold elections, follow parliamentary procedures, and organize debates. Elected officers represent their clubs at ASPIRA headquarters in Washington D.C. The school dropout rate for *Aspirantes* is half the rate for other Hispanics. Ninety-eight percent of the students in the Public Policy internship program go to college. An ASPIRA representative attributed the success of ASPIRA clubs to two main reasons: counselors who understand the Hispanic community and a philosophy that emphasizes the potential of young Hispanics.

Clubs like those organized by ASPIRA are not beyond the capabilities of schools. Each school must look at patterns of enrollment in extracurricular activities and wonder if there are other activities that should be offered. When significant minorities decline to participate, it is time to do something. They might be losing academically as well as socially.

THE CO-CURRICULUM

Students are highly motivated to work and learn in the context of extracurricular activities. Educators who recognize the power of extracurricular activities and use it to advantage are likely to speak of the "co-curriculum." Co-curricular activities have an educational purpose. They are really a part of the curriculum, but the learning that takes place in the co-curriculum is so different from the learning we normally associate with the curriculum that a separate term is appropriate. Besides, if students thought that we were absorbing activities they cherish into the curriculum, they might rebel. So "co-curriculum" is a convenient term. It suggests that the co-curriculum supports the curriculum without being a part of it. It is possible that schools of the future will abandon the distinction when the curriculum and the co-curriculum are closer in methodology and effect. Now, however, they are separate, but closely related. We suggest that anyone examining the co-curriculum begin by making a catalogue of the various activities offered to students. We have listed some of the categories, along with questions that might be asked in a self-evaluation.

Athletics

Interscholastic competition is not a major concern in elementary schools. Younger children tend to play games outside the school in leagues organized by community groups. Community programs are less plentiful for older children, however, and by the time they reach high school, students depend upon schools for the facilities and organization needed for team sports. Nevertheless, there are many athletic programs available to young people in urban youth clubs, and those whose parents can afford the membership fees play lifetime sports, such as tennis and golf, in private clubs. Americans love sports, and children play sports wherever and whenever they get the chance. For many, the main chance comes at school.

Athletic programs have a symbiotic relationship with their host schools. No matter how the program has evolved, it seems to be necessary just the way it is. Although the purpose of athletics is often questioned—usually when a team is exceptionally good or exceptionally bad—the answer is soon forgotten. Perhaps athletics are meant to teach physical fitness, discipline, teamwork, leadership, and sportsmanship. But we have never met an athletic director who assesses student achievement of any of these goals. Athletic directors, coaches, players, and fellow students all want their teams to win—quite justifiably, since contests in which the competitors are not trying to win are ludicrous. Achievement of every other goal is compromised if it does not contribute to the primary purpose of winning. Participation of large numbers of students is widely valued, but the weakest players sit on the bench until the game is clearly won or clearly lost. Team leaders are highly prized, but only insofar as they contribute to winning. Sportsmanship is widely valued, but foul play, foul language, and fights occur in interscholastic sports when competition is fierce, even though coaches and school administrators publicly discourage such behavior. The rules and guidelines of interscholastic athletic associations are a necessary restraint on rampant competitiveness. Athletics seem to have a life and logic of their own.

Surely, athletics are subject to control from within the school. Must a program cater only to the best athletes? If athletics benefit some students, why not all students? If fitness is a goal, are the unfit allowed to participate? Since relatively few students excel in the "major" sports like basketball or football, are there equal opportunities and just as much encouragement for those who want to practice water sports, or racquet sports, or noncompetitive sports? And if large amounts of money are spent on interscholastic competition, are equal amounts of money spent on other pursuits that are just as worthy, such as starting a business, parenting, money management, or community service?

Clubs

Clubs come into being when enough students want to participate, when teachers and administrators feel that the proposed activity is worthwhile, and when all the necessary resources are available. Clubs fail, or fail to get started, when any of these conditions is not met. A necessary resource is a teacher to sponsor the club. Even if a teacher is interested and willing, the principal might not have the funds to pay that teacher for taking on an extra duty. If the teachers' agreement with the school requires extra pay for extra work, then teachers are in no position to volunteer. Clubs require a hefty investment of scarce resources.

There are academic clubs, social clubs, recreational clubs, and service clubs. In practice, however, any club might qualify for more than one of these categories. If the school has an International Club, for example, it might offer support for immigrant students as well as tutoring in English. A Computer Club might be academic as well as recreational. No doubt there are clubs that do not fit any of the four categories. Clubs are an institutional response to a need—or, if not to a need, at least to a wish. A club might form at a time of crisis. After repeated incidents of racial prejudice, perhaps, a club is formed to help minority students deal with the problem. Or a club might take the form of a class. Students wish to study something, and a teacher agrees to teach it, but for some reason the class is not suitable for inclusion in the curriculum. Maybe the subject is photography, and the students wish to meet informally, without grades and tests and mandatory attendance. Whatever the shape and purpose of clubs, they can be a powerful presence in the school community. Or they might serve mainly to fill in space on a college application.

What are the policies for clubs in the school? Are useful and educational clubs encouraged? Are clubs evaluated? Is there competition for limited resources? Are resources well invested? Are there students who need a club that currently does not exist?

Assemblies

Small schools with a big auditorium are blessed with a wonderful resource. Independent schools make good use of their chapels and theaters. If they do not have a space reserved for assemblies, some schools make do with cafeterias and gyms. We were at a small independent high school on the first day of the Gulf War, in January 1991. The head of the school had gathered all the students and teachers in the gym. Everyone sat on the floor. Some students had questions; others had comments and speeches they felt compelled to make. It was an occasion of national and international significance, and the school dealt with it as a community. Regular assemblies help create that spirit of community, even if students have to sit on the floor.

The auditorium is a huge classroom. The principal or head of the school presides and sets the tone for all assemblies. Students learn to speak before a large audience by making brief announcements, but sooner or later they have opportunities to speak at length about topics of general interest. In addition to regularly scheduled school assemblies, a series of special assemblies throughout the year becomes a noncredit course in the humanities. Local and national leaders, scientists, historians, journalists, astronauts, and authors might come to talk or debate with the students. The auditorium also connects the school with the surrounding community, especially if it is used for town meetings or other community functions. Students are encouraged to attend events sponsored by community groups, and members of the community are encouraged to attend events sponsored by the school.

If the school is too big for assemblies as we describe them, what about smaller groups? Middle schools are learning the value of schools within schools—"houses" or "families" with relatively few students, few teachers, and a strong sense of identity. These groups fit into smaller spaces and can meet in hallways if the students and teachers are willing to sit on the floor.

Who plans assemblies for the school? Are regular assemblies preferable to morning announcements on the PA system? Are special assemblies a low-priority chore for a busy administrator, or are they carefully planned by an interdisciplinary committee of teachers and students? Is time set aside for assemblies, or do they always interrupt the schedule of classes?

Service Organizations

Students are usually eager to do the work of adults or to help adults accomplish something useful. Even very young students respond enthusiastically to jobs perceived as useful, like cleaning the chalkboard, operating a stopwatch, or shelving books in the library. Capable and committed students can serve the school and community in many ways. Some service organizations mobilize their resources for selected worthy causes. They might pitch in to clean up a public space or raise money for a good cause. Others offer specialized services, like tutoring, consultation in the computer center, or supervision in the weight room. Students can become so helpful that they are inadvertently exploited. Teachers learn to rely on the student who makes overhead transparencies, delivers a projector to the classroom, programs VCRs, edits tapes, and seems able to repair anything with a pair of pliers and a paper clip. No teacher realizes that all the other teachers are asking for the same student's help, and consequently he or she spends more time helping than studying. Service organizations should make sure that their service is beneficial for the volunteers as well as the community at large.

The community beyond the school offers students endless opportunities to be useful. The dividend from community service is twofold, of course. The volunteers benefit as much as the people they help. Children and staff at the Community Service Project in Rockland, Maine, put out a regular newsletter. In one issue (1989) a 12-year-old wrote:

> Instead of wasting my time getting in trouble, I joined the Community Service Project. I put all of my energy into the organization that I thought could use it. All summer I helped out the elderly and they greatly appreciated it. You feel good after helping out a person who really needs it. And the older people really need the help.

A 15-year-old wrote:

> I am here to help old people out on things they can't do. I like working for people that have had trouble doing things by themselves because they are too old to do things. I like to work at Projects

because I don't have to sit home and be bored watching television and falling asleep. I like doing it because you can do apprenticeships and you can go on trips if you have enough hours.

Students are eligible for apprenticeships after twenty hours of community service and two training workshops. The program director places students in an apprenticeship suitable to their interests. Each apprentice has a mentor. Students choose work as varied as jewelry design, cooking, teaching, and social work. A 15-year-old-apprentice wrote: "My apprenticeship was at a place where they counsel and treat alcoholics. When I get older I hope to go on with this. I am planning to go to college when I get older and study this subject. The apprenticeship was fun and I learned a lot about alcoholism." After thirty hours, volunteers qualify for a "Reward Trip." Adult volunteers accompany students and staff on an adventure, a cruise along the Maine coast or a camping trip to Baxter State Park.

Community service projects might employ students as unskilled laborers or might take advantage of skills that students have acquired through special training programs. Students who volunteer to be emergency medical technicians in Darien, Connecticut, take a thirty-six-week course. An adult with the service says, "The minute the buzzer goes off, they're no longer teenagers. They're well-trained, well-disciplined ambulance personnel." Twenty-eight graduates of this program have become physicians (Ciabattari 1990).

Is the school providing opportunities for service? Are the jobs available to students truly useful? Are there intrinsic and extrinsic rewards for service? Is there a variety of service projects available, permitting different levels of commitment and skill? Are there opportunities for growth? Do students find a use for skills they have learned in the classroom?

Publications

Even if they are handwritten and pinned on a bulletin board, publications provide on-the-job-training for students interested in publishing. There is much to learn about writing, layout, and illustration, yet elementary students using crayons can produce excellent publications. We attended a first-grade writing workshop in which each student selected one story from a portfolio of first drafts and carefully rewrote it with correct spelling and colorful illustrations. When these stories were bound and catalogued, other young students enjoyed borrowing them from the library. Those who start early become very proficient by the time they are high school seniors, if the schools they attend allow them to grow. High school students in Pittsburgh started a city magazine and published it successfully for three years, but eventually they succumbed to the competition of another magazine published by professionals. Attracting and organizing a staff, encouraging contributors, making sure that students learn, setting standards, and facilitating relations with the adult world are the responsibilities of teacher-advisors. Any of these responsibilities may be delegated to capable students, but students must always do the writing, the layout, and the editing.

Are the school's publications "authentic" in the sense that an audience actually reads them, or are they "pretend" publications read mainly by the writers? Do they contain information and ideas about the world outside the school? Do the principal and faculty advisor of each publication agree on a standard of excellence? Do the editors and faculty advisor agree? Do the staff and the student body agree? Who does most of the work—the advisor, the editors, or a large staff of writers, artists, and photographers? If the work done by students is excellent, are the facilities and financial support provided by the school equally excellent?

Performing Arts

Almost all schools have extracurricular programs in music, dance, and drama. The arts are thought to be legitimate subjects for study in schools, although they are not always given the status of "major" subjects. The visual arts are usually squeezed into the regular schedule of classes, but rehearsals for plays and concerts tend to last longer than the usual forty minutes. They bring together shifting groups of students for varying lengths of time, and they continue for about six weeks—not a whole term. Hence, performing arts become extracurricular activities. Generally they are welcome in a school, although the pressures of performance can be stressful for students. In fact, an ambitious production undertaken by a demanding director can be stressful for the whole school and everyone in it.

Performances, like publications, can be "authentic" or "pretend."

Authentic performances engage an audience the way audiences are engaged by professional actors, musicians, or dancers. Something is communicated through the art. "Pretend" performances might be enjoyed, but the audience tends to be more interested in the performers than the performance. Only highly skilled student performers can pull off authentic performances of works in the professional repertory, of Shakespeare and Beethoven, for example. Authentic performances are supported by educational programs that teach the basic skills of acting, singing, dancing, or music. A good test of authenticity is a tour, even to one other school. If an audience of people who do not know the performers are enthralled, the performance is undoubtedly authentic.

The student audience is an important part of a performing arts program. Students can be cruelly critical of other students, in the auditorium as well as in the classroom. Few artists will willingly subject themselves to derision. Even seasoned performers will balk. We were in a high school theater once when a traveling company performing *Macbeth* interrupted the play and assembled on stage to talk with students about their bizarre and inconsiderate behavior in response to every enactment of violence. In the same school, students performing *King Lear* were ridiculed, yet the following week in another school they received a standing ovation. If performances are to work at all, teacher directors and student actors must select a program appropriate for its intended audience, but audiences also have an obligation to listen and applaud respectfully. Parents, teachers, and administrators can support the performing arts by teaching students to be appreciative.

What is the purpose of performance in a school? When a music teacher, a drama teacher, or dance teacher is hired, is any thought given to an educational philosophy of the performing arts? Are teachers developing the skills, understanding, and confidence of the performers, or are they controlling every move that the students make? Do performances in the school fulfill the function of the theater and the concert hall in real life? Are beginners encouraged to participate? Are different kinds of performance appreciated and encouraged? Are the performing arts related to anything else in the curriculum? If the school is small and resources are limited, would a regional performing arts program serve the students better than a school-based program?

THE WHOLE SCHOOL

Whenever a problem threatens the present or future well-being of children, schools are expected to respond. Some of these problems— chemical dependency, AIDS, racism, domestic violence, to name only a few—are way beyond the capacity of schools alone to solve. Not only schools, but all our agencies for health, welfare, and justice are reeling from the severity of such problems. Lacking the leadership and liaison needed for massive cooperative efforts, each agency does the best it can. Given the challenge of teaching students to read and write and calculate, learn huge amounts of information, think critically and creatively, appreciate the values of the culture, appreciate the values of other cultures, master the skills of the workplace, and persevere through twelve to twenty years of education, schools might not have the energy, resources, or expertise to mount additional campaigns. Because they are compelled to do something about everything, schools buy new textbooks, install metal detectors, organize inservice for teachers, open child care centers, teach parenting courses, distribute condoms, provide counseling for grief-stricken students, and more and more, all of which are helpful but probably not enough. In an article in *Phi Delta Kappan,* James Banner (1992) suggests that schools jettison everything but the academic program and send students to a "parallel school" for everything else.

We agree that schools cannot do everything, and as visitors in schools we share a sense of futility with principals and teachers who are doing the best they can, knowing that band-aid solutions cannot have much effect on epidemic social problems. Yet we cannot imagine a school that has been divorced from "everything else." We see a need to unify the educational experience rather than divide it. Each student is one person. One person wakes up every morning and puts on familiar clothes, goes to a familiar school, finds familiar friends, faces familiar terrors. The little girl who sips a rum-and-coke on the school bus is the same little girl who sits in math class and pretends to have done her homework. The African-American wrestler trying to understand his feelings about wrestling white opponents is the same African-American student reading Toni Morrison's *Song of Solomon* in English class. The sixth-grader who can define the term "virus" on a science test is the same sixth-grader whose next-door neighbor is dying of AIDS. Students enter different classrooms, make different friends, like or dislike different teachers, solve different problems, foresee different careers. Diversity is everywhere and inevitable. But each individual student is trying to make sense of it all. Other students have different resources and different problems, and all are trying to make sense of their lives.

Rather than compartmentalizing all the experiences in school, we should be helping students integrate and understand their experiences. The learning that takes place out of class is just as important as the learning that takes place in class. Anything that is learned in class alone and does not spill into the rest of the student's world is "inert" knowledge, useful mainly for passing tests. To help students carry what they learn in school into the world and, just as important, what they learn about the world into the school, we must offer a transactional experience.

Extracurricular activities have always been a bridge between learning and living. Acting in a play, writing for the school newspaper, or playing for a team are real-time activities. They are social activities. Through group participation, students form alliances and friendships that continue through evenings and weekends. Although tasks are prescribed, they permit a level of independence and personal decision making not usually experienced in the classroom. And these activities have outcomes—a performance, a story, or a game—of immediate value and interest. They are products to be proud of. Classes, on the other hand, are oriented to the future rather than the present. Classes are dominated by teachers. Interaction among peers is highly constrained and very different from the comfortable interaction of friends outside the classroom. Papers and tests—products representing considerable effort—are soon discarded. Students have a life, and they also have school. Extracurricular activities fall somewhere in the middle.

The transitional quality of extracurricular activities is not always exploited. Only a fraction of the student body might be included in the offerings. To involve more students, new activities might have to be added or existing activities modified. Some may be set up in such a way that membership is limited—either deliberately, for good practical reasons, or inadvertently. When faculty advisors and coaches are fully occupied in the center of things, as often they must be, they may not have the time or the incentive to bring along interested novices who come to see what is going on and go away again if they are not welcomed. Also, the relationship between extracurricular activities to the curriculum is not always examined. Conventionally, some extra-curricular activities are closely related to the curriculum, while others are remote. The newspaper is often supported by a journalism class. Performances are often supported by acting, singing, and dancing classes. The Debate Club makes extensive use of the library and employs many of the skills that are taught in English and social studies classes. Although physical education teachers quite properly insist that physical education is separate and distinct from athletics, PE classes do introduce students to skills that are used in serious competition.

Extracurricular activities provide links between the curriculum and the rest of the student's life. These links can and should be strengthened. When a school thinks of integrating its resources in order to help students integrate their experiences, distinctions like "curriculum" and "extracurriculum" begin to blur. Although the various components of the school may remain separate in operation, they come closer in purpose. The Oasis project in middle schools in Pittsburgh, Pennsylvania, for example, operates under the aegis of vocational education. Twenty-four eighth-graders in each school learn shop skills by making a tool box. Then, under the guidance of a teacher-contractor, they take their skills and their tools into the community to do useful work. All the students in the program have been identified as at-risk of dropping out in the seventh grade. All remain in school throughout the eighth grade, taking three academic courses in addition to the Oasis project. In the middle school we visited, sixteen of the twenty-four Oasis students had been cited for outstanding citizenship; eight were on the honor roll. Follow-up studies show that former Oasis students have a better attendance record than the general population of their classmates. This vocational education-community service program serves a distinctly academic purpose.

Schools cannot deal with enormous educational and social challenges by adding more and more specialized programs. The school as a whole has to respond. Take, for example, the problem of domestic violence. It appears to be an enormous problem that snowballs from one generation to another and causes untold suffering. The effects of domestic violence ripple through the society in the form of substance abuse, sexual abuse, assault with a deadly weapon, and other horrors. The least a school must do is report cases of suspected child abuse. If the school as a whole responds to the problem, however, its response will be more than minimal. Teachers will talk with young children about trust and the keeping of secrets. They will teach children what to do and whom to tell when an adult makes them feel bad. Children of all ages will learn about alternatives to violence as a means of getting what they want. They will learn about sexual harassment and discuss acceptable and unacceptable behavior with members of the other sex. Students in English and social studies classes will read stories and essays about interpersonal violence. They will share the insights they have gained from experience and synthesize what they already know with what these disciplines have to offer. Above all, the culture of the school will discourage abusive relationships.

It is not necessary to stop teaching U.S. history in order to discuss interpersonal violence with children. It is not necessary to stop teaching algebra. Children in any classroom can learn to take turns, listen to others, and examine the consequences of selfish behavior. While they are learning history and algebra, they can learn to cooperate and to value cooperation. They can learn that the adults in the school care about them, not because the adults say that they care, but because the adults treat them with respect. Teachers can show their respect by listening whenever students are trying to communicate. Students must not be allowed to give up trying to explain their feelings and their points of view. When they start to believe, "It's no use; the teachers never listen," they cannot believe teachers who say, "Talk about it, work it out, violence doesn't solve the problem." Somehow teachers have to avoid situations in which they are barking out commands: "Stop talking, sit down, I don't want to know, do it because I say so." Order is better than chaos, of course. Sometimes adults have to exert the power of authority, of a loud voice, of outrage, of anything available at the time, to establish order. If, however, the culture of the school does not include a steady diet of cooperation, then the students are not likely to learn much about alternatives to violence.

Teachers teach explicitly when they explain concepts and rules and relationships, give homework assignments, and correct tests. They teach implicitly through their own behavior and the behavior they encourage in students. Learning is enhanced when implicit teaching and explicit teaching are consistent. It is virtually impossible to discuss literature without discussing violence. Connecting implicit lessons about violence with explicit lessons about literature should present English teachers with no trouble at all. Similarly, history offers countless opportunities to study the causes and consequences of violence. In no way will it detract from the students' understanding of history to connect their own knowledge about violence with knowledge about violence in history. Mathematics, on the other hand, offers relatively few opportunities for explicit study of violence. Nevertheless, a math teacher can be quite explicit about rules and expectations in the class-room. The value of cooperation in group problem solving can be discussed openly and productively without straying too far from the particular math problem to be solved. Considering the great range of human experience that falls within the realm of the academic disci-plines, a whole-school response to an educational challenge need not jeopardize the continuity and integrity of the curriculum.

Nevertheless, the school as a whole cannot respond to everything. A total response requires frequent and sustained communication, a modified curriculum, analysis of sudent-teacher interaction. If new programs are to have an impact, they must link and extend the capa-bilities of existing programs. Clearly, a strong sense of priority is crucial. Instead of undertaking to do something about everything, each school might try doing everything about something. This forces a momentous choice that demands care, analysis, and forethought—a level of preparedness warranted by the huge undertaking.

Having learned to focus its efforts, the school will find that its resources are not exhausted. The capability to deal thoroughly with one problem will produce the resources to deal with another. Let us imag-ine that a whole-school response to domestic violence is well under-way. Teachers now give class time to interpersonal violence and its consequences, in society at large and in the more immediate context of the local community. Students in discussion groups have talked about abusive relationships as experienced by teenagers. Counselors have been mobilized to help victims and perpetrators in the student popu-lation. Teachers and administrators have examined their own use of power so that they can understand the message implicit in their behav-ior. Once these and other mechanisms are in operation, they might serve a second purpose, and a third.

It becomes evident that a number of students in the school are suffering from eating disorders such as anorexia and bulimia. Teachers are already working on the assumption that knowledge helps students understand themselves and their environment. The methods used to help students understand domestic violence can also help students understand eating disorders. In health they learn about nutrition and malnutrition. In science they learn about the interdependent systems of the body. In geography they learn about famine and its toll of human suffering. In literature they meet characters whose self-image is distorted by the expectations of others. In social studies they examine the images of "ideal" women in advertising and entertainment. Students who live in a climate of trust and cooperation, as opposed to a climate of fear and harassment, will want to help friends who are victims of self-abuse. Once networks between schools and other social service agencies have been established, they can be used for students and families with various needs, not just one need.

To respond thoroughly to anything, a school must preserve a degree of flexibility. An overburdened curriculum that is strictly imposed on teachers does not allow them to respond to the children in their classrooms, who are not the same as other children in other classrooms. A negotiated contract that demands the *same* conditions for all teachers rather than *fair* conditions for all teachers inhibits the ingenuity of administrators and teachers working together. Calcified notions about what a school "is supposed to do" open up rifts between the rigid curriculum and the changing lives of students entering the school year after year.

The school must think of itself as a whole organism. We once helped mediate an argument between elementary science teachers and a caterer who had been contracted to provide food services in the cafeteria. The teachers had been emphasizing the need for a proper diet in science classes, but the children were encouraged to spend money on chocolate and cola as they filed through the lunch line. In a high school, teachers trying to raise the self-esteem of girls found themselves in conflict with coaches who were trying to raise money for the girls' athletic program by holding a "slave auction." To the sounds of exotic music, the girls "sold" themselves to other students, mostly boys, as "slaves" for a day. In a boarding school that was proud to have a "multicultural" curriculum, all the members of the International Club were foreign students—not one American. In a big urban high school, students in an Advanced Placement English class were reading *To Kill a Mockingbird*. Teacher and students discussed the racial prejudice in the novel. No one mentioned that 13 percent of the students in the AP class were African-American, but more than 50 percent of the students in the school were African-American. In another large urban school a remedial reading program was dropped for lack of funds, but the School Board raised enough money from local businesses to save the athletic program.

On the brighter side, many schools have educational programs that integrate the classroom and the world outside the classroom. Many schools support and extend explicit instruction by developing a complementary school culture. In 1987, after a student was murdered, New Utrecht High School, New York, started a Mediation Center, where students in conflict with another student or with a teacher may go for help. Mediators at the center are students who have been trained in conflict resolution. Through mediation they see that both sides in a dispute are listened to, and then they help the disputants to negotiate a resolution. In a three-year period the number of students suspended was reduced from fifty-one to twenty per year (Scherer 1992). The importance of the Mediation Center in the school community shows students that peaceful negotiation of conflict is highly valued. The training of student mediators and their impact on the community demonstrate for all students that they can make a difference through peaceful interaction in which the rights of both parties are respected. Students in an ecology class at Oakmont High School in Asburnham, Massachusetts, collaborate with a local developer. They study parcels of land that he has purchased for development. With the help of their teacher and specialists employed by various state agencies, they study the vegetation, soil, bedrock, water, animal life, drainage, topography, erosion—everything needed to understand the ecology of the site and the implications of building on it. They gather useful information for the owner and confer with him as he decides how to develop the site. At Santa Fe Preparatory School, New Mexico, all the students participate in a community service program in which they must earn a certain number of credits in order to graduate. While many of the services provided by students require fairly general skills, some require specialized knowledge or skills they have learned in the classroom. Those who visit elderly people in nursing homes have a wonderful opportunity to converse in Spanish, since Spanish is the first language for many of the residents. Other options employ skills that students have learned in science, English, drama, art, and mathematics.

Steven Nielsen (1992), assistant principal at Rincon Valley Junior High School in Santa Rosa, California, has written a helpful account of a whole-school response. Rincon Valley has made a major, proactive effort to prevent the formation of gangs. The principal had emphasized campus safety even before the first signs of gang activity. Administrators were aware of and had implemented safety guidelines provided by the California State Department of Education (1989). Collaborative councils involving students, teachers, administrators, and parents were already in existence. A number of school personnel had been trained to help at-risk students. When insignia associated with gangs began to appear, particularly during one episode in which students were threatened with violence, the school as a whole decided to take preventive action. Although some people were not alarmed by the prospect of gangs in a middle-class town of 100,000, the school had been forewarned by the National School Safety Center (1989) in a publication made available to schools. Gangs have a strong appeal to young teenagers who lack interest in socially sanctioned activities and feel alienated from their families. Gangs support rebelliousness and offer a different kind of belonging. In urban areas where drug traffic is heavy, gangs are likely to be drawn into the network of distribution. The support provided by a gang enables individuals to start the sort of criminal activity needed to finance an expensive and illegal habit.

Administrators and counselors at Rincon Valley use a profile to identify students at risk of joining a gang. They distinguish between gang members, students who want to be gang members, students closely acquainted with gang members, and students adopting bits of gang-related behavior with no intent to join a gang. All gang-related behavior warrants intervention. Graffiti are removed as soon as they appear. Insignia displayed publicly are photographed and made available to parents, so that parents will recognize the same insignia if they appear in students' homes. Students wearing bandanas and other items made popular by gangs are asked to desist, and parents are asked to cooperate. Teachers, however, tend not to criticize students for appearing to admire the lifestyle of gang members. It is felt that a teacher's attentions can make gang-related behavior even more attractive to rebellious adolescents. Interventions are made by counselors and administrators, usually with parental involvement. Serious cases might involve the police and the courts. Two police officers are assigned to provide liaison with secondary schools in Santa Rosa. Probation officers work closely with school and family counselors. Meanwhile, the school sponsors a variety of service activities that encourage students to make a positive contribution to the community. Clubs and classes undertake projects to benefit the homeless, the elderly, and the environment. To help students develop a stronger sense of belonging, the entire school, including teachers, counselors, and administrators, has been organized into teams. Closer relations develop when small groups of students take all their classes from the teachers on their team.

Coordinating a school's resources to this degree involves just about everyone associated with the school in a common endeavor. It cannot be accomplished without cooperation, and cooperation in one effort creates interactive networks that facilitate cooperation in other efforts. The Youth Advisory Group at Rincon Valley Junior High School now meets regularly with equivalent groups in other middle schools to form the Junior High School Proactive Task Force. This body has made racial stereotyping and prejudice its principal concern. At Rincon Valley, cooperative networks established to counteract gangs are now at work to counteract racism. Members of the Youth Advisory Group and a student leadership class are planning a curriculum to help seventh- and eighth-graders examine the issues of stereotyping and prejudice. Students will teach the classes, using skits, activities, and topics for discussion that they have devised. The Youth Advisory Group also hopes to commission a mural. All the students will be invited to contribute ideas, and the mural will be designed and painted by student artists. Its theme will be ethnic and cultural diversity, united in a common cause at school.

When a school sets a high-priority goal and pursues it vigorously, the pursuit of other goals cannot be postponed. The rest of the school continues. Other problems occur. Other decisions have to be made. A study of eighteen high schools in the process of change (Stiegelbauer 1984) shows that the factors influencing change vary from one school to the next. Although the decisions made by administrators are a fairly constant influence, these decisions are often made in response to events over which administrators have no control. One superintendent resigns, another takes over, an unexpected source of funds becomes available, parents demand that something be done, the budget is cut, students find a new way to misbehave, the football team joins a different league. Decisions affecting the future of the school are made every day, day in and day out. The band needs a new director, but the candidate the Booster Club wants is not the best all-round music teacher. The children have always learned Christmas carols and have sung at the mayor's Christmas party for the homeless, but now a small group of parents has protested that this is a violation of the First

Amendment. Proponents of a grade point requirement for playing on a team argue that athletes will benefit in the long run, but the proposed requirement will almost certainly cause some current students to drop out of school. Highly developed, cooperative networks holding the school and community together are more likely to grow through long-range proactive efforts, but they sure help in a crisis.

SUMMARY

Although extracurricular activities sometimes seem to threaten the academic program, they are an important part of school life. The powerful appeal of extracurricular activities suggests that they are sometimes seen by students and parents as more important than classes. Since extracurricular activities are costly, their purpose and operation must be examined. Only then can each activity be evaluated and held accountable.

Many extracurricular activities further student achievement of academic goals. They provide transitional experiences for students, linking the school to the rest of a student's life. They offer students opportunities to use knowledge and skills learned in the classroom. In addition, they help students develop personal qualities that are hard to teach in the classroom. When schools realize the educational advantage of extracurricular activities, the term "co-curriculum" is often used. Although the co-curriculum is separate from the curriculum, both lead to fulfillment of the mission.

Developing a harmonious relationship between the curriculum and the co-curriculum leads to a "whole-school" concept. Many of the problems that face schools are too complex and too deeply embedded in the greater community to be solved by any single program. To have an impact, schools must set priorities, mobilize all resources, and act as a whole organism. Then students, teachers, coaches, counselors, administrators, and parents all work together to achieve a specific purpose. Even so, schools might need to enlist the help of social and civic agencies in the larger community. When a school has developed this whole-school image, opened channels of communication, established cooperative networks extending into the community, and mounted a campaign to meet one challenge, it is well organized to meet other challenges that are sure to come along, planned or unplanned.

REFERENCES

The ASPIRA Association. (1990). *Latinos and the Drop-Out Crisis: The Community Solution.* Washington, D.C.: The ASPIRA Association.

Banner, J. M. (1992). "The Parallel School." *Phi Delta Kappan 73*:6, 486-488.

Ciabattari, J. (November 25, 1990). "These Teens Save Lives." *Parade Magazine,* 17.

California State Department of Education. (1989). *Safe Schools: A Planning Guide for Action.* Sacramento, Calif.: California State Department of Education.

Community Service Project. (1989). *Fall Newsletter.* Rockland, Maine: The Community Service Project.

National Association of Secondary School Principals. (1992). "Student Activity Programs Enhance Education Experience for Nation's Youth." *NASSP Bulletin 76*:542, 60-65.

National School Safety Center. (1989). *Gangs in Schools: Breaking Up Is Hard to Do.* Malibu, Calif.: Pepperdine University Press.

Nielsen, S. (1992). "The Emergence of Gang Activity: One Junior High School's Response." *NASSP Bulletin 76*:543, 61-67.

Scherer, M. (1992). "Solving Conflicts—Not Just for Children." *Educational Leadership 50*:1, 14-18.

Springstead, E., L. Miller, D. Hinojosa, and R. Diersing. (1981). *Migrant Drop-Out Study, 1980-81: Final Evaluation.* Education Service Center Region 2, Corpus Christi, Texas. (ERIC Document ED247039).

Stiegelbauer, S. M. (1984). *Context and Co-Curriculum: Situational Factors Influencing School Improvements in a Study of High Schools.* (R&D Report No. 3186). Austin, Texas: Research and Development Center for Teacher Education.

5

TEACHING AND LEARNING

Teaching is as close as we can get to the heart of the matter, which is learning. Although we can teach students how to learn, we cannot do the learning for them. Teaching is all we can do. Here, above all, we must do our best.

It helps to remember that teaching is functional. It has a purpose. There is no point in talking about "good teaching" or "good teachers" without reference to learning. It is pointless to debate the characteristics of "good teachers" without raising closely related issues of objectives and assessment. What are the students supposed to learn? What are they actually learning? How do we know what they have learned?

Unexamined assumptions about "good teaching," however well intended, might waste students' time. We once evaluated a highly regarded English course that had been taught by the same teacher in an independent school for six years (McQuade 1980). This course, called "Editorial Skills," was supposed to teach grammar and diction to students who would go to college but whose command of English was not yet considered excellent. The teacher was widely recognized as a "good teacher." He was awarded a master teacher's "chair" of English during the six years in which he taught Editorial Skills. Everyone was satisfied with the course—students, parents, faculty, and administration. Everyone thought it taught useful skills that would help students become better editors of their own writing and help raise their scores on College Board tests like the SAT and the English Achievement. Students found the course challenging and worked hard, motivated in part by a system of diagnostic tests and individualized instruction. The final examination was comprehensive and rigorous. However, when the English department began to target students who had scored below a certain level on standardized tests of English, students who had passed Editorial Skills became candidates for remediation. Something was wrong. We tried in various ways to discover what, if anything, was learned in Editorial Skills. We compared SAT scores before and after the course. We compared writing samples before and after. We compared the difference between the SAT scores and Achievement scores of students who had taken the course and of other students in the same graduating class. We gave a final examination on the first day of class and a similar final on the last day of class. By every measure, the students were able to do as well before taking the course as they were after taking the course.

Was this good teaching? Only the teacher's willingness to evaluate the course and to look for more effective alternatives can be considered good teaching. By every measure we could devise, the course was a waste of the students' time. A friendly classroom, frequent tests, and the deceptiveness of short-term memory all contributed to an illusion that the students were learning. So long as they were receiving satisfactory grades, merely "exposing" them to grammar was considered sufficient.

OBJECTIVES AND ACTIVITIES

Which comes first to a songwriter, the words or the melody? Sometimes the words come first, sometimes the melody. Which comes first to a teacher, the objectives or the activity? Sometimes objectives come first, and the teacher wonders how students can be taught to achieve them. Sometimes the activity comes first. The teacher thinks, "Wouldn't it be neat if . . . !" Then the teacher wonders, or *should* wonder, "But what will the students learn if we do this?" Often the objectives and the activities are given to the teacher in the form of textbooks and teacher's manuals. Then the teacher is said merely to "deliver the curriculum." However it happens, instruction must have a purpose. The purpose must never be taken for granted.

Everyone in education agrees that there is no teaching without learning. Yet instructional activities are sometimes adopted for their own sake, regardless of outcomes. A field trip to the science museum, a visiting poet, an ethnic food festival, distinguished alumni invited to talk about their jobs . . . the purpose of instruction sometimes seems to be self-evident. To ask, "What are the students expected to learn from this, and how will we know what they learn?" might sometimes seem to be superfluous. Yet such questions must be asked and answered continually—especially when the answers seem obvious. When the purpose of instruction is taken for granted, assessment is too easily neglected. Once we were with a physics teacher on a "busman's holiday" at the Franklin Institute in Philadelphia and noticed some children of middle school age swinging on ropes that hang from a huge lever attached to a huge weight. They could swing from the ropes closest to the fulcrum of the lever, but not from the rope at the far end. "What happens when you pull on that one?" the teacher asked. They stopped swinging and tugging for a moment but did not seem interested in the question or the stranger who had asked it. Instead, they ran to play on the pulleys. These kids having fun taught the physics teacher a lesson about field trips to museums. Although research shows that students tend to remember the science they learn in museums (Holliday et al. 1985), that does not mean that all students turned loose in science museums will learn about science or that anything they do learn will be revealed on the next science test. The purpose of instruction, the method, and the means of assessment must all be related.

The purpose need not always be conceived in terms of "instructional objectives." There are occasions when an objective like "Explain the mechanical advantage of a lever in terms of force and distance" is helpful, but a field trip to the science museum is not likely to be one of those occasions. In addition to the precisely defined objectives we assess in chapter tests, there are overarching goals that students with various interests and personalities achieve in their own wonderfully adaptive ways. The purpose of the trip to the science museum might be broadly conceived and loosely defined: "To stimulate curiosity . . . To acquire knowledge about a topic of interest." Whatever the purpose, it must be clear to the teacher, who explains it to the students and helps them formulate strategies for achieving it. Other teachers in the school should also know the purpose of the field trip. They will be much happier if they know what benefits justify the time lost from their classes. And parents should know the purpose. Parents are in an excellent position to reinforce the learning of their children. If encouraged to participate, they will do more than ask, "Did you have a nice time at the museum?"

The purpose suggests the means of assessment, and, reflexively, the means of assessment further defines the purpose. After a trip to the science museum, each student might be asked to describe an exhibit and to explain the scientific principles learned from it. After hearing these presentations, the teacher will be in a good position to appraise the effectiveness of the instruction and to improve it, either by adding follow-up activities that now seem appropriate or by modifying the plan for subsequent groups going to the museum. The trip might be improved, for example, if each student previews all the exhibits before choosing one exhibit of particular interest. Each student might be asked to return to his or her chosen exhibit and to take notes while studying it in more detail. Curiosity might be furthered if the students prepare questions about the science represented in their selected exhibits and seek answers to their questions in the classroom, the laboratory, and the library. If asked what would help them learn more from the trip, the students will almost certainly have more suggestions to offer.

To emphasize the importance of outcomes and to evaluate instruction according to its purpose is not to imply, of course, that ends *always* justify the means. The *New York Times* of April 12, 1991, described a controversy over a science teacher who had violated the school's standards of safety and professional conduct while "making learning fun" for his students. For instance, he arranged a flight in an airplane during which physics students conducted experiments related to gravity. For that he was fined $1200. According to students, this teacher made them want to come to class, study harder, and continue in science. These are highly desirable ends, but they do not justify any means of instruction that endanger students. The incident does illustrate the need for assessment. If, in fact, this teacher has achieved these highly desirable outcomes of motivation and interest while also meeting the school's objectives in science, then there is much to learn from his methods. Can the same ends be reached by methods that are safe? That school is in an excellent position to find out.

DECISION MAKING

Teaching is creative. Teachers have limitless permutations of methods, styles, and materials to choose from, and if the classroom permits any degree of spontaneity at all, every lesson will be different. Some teachers will get certain consistent results by combining relatively few components repeatedly under similar circumstances, like a painter with a limited palette. But twenty or more students gathering day in and day out, year upon year, in a typical classroom will challenge a teacher's every resource. Every lesson presents a problem to solve, and dozens of mini-problems occur along the way. Richard Shavelson has characterized the number of instructional decisions made by a teacher as infinite. He sees decision making as the most basic skill in teaching (Shavelson 1973; Shavelson and Stern 1981). Hundreds of daily decisions are improved if the teacher has a rich repertoire of strategies and techniques to draw on (Fogerty, Wang, and Creek 1983; Westerman 1990). Bruce Joyce and Richard Hodges (1981) suggest that flexibility in decision making should be the core of a teacher education program.

Effective teachers do not follow lesson plans that have been tested in schools of education and recommended for general consumption. They use what they know about the students in their classroom and select methods and materials that are most likely to help the students arrive at accepted goals for learning. They monitor the students' progress, and when difficulties arise, they try something else that is likely to work.

If students are not learning what they are supposed to learn, it is fruitless to go on doing the same thing while complaining about the students. The failure of students to learn might not be the teacher's fault, but that does not mean that the teacher may therefore abdicate responsibility. The teacher might be doing exactly what he or she has been hired to do and doing it just as it has been done for years. Demographic, socio-economic, or cultural changes might have brought students with different values and expectations to the classroom. Their prior education might be deficient. They might not have prerequisite learning skills. There might simply be too many students in the classroom. Regardless of the cause, *something must be done* to remedy the problem. After much thought, consultation, and collaboration with colleagues, administrators, and parents, the teacher might even be advised to go on providing precisely the same type of instruction that was found to be deficient for a certain group of students. In that case, the students who were not learning must be given another, more appropriate environment where they *can* learn successfully. Long before their own resources are exhausted, teachers must talk about problems with colleagues and supervisors, even if only one student in a class is failing to learn. If instruction in the classroom does not change, something else must change. A combination of changes in the classroom *and* elsewhere in the student's life might be necessary.

Requiring teachers to cling to one method and one package of materials severely limits their capacity to respond to the needs of their students. Although no two teachers can teach the same curriculum in exactly the same way, rigid teacher evaluation and other pressures can limit their options. Minor adjustments to the curriculum are not always sufficient. Teachers must have the latitude to introduce supplementary instruction and, with support from the administration, to cut and paste a new curriculum that works.

Because teaching must serve a purpose, methods of teaching will vary radically as teachers and students pursue the various goals of learning. At different times in the same week a teacher might lecture, ask questions, answer student questions, moderate a discussion, read student work while the students conduct their own discussion, demonstrate a procedure, observe an investigation, set a problem to which the answer is already known, or set a problem to which the answer is unknowable. Different subjects demand different skills, and therefore some methods are particularly suited to certain subjects but not necessarily to other subjects. Playwriting is not the same as acting, and hence the same teacher might allow students more independence and individual initiative in a playwriting class than in rehearsals for a performance. Football is not the same as soccer, and hence the football coach might be more authoritarian than the soccer coach. Reading is not the same as music, and hence the reading teacher might encourage students to talk more about stories than the music teacher permits them to talk about songs. Teaching vocabulary in science, when students can form strong associations between new words and their hands-on experiences, is not the same as teaching vocabulary in English, when new words are derived from a wider range of experience, some of which must be vicarious. And teaching students to think in mathematics, when hypotheses can be tested by calculations, is different from teaching students to think in biology, when hypotheses are more often tested by experiment. Elementary teachers, who teach all subjects, must be geniuses of flexibility.

NECESSARY CONDITIONS

Every classroom, every teacher, and every student is unique, yet there are also some common features of instruction that teachers may modify but cannot eliminate. Teachers, and anyone supervising teachers, must pay particular attention to the necessary conditions of instruction. How well are they used to further learning?

Expectations

Expectations are inescapable. If a teacher does not expect students to learn, the teacher is doing something other than teaching. The power of expectations was demonstrated in the famous "Pygmalion" research conducted by Rosenthal and Jacobsen at Oak School in California (1968). Researchers tested all the students in the first six grades. Teachers were told that the tests had identified certain students who were capable of higher achievement than they had managed thus far. The students so identified, however, had actually been selected at random. Nevertheless, by the end of the year these selected students made greater gains than students who had not been selected. Teacher expectations had transformed them.

Since then, teacher expectations have been the subject of continuing research (Cooper and Tom 1984), and it is now widely known that expectations can have both a positive and a negative effect on student achievement. Students from whom teachers do not expect much do not achieve much; students from whom teachers expect more tend to accomplish more. Prophesies become self-fulfilling because the expectations of teachers lead to discriminating treatment, and discriminating treatment affects the self-image and motivation of the students (Good and Brophy 1987). The practice known as "tracking" is discriminatory in this way (Oakes 1985, 1991). When students are placed in the bottom track, their placement, no matter what the purpose, tells them that not much is expected of them. But students are not alike, one might reason, and students at any point in their school careers, even the first day of kindergarten, have already achieved at different levels. How can we provide instruction appropriate for different backgrounds and levels of achievement unless we have different expectations? If expectations are based on sound professional judgment, one might argue, low achievement only confirms the teacher's ability to predict. We advocate the opposite: If a teacher does not expect the students to succeed, they would be better off with another teacher.

Should teachers know about past performance? Teachers who say, "I don't want to know what my students did last year; the knowledge might lower my expectations" deny themselves information that might be critical to success. Teachers must gather as much data as they can from student records. These records seldom contain enough useful information—too much information is hard to imagine. Knowledge of past performance helps the teacher teach the students instead of just teaching the curriculum. Students are best served if they learn to relate new knowledge to what they already know, if the methods by which they are taught are well matched with their learning styles, if teachers are willing to try something different instead of doing the same things that have not worked in the past. Moreover, teachers do not escape the expectations trap by refusing to study student records. Current performance has just as much influence on teacher expectations as past performance, and if the teacher has not chosen teaching methods that are right for the students, current performance is apt to be low. Teachers must have information about their students *and* expect their students to succeed.

Here is a general strategy that is useful at every level in every classroom:

1. Address each student's strengths and weaknesses with appropriate instruction.
2. Teach and assess a variety of skills and capabilities, so that success or failure does not depend upon a few things that only some students do well.
3. Expect every student to achieve excellence—but not the same excellence.

Each teacher tries to find the best instruction by accommodating different learning styles, arranging tutoring for certain students, organizing cooperative work groups, meeting with parents to discuss a student's habits of doing homework, conducting drill sessions for students who need them, and so on. At the same time, other teachers and administrators working in concert make sure that all the resources of the school are used to support learning, that someone is counseling the troubled student, that students who do not read well have opportunities for learning orally and kinesthetically, that high achievement in arts is valued as much as high achievement in athletics, that structure is provided for students who do not have structure elsewhere in their lives.

Each teacher encourages a variety of skills in each subject. A teacher might reward creative practical applications of mathematics as well as quick and accurate calculations, might teach various types of writing about all sorts of experiences, might assign data-gathering projects as well as problem-solving projects, might permit oral and graphic presentations in addition to written tests, and so on. The whole school, meanwhile, encourages a variety of skills by having a rich array of programs in shops and studios and gyms for students with manual and physical skills, civic and entrepreneurial opportunities for students with interpersonal skills, community service for students with the motivation and compassion to help others, exhibitions and performances for students who can paint, act, play, and sing.

Similarly, each and every teacher can help students find their unique geniuses. The expectation that students will achieve the objectives of instruction is fundamental but not in itself enough. Achievement must also reward students for the effort of learning. Weak students especially suffer classes from which creativity, variety, and challenge have been removed and only the dullest worksheets remain. If students in eighth grade sit down each day to face columns of arithmetic problems, they have probably never done anything else in mathematics. The expectation that they will at last learn to multiply decimals is necessary but insufficient. Students who have not mastered arithmetic have not forsworn human ambition. The expectations of teachers must in some way mesh with the aspirations of the students. The supposition that students have to learn another concept or master another procedure before they can think is without foundation. Young children coming to school for the first time use language and mathematics to solve problems and to communicate their own discoveries (Resnick 1987). They are strongly motivated to be capable and independent people. It does not make sense to remove this motivation from the classroom, especially classrooms in which weak students most need to labor.

When students of any age are interested in what they do, when they consider the task worthy of their efforts, they are capable of extraordinary accomplishments. A group of fourth-, fifth-, and sixth-graders in Brooklyn, not chosen because of any particular talent, met regularly after school to learn more about science. At the end of a year, all passed the New York Regents' examination in biology, a test intended for high school students (Johnson 1990). Students at Nashoba Valley High School in Massachusetts serve their community as emergency medical technicians. When a call comes for help, they drop everything and go, perhaps to save a life. The Rochester, New York, public schools can assemble an orchestra and soloists to perform the concertos of Mozart, Beethoven, or Tchaikovsky. At St. Johnsbury Academy in Vermont, a group of "vocational" students, who had not thought of themselves as "college material," built an electric car and entered it in competition against college and commercial teams. The St. Johnsbury car won. Students rise to the highest expectations.

Sequence

Learning takes time. There must be a series of events. Teachers organize these events into manageable steps that lead students to achievement of course objectives. Sequence is guided by analysis of the objectives and assessment of the students' readiness for each succeeding step. If the curriculum provided for the teacher moves too quickly to a step the students are not prepared to take, the teacher must be free and able to modify the curriculum by slowing it down or adding intermediate steps. If the curriculum bores the students with too much practice at a level they have mastered, the teacher must feel free to move along.

As teachers develop a deeper understanding of the disciplines they teach, they discover new steps they had not clearly identified before or combine steps in new ways that stimulate the interest and motivation of their students. The steps in any routine process eventually become automatic. Experts who have learned to conceptualize in great chunks of knowledge and to move in leaps and bounds forget how hard it was when they were novices to master each little step along the way. Teachers, on the other hand, must empathize continually with the learner, to see each lesson from the learner's point of view.

Sequence is unavoidable, and manageable steps are essential. Even so, students easily lose sight of the whole. While experts focus on the whole task, breezing unconsciously through zillions of little steps, students who learn each little step with difficulty cannot see the whole picture. Thus, teachers must constantly relate the parts to the whole. As soon as possible, and as often as possible, students need to consolidate the discrete skills they are learning into summary tasks that start to look like the work of an expert.

Teachers who are following a curriculum they have not helped to create might too easily take for granted that "it works" as it is supposed to work. Some might assume that students who do everything they are supposed to do will achieve the desired outcomes inevitably. In fact, students tend to follow instructions, do the homework, and take the tests without any clear notion of the long-term goals of instruction (Bereiter and Scardamalia 1989). The teacher's job is much more than simply "delivering the curriculum." Through assessment, the teacher monitors the appropriateness of each step, subdividing, omitting, or combining steps to facilitate learning and motivate the students. The teacher must also understand the whole task, the terminal objectives of the curriculum, and make sure that students are continually integrating the sequence of steps into successive approximations of the whole task. If students are graded only on quizzes and tests throughout the year, and an average of these grades determines the final grade in the course, it is possible that no one, neither the teacher nor the students, will ever see the whole that was envisioned by the authors of the curriculum.

Teachers who have had a role in the process of making the school coherent, described in Chapter 1, are likely to have a good idea of where they and their students are going. But every teacher who comes to the school cannot participate in that first wave of creation. Teachers hired subsequently will be chosen for their sense of direction and then introduced to the school through a process of orientation, described in Chapter 7. Orientation calibrates their sense of direction, aligns it with the compass points, compares the map with the territory, and helps new teachers get their bearings. Only if they know the goals of the school, the objectives of the courses that they teach, the purpose of the materials they use, can they help the students follow a sequence and pull it all together.

Making Meaning

No matter what the teacher does, each student, individually, extracts what he or she is able from the class, organizes the pieces, and decides what it all means. Asked what they have learned, students are likely to come up with different, sometimes contradictory accounts (McQuade 1990). Central to the message that modern cognitive psychology has to offer is the independence of every intellect (Resnick 1987). No teacher under any circumstances can ever assume that because it was taught, it was learned.

The independence of each individual's learning has at least two implications for instruction. *Before* students are held accountable for learning, the teacher must help them construct the meaning of instruction and then find out if the meaning each student has constructed is satisfactory.

Meaning is not a right or wrong answer. Students gather data from texts, films, library research, lectures, discussions, questions, answers, and calculations. Deliberately or automatically, they bridge gaps in their knowledge with inferences, which may or may not be accurate and may or may not prove helpful to the cause of understanding. Each student forms a tentative idea of meaning and grasps it with some degree of clarity and confidence. "Meaning" might be an original interpretation of events around which there is no established scholarly consensus, or "meaning" might be the student's understanding of a scientific theory. In either case, "meaning" for the student is like a hypothesis, which may or may not survive as the student gathers and integrates additional data. Reinforcement from the teacher is one source of data. "Good idea." "Right." "Interesting idea." "Grade A–." "You don't seem to have mastered the facts of this case." "Think again." Whether students are putting together their personal interpretations of a poem or using widely accepted scientific knowledge to explain the results of an experiment, the teacher must find out what meaning each student has managed to construct, and, if necessary, help each student improve on it.

Some of the conventional methods of checking on meaning are flawed. Questions asked orally of the whole class are often answered one at a time by various students—perhaps a small minority of the class. The *teacher* has a purpose for the questions and knows how the various answers contribute to a coherent body of knowledge. The *students,* on the other hand, have neither the teacher's sense of purpose nor the teacher's knowledge, and hence the separate answers do not make sense to the students as they make sense to the teacher. Even if the teacher summarizes a classroom "discussion" of teacher questions and student answers, the summary is yet another piece of discourse for students to interpret with varying degrees of success. "Objective questions" are a common feature of classroom tests, but even a student who can answer ten or a hundred questions on a test might have formed an erroneous version of the whole. A fifth-grader might remember details about Paul Revere, Crispus Atticus, and George Washington but think that the War of Independence was fought between the United States and Spain. A biology student might pass a multiple-choice test on adaptation while believing that hummingbirds developed longer beaks because they "needed" to reach deeper into flowers for food. Students must be expected to summarize data and to represent chunks of knowledge in their entirety. In this way, teachers can help each student correct erroneous ideas and strengthen flimsy interpretations before they are fully accepted into the student's view of the world.

Asking students to write a summary is a simple and direct way to find out what they have learned. They can summarize stories, poems, chapters, procedures, arguments, films, discussions, and so on. At least at first, their summaries are likely to be deficient. Teachers at all levels should explain what they expect in a summary and provide examples of satisfactory summaries. It would be a great mistake to teach "how to summarize" only in English or language arts classes and then expect students to employ their summarizing skills in all classes. By teaching students how to summarize in all classes, teachers can teach them what to attend to in class, how to use the textbook, how to organize the basic principles of the discipline, how evidence is related to conclusions, how the bits and pieces of their knowledge are interrelated. All this entails specific content. Needless to say, knowledge that has meaning *in toto* is more easily remembered and more useful than incoherent bits and pieces of knowledge.

Written summaries are not the only means of representing meaning. Concept maps are often recommended (e.g., Marshak 1986), although their use in classrooms is not yet commonplace. Some teachers provide concept maps to help students follow a sequence of instruction, unit by unit, throughout an entire course (Cliburn 1986). But students can also create their own concept maps (White and Gunstone 1992), either individually or in groups. Given the "key words" from a chapter of text, students in small groups will engage themselves in very productive discussion as they arrange and rearrange concepts into a satisfactory map. The finished product will quickly reveal their understanding or confusion.

Another alternative is the "summary task." Here are some examples:

List the reasons for and against the creation of a national bank in 1791.

Trace the path and the fate of a cookie from ingestion to excretion.

List and categorize the types of problems for which it is important to know the differential and the types of problems for which it is important to know that the differential is equal to zero.

Using the correct terminology, label all the traces of ancient glaciers that you can find on this topographical map. Explain how the glaciers left these traces on the landscape.

Time

Research in effective schools shows that time is a crucial variable in learning. Up to a certain point, the more time a student is actively involved in learning, the higher the achievement (Fisher et al. 1978). This relationship of time to achievement is all the more interesting when one realizes how much the time of involvement in any given subject varies from class to class and school to school. In some schools, amounts of time allocated to reading and mathematics are double and triple the amounts allocated in other schools. Schools allocate time in the form of a schedule, and within that framework, teachers further allocate time to classroom activities. Some of these activities will involve the students in learning, but some, like taking attendance, settling disputes, or record keeping, will not. In elementary schools, teachers borrow time from one subject to give to another subject, and, depending upon the teacher's ability to maintain a balance, the practice might cause a mounting debt to one subject, particularly one the teacher does not value (Schmidt and Buchman 1983). As teachers know, school administrators frequently take back scheduled time to accommodate special assemblies, field trips, and occasional crises that warrant the cancellation of classes.

A school's schedule is a platform of priorities. There is only so much time available. In trying to accomplish too much, schools are in danger of doling out time so frugally that students cannot achieve excellence in anything. Our advice is to give plenty of time to goals of the highest priority and then, through vigilance and supervision, to protect that time against erosion. Every proposal to rearrange student time should be evaluated in light of the school's goals.

A coherent curriculum helps a school gather time and focus its power where power is most needed (see Chapter 1). For example, the mission of The Gow School in South Wales, New York, is to prepare dyslexic boys for further education. One of its highest goals is "to analyze and understand the use of language in all areas of endeavor and to arrive at effective strategies for improvement in listening, speaking, reading, writing, and spelling." From the school's inception in 1926, there has been a special language program for all students. "Reconstructive Language," as the program is called, is taught daily in small groups of no more than six students in a classroom. Recently, however, the headmaster and faculty have realized that students will learn to use language even better if the goal is addressed in every class they take at Gow. Hence, the science department has adopted these goals:

> Learn strategies for building vocabulary, taking notes, and organizing information.
>
> Improve ability to read texts and articles, to write scientific reports, to read and interpret charts, graphs, and tables.
>
> Discuss and debate controversial issues in science.
>
> Research topics of scientific interest and deliver written, visual, and oral reports.

The mathematics department has adopted these:

> Apply the techniques of "Reconstructive Language" to reading in mathematics.
>
> Employ the language of mathematics in class discussion.
>
> Learn to use the conventions of data analysis, graphing, inductive and deductive thought, analogy, and proof in oral and written communications.

Because every department has goals for language development, the amount of time given to language learning has been greatly amplified. Horizontal coherence increases the learning time allocated to high-priority goals.

Time allocated is one thing. Time of involvement is another. Allocated time is easily squandered. We have observed teachers taking time to tutor a single student while twenty or more other students wait in a sort of idle bliss. Unless taught to do otherwise, students delivering oral reports tend to address the teacher, the only person in the classroom who listens attentively, asks questions, and uses the information to form new ideas. Students in math classes often are told to put problems "on the board" and then to explain what they have done, while all the students who have solved the problems merely wait. Teachers intending to increase their students' time of involvement will soon learn to avoid these pitfalls, and a friendly observer helping to keep track of time in the classroom will prove to be most helpful.

Routine

The routines in our lives help us feel secure and comfortable. We devise procedures for taking a shower, making breakfast, getting to work. The procedures work well, or well enough, and feeling no need to improve them we repeat them again and again. Rather than examining and redesigning what we do each day, we save our creative energy for more important things. Routines also have a potential to be boring, however. If everything in our lives becomes routine, we lose the variety and excitement of the changing world around us.

In the classroom, routines help teachers manage groups of students efficiently. Routines for distributing materials, for setting up and cleaning up the lab, for taking attendance, for taking tests, for dividing into groups, for transitions from one activity to the next, all help to smooth the mechanics of the classroom and save time for the more productive tasks of teaching. But routines are not just a feature of class management. They are just as pervasive in methods of teaching.

It is quite logical when something works well to do it again. Rather than slip into repetition because all the good ideas have been used up, or energy is low, or the workload has tripled, teachers might more profitably cultivate classroom routines, study them, enhance them, and see how much learning they can squeeze out of them. What students do in the classroom is what they are learning to do. As a PE teacher once told us, practice does not make perfect—practice makes permanent. Classroom routines should be planned carefully, evaluated often, and ruthlessly improved.

One pervasive routine is known as "seatwork." Students at all levels know the seatwork routine. "Open your workbooks to page _____ and do the exercises from _____ to _____." Seatwork of this type is usually designed to isolate a component skill and provide enough practice to make it automatic. Students do a series of calculations until they are allowed to stop and check the answers. They draw lines to connect the right numbers with the pictures. They read and reread passages of prose to find answers to questions printed at the end of each passage. They do the even-numbered problems in class and the odd-numbered problems for homework. This type of practice is almost always tedious, although some successful students might find in seat-work a sort of numbing comfort that they claim to like.

Component skills are taught and practiced so that sooner or later they will come together in some form of mastery. Basketball players practice passing and catching and foul shots and lay-ups and picks—again and again. Their skills come together in games that reward and justify the practice. If they were denied the opportunity to play basketball, their willingness to practice would almost certainly diminish. Low-achieving students are not usually forced to practice basketball, but they are given endless seatwork that they cannot do well—and rarely have an opportunity to play in a game. The classroom equivalent of "playing in a game" is a real-life task like reading for pleasure, or writing a real argument to persuade a real audience, or solving a problem that makes life a little better.

Because the seatwork routine is decontextualized, "practice skills" are not identical to the "real skills" needed in performance. Again we can learn from the coaches who say of a player, "Great in practice, but can't put it together in a game." The difference between practice and performance is also recognized in the arts. A young pianist struggling to interpret the "Moonlight Sonata" for an audience is doing something entirely different from playing scales. Similarly, a young scientist who is struggling to interpret an article in *Scientific American* because it contains useful or interesting information is doing something entirely different from answering questions at the end of the chapter. If decontextualized practice helps students to perform a real task, they should understand the relationship between the practice and the performance. They should also be given opportunities to perform the real task so that they *feel* the improvement that practice has helped them to achieve.

The problem of teaching decontextualized skills is further compounded when teachers make success in practice the only goal of learning and then teach students "short cuts" and "easy ways" to get through the practice. Young math students learn to add two-digit numbers without regrouping before they learn to add two-digit numbers that require regrouping. One first-grade teacher we observed taught students to cover the tens column with a finger while adding the numbers in the units column, and then to cover the units column while adding the numbers in the tens column. She wanted the students to see that their knowledge of single-digit addition was applicable to two-digit addition, and, indeed, using the method of covering the columns, they were able to treat two-digit addition as two separate instances of single-digit addition and achieve a high degree of success. Then they learned to "carry " when the numbers in the units column added to more than ten. Now, when they covered the units column with their fingers, they sometimes had three numbers in the tens column to add. They learned to do this and usually arrived at the "right" answer. As they sat at their desks day after day, however, working on two-digit and then multi-digit addition problems, and then moving on to subtraction problems, they came no closer to understanding the theory of numeration, the principle of regrouping, or the quantities represented by the whole numbers they were systematically decimating with their fingers. Practice makes permanent. Classroom routines have to be examined very carefully to make sure that what the students are learning does, in fact, contribute to expertise in the discipline.

Potentially boring, potentially detrimental to the highest goals of learning, routines are nonetheless powerful and can be very helpful. Good routines add significantly to time of involvement. If students know the routines they do not need new directions every day. They become increasingly independent as they decide when to cease one familiar activity and shift to another. It is always thrilling to see students arrive in a classroom or a lab and, without any signal from the teacher, without even waiting for the bell to ring, form into groups and start to work. To help promote independence, it is worth discussing the procedures of the classroom with students, letting them know how they can use their own resources to best advantage. They should know why the routine has been chosen and how it contributes to expertise in the discipline. A French teacher we know has a "journal" routine in one of her classes. Once a week, each student in the class tells the other students about something that has happened in his or her life. At some point during or after this shared experience, every other student in the class is expected to ask a question, also in French. Many of these questions were trivial at first, the meaning of a word or the name of someone who had been mentioned but not named. When the pattern of questioning became repetitive, the teacher pointed out that the purpose of the routine was to engage every student in the conversation and not merely to satisfy the requirement of asking a question. They had to be interested in knowing the answer. The students said it would help if the experiences they shared in "journal time" were more interesting in the first place, but their limited ability in the language confined them to superficialities. They wondered if keeping a written journal would help. They could take the time to look up new words, confer with the teacher, and maybe pursue a topic for several days or weeks in succession. Then they would be better prepared to talk about something interesting in journal time. The teacher agreed that a written journal would greatly enhance their learning, and the students agreed to make their weekly conversations as "genuine" as they could. In this example, teacher and students worked together to increase the yield of a classroom routine.

Routines save a teacher from the formidable task of planning every lesson completely from scratch. Only the content need be changed from day to day or week to week. If, as in journal time, the students generate the content, the teacher's responsibility for planning is further reduced. The point is not to escape from work, but to contain the work within manageable bounds while providing excellent instruction. If student contributions are properly monitored, the more they do, the better. One of the tenets of the Coalition for Essential Schools is "Student as Worker"—the students learn actively rather than waiting passively for the teacher to "deliver" the curriculum (Sizer 1986). Through classroom routines, teachers might save time in which to plan other activities to be introduced when the current routines have worn thin. Any new activity that works once might work again, and again. But only so long as it works!

Assessment

We discuss assessment more fully in Chapter 6 but must introduce the topic here because assessment is another necessary feature of instruction. If curriculum provides the teacher with a chart, assessment provides the compass, the sextant, and the log.

It helps to recognize two types of assessment, formative and summative. A "test" usually means summative assessment. Something has been taught, the students are tested, and their achievement is recorded. There is no further instruction at this point; the class moves on to something else. If, however, information gained from the test helps the teacher and the students make decisions about further instruction—what to review, what to emphasize, what to supplement, what to continue—the assessment is formative. Ample formative assessment does wonderful things for instruction. Well done, it cements the alliance between the teacher and the students. Students do not feel punished for their weaknesses, because the discovery of weakness leads to learning, which leads to strength. Even if they perform poorly in the end, they are likely to feel that the teacher has done everything possible to help.

Quizzes leading to a unit test are formative if the teacher helps students overcome any difficulties that the quizzes reveal. Practice tests and worksheets are usually formative, but they should not result in short cuts and easy ways to get through the test. A written draft that will later be revised is formative. The student receives feedback from the teacher and classmates, and this feedback helps the student produce a better piece of writing. A portfolio is formative. The student and the teacher together analyze strengths and weaknesses in the portfolio, and together they work out a plan for improvement. Written summaries, concept maps, and "summary tasks" that help students consolidate and represent their accumulating knowledge are formative. Debriefing a test is formative, but not if the purpose is merely to tell students the right answers—the coach and the players do not study films of the game to find out the score. Debriefing evaluates the effectiveness of the strategy and tactics that were used and should result in a plan for subsequent practice sessions.

All assessment, even a final exam, can be useful to teachers. Students move on after taking a final exam, but the teacher probably stays at the same grade level and teaches the course again. Analyzing student performance at the end of one year will lead to better teaching the following year. Assessment has limited value, however, if it does not assess student achievement of the full range of objectives set for the course. We cannot expect students to learn to think if they need only to memorize in order to pass the tests. We cannot expect them to learn to solve problems if they can pass the course without solving problems. We cannot expect them to value learning if passing the course accomplishes nothing important in their lives.

Homework

Both home and work are necessary. The location and the activity are so commonly associated that homework also seems necessary. Many students, unfortunately, do not do homework. We are often dismayed to see large numbers of students leaving school empty-handed at the end of the day. Students who do homework enjoy higher academic achievement than students who do not (Walberg 1984, 1985). Time spent doing homework is pure time of involvement. It is worth waging war to get students to do homework.

All we have said of work in the classroom applies also to homework. The difference between the confined classroom and the unconfined environment outside the classroom is worth exploiting, however. If we want learning in the classroom to have meaning in the lives of the students, homework is a likely vehicle for this transfer. If, on the other hand, homework is just like the seatwork done in class, learning closes like a textbook and stays closed until the student is told to do the next assignment. While we call it *home*work, homework can actually be done anywhere. It can be done in the lab, the library, the museum, the streets, the field, the forest, and the stream; it can be done alone or in groups; it can involve parents, friends of the family, mentors, and all the resources of the community. It can be done in short assignments one day at a time, or one project can hold a student's interest for months.

The following examples serve to illustrate the variety of possible homework assignments:

Bring a favorite toy, game, book, or family picture to class and describe how you feel about it.

Interview people in the family or neighborhood and bring the results to class. The class will organize the information in tables and graphs and write an article for the school newspaper.

In groups, make a slide "video" to accompany a reading of a poem.

List the products found under the sink at home. List the ingredients of each product. Bring the lists to class for classification and further study.

Keep a journal of quotations and questions as you read the next assignment. Bring your journal to class for discussion in small groups.

Choose an object that is more than a hundred years old. Do the necessary research to discover how historical events influenced the creation and subsequent history of the object. Present the object and your discoveries in an oral report to the class.

Prepare a beginner's lesson to teach your classmates how to do something that you do well.

Amnesty International organizes letter-writing campaigns. Write letters in English or another language.

Interview someone who uses mathematics. Find out what mathematics he or she uses and ask why the mathematics is useful. Write a report on the interview. Illustrate the report with mathematical examples.

Write a computer program to solve specific types of problems encountered in science class.

Draw a map of your neighborhood. Make copies. Enter color-coded information related to businesses, housing, motor traffic, pedestrian traffic, crimes committed, etc. Compare your neighborhood with the neighborhoods of other students in the class. Write an essay about your neighborhood.

Teachers, administrators, and counselors in elementary and middle schools should make every effort to involve parents constructively in the homework of their children. Young children rely on parents to provide a location and a time for homework. Parents who are well informed about the purpose of homework can do more. They can promote learning by taking an interest and rewarding their children for work well done. Parents learn different approaches to supervision as their children grow older and become increasingly independent. Parents would find it very difficult to start supervising the homework of a high school student if they had not already developed an understanding of their respective roles. A "homework clinic" at the school even one evening a week would be a useful service to offer. Helping a parent help a child do homework might have lasting impact on the child's career.

MODES

Because we have the opportunity to visit a variety of schools, each unique, and observe in hundreds of classrooms, each unique, we are

Student-Centered Discussions

1. Students are told the topic, format, purpose, and date of the discussion.
2. They are expected to prepare. They are given the task of gathering data—not all from the same source. Discussions are a means of sharing information as well as sharing opinions.
3. They write in advance of the discussion. The writing may be done in class and should be brief. They write to prepare a preliminary point of view, not to produce an essay.
4. More students participate and have more to say if the discussion takes place in small groups. Whole-group discussion may follow group "reports."
5. Students are more likely to sustain a discussion if it has a purpose—a proposal to present to the whole group or a majority and minority report.
6. Students take notes on the discussion. They refer to their notes as they respond to points made by other students.
7. Each small group is responsible for reporting to the whole group.
8. The whole group may discuss the various points of view presented.
9. Information and insights gained from such a discussion are consolidated if students write about the topic they have discussed. There may be other discussions on related topics before the writing assignment is complete.
10. The teacher conducts a debriefing session, analyzing and exemplifying the skills of discussion. Students suggest ways to improve future discussions.

FIGURE 5-1 Suggestions for Stimulating Student-Centered Discussions

keenly aware of the great diversity of teaching methods and teaching styles. Each individual teacher might have a limited repertoire that he or she draws upon repeatedly, but collectively the possibilities are endless. The extensive analysis and improvement of educational practice that we describe in this book—coherent goals and objectives, colleagual curriculum development, assessment to improve instruction, a climate of professional growth—will eventually confront teachers with challenges they have not yet undertaken and problems they have not yet solved. A repertoire that includes at least the major modes of instruction will prove invaluable.

These modes are neither good nor bad in themselves. Like tools of a trade, they are all excellent for some purposes and next to useless for others. An intrepid homeowner will tackle almost any job with a screwdriver and a hammer, but when we call a plumber or electrician we expect the professional to show up with the right tools. It is absurd to take on the complex job of teaching with only one tool, "direct instruction," "cooperative learning," or "the Socratic method." It is equally absurd to expect a teacher to try out all the tools, one after another, hoping that one of them will accomplish something. What, exactly, has to be done? What is the best tool for the job?

Discussions

Discussions are harder to find than one might suppose. Before we enter classrooms to observe, we usually ask teachers what we are likely to see. When we are told that there will be "a discussion," we are not sure what to expect. Discussion shades into recitation. The teacher asks a question; students raise their hands; the teacher calls one student by name; this student offers an answer; the teacher considers the answer and either accepts it or looks interested in hearing another; the teacher elaborates; the teacher relates the elaborated answer to new information; the teacher asks another question. If the questions are answered briefly, with factual information, "recitation" is probably the best description of what is going on. If the questions are answered by a succession of students, at length, with conjectures that are then challenged by other students, then the proceedings come closer to "discussion." When "recitation" questions and "discussion" questions are presented in the same context, without differentiation, students are understandably con- fused by the mixture of expectations. They find silence or short, tentative answers to be safer than hearty participation. When we ask teachers what sort of discussions they would like to promote, their wishes tend toward a common ideal: a specific topic or theme, all students participating, remarks relevant to the topic, opinions offered with evidence, students listening and talking to one another, teacher facilitating.

We advise teachers to go for the ideal, all at once (see Fig. 5-1), rather than trying to coax longer answers out of students in a recitation format. Preparation is essential. Students should know in advance what they are going to discuss and why the topic is important. They should know the format of the discussion and what is expected of them. If they are told to gather information, take a position, and come prepared to participate, they are more likely to talk more and talk effectively than in unplanned discussions that teachers try to generate spontaneously. Discussions may involve small groups or whole groups. The size of the group, the amount of individual participation, the available time, the extent to which students care about the topic, and the outcome—whether it is purely hypothetical or a decision with consequences—are all important variables to consider in advance.

Well done, discussions teach students to communicate their opinions persuasively, to listen to other opinions, to collaborate, to sort out subordinate and coordinate relationships between ideas. Students learn how other students think. They learn that thinking is not always logical and not always sincere. They learn to couch an argument in terms that their audience will understand and at least consider. Discussions are hard to control and hard to follow. To make meaning out of discussions, students have to gather bits and pieces of information and organize the fragments into something coherent, especially if they are expected to produce some sort of summary. Students rarely emerge from discussions all having learned the same thing.

If the school and the course have goals for communication, reasoning, and problem solving, these can be achieved at least partially through discussion. To help the students become good at discussion, teachers should take time to discuss the discussions. How do individual students feel about the outcome? How did each student contribute to it? What else could have been done? What discussion skills were observed? Was the discussion cooperative or competitive? Were students aware of following any particular strategy? What strategies might be useful in the future?

Lectures

The legendary professor of dullness delivered the same lectures from the same notes year in and year out. Nevertheless, a good lecture is worth repeating. As lecturers remember more of the details of a lecture and rely less on their notes, they develop more effective gestures, weightier pauses, funnier jokes. Good lectures, of course, are more than entertaining. They embody the style and cognitive structures of the discipline. They legitimize the lecturer's inclination to show off a little, because the lecturer is supposed to be an exemplar of scholarship. While lectures may be revised each time they are delivered, eventually they wear out. The discipline changes. The lecturer moves on to new interests and new discoveries. The scholarship that led to a well-constructed lecture in the first place—and to each decision to repeat it—eventually leads to its demise.

The worst lectures are discussions that have fizzled out, leaving the teacher to talk "off the cuff." Perhaps the teacher asks questions and weaves the answers into a network of loose associations. Perhaps the students ask questions that lead the teacher further and further astray. Time passes, and sooner or later the bell rings.

The limitations of lectures are fairly obvious. The lecturer, caught up in the structure and delivery of the lecture, is largely unaware of the thoughts and feelings of the audience. Even if the lecturer invites the audience to interrupt, only occasional questions are possible, and the lecturer must return to the logic of the lecture. The lecturer is compelled to get it all said, and the audience, not knowing what is yet to come, feels that the most cooperative thing to do is wait and listen. Students in the audience construct the meaning of the lecture as it unfolds, taking notes, relating new information to information they already possess, but if they have trouble following the gist, or trouble concentrating, there is not much they can do. While certain lectures at certain points in a student's career might precipitate cataclysmic insights, the principal challenge for the student is comprehending, integrating, and remembering what is said.

To realize the value of lectures, teachers should prepare carefully and make the lecture as interesting as possible. A lecture should connect strongly with what the students already know. Its constituent parts should be clear, and its organizing principles should be unmistakable. If the teacher lectures often, the students should be taught how to listen to lectures. Teacher and students should discuss the format, style, and purpose of the lectures. The students should learn to follow and record the sequence of ideas and to look for the logic that binds the ideas together. When the lecture is over, the knowledge gained through the fairly passive process of listening and note taking can be activated through questions, small-group discussions, or a writing assignment that requires the students to make meaning of the lecture. Written summaries are particularly useful to the lecturer who wants to improve the clarity and impact of the lecture before delivering it again.

Convention suggests that lecturing is more appropriate for older students. College professors deliver lectures, whereas elementary teachers give "little talks." Perhaps college students who set their own goals for learning are more likely than young students to activate the knowledge they have gained from listening. Nevertheless, lectures can be just as useful and inspiring in the lower grades as they are in college. One third-grade teacher we know has a fairly constant stream of guest lecturers come to her classroom. For a period of time every year, for example, every student in the class is a "doctor." The teacher calls the students "Dr. Thompson," "Dr. Hernandez," and so on, and they join happily in this pretense. They are all specialists—"cardiologists," "orthopedists," "brain surgeons"—and they work in teams to produce life-size diagrams of the organs and systems related to each of their specialties. The room is crammed with anatomy books. A skeleton is always present. Physician friends and parents, some of whom are the real-life doctors of the students, come to "do rounds." The student "doctors" lay out their diagrams and give progress reports on what they have learned. The guest specialists give "little talks" about the subject of their expertise. Before each guest leaves, the teams of students are already integrating this latest information into their work.

Collaborative Learning

Collaborative learning often requires students in small groups to make a decision or solve a problem, and then to deliver an oral report in the classroom. The report to classmates may or may not be followed by a written report addressed to an audience beyond the classroom. The teacher defines the task, makes the rules, provides organizational materials, and stays in fairly close communication with each group to observe progress and, if necessary, to help. Students collaborate to choose and refine a topic, develop strategies, plan the product, and share the labor of production. Learning to be good at the process is considered an end in itself (Johnson and Johnson 1987a). Collaboration among peers is a mode of operation in business, research, media, and the professions. Learning to collaborate, therefore, is preparation for the world of work.

It seems that certain tasks are done better collaboratively than alone, and research in education supports this contention (Johnson and Johnson 1987b). We find no evidence to suggest, however, that *all* tasks are done better in groups or that any group under any circumstances produces higher-quality work than does an individual. Teachers who adopt the method need not deny the value of individual work or forswear competition.

Not all learning done in groups is collaborative, as the term is currently understood. Small groups doing seatwork while the teacher works with one group is not considered collaborative learning, because students in each group are merely sitting together. A foreign language class divided into groups to drill and memorize the conjugation of verbs is not considered collaborative learning, because the prescribed task leaves no room for individuality. For the same reason, the conventional science lab in which partners follow instructions in the lab manual is not considered collaborative learning. Tasks for collaborative learning tend to be complex. They require groups to formulate strategies, to plan ahead, and to deal with issues of individual and group responsibility. Because collaboration entails negotiation, students must explain their ideas to other members of the group and evaluate their opinions in the light of other, conflicting opinions.

For all these reasons, collaborative learning is linked to the acquisition of higher-level thinking skills (Skon, Johnson, and Johnson 1981). In long-term studies conducted in different classrooms, both elementary and secondary, students who had learned through group investigations (see Fig 5-2) did better on tests of higher-level thinking than students who had learned through whole-class instruction. They also learned as much information, and in some cases more information, than students in conventional classes (Sharan and Shachar 1988; Sharan and Sharan 1990).

These studies were conducted in schools where teachers had spent some time learning how to manage collaborative learning groups. Teachers who attempt it without the benefit of training and supervision may be disappointed. In one middle school classroom we observed, students were given the task of deciding where the dramatic climax of *Julius Caesar* occurs. Some students in each group talked sporadically about Julius Caesar while other students listened, but everyone joined in off-task conversations about shopping, absent friends, movies, or last night's basketball game. Finding the dramatic climax of *Julius*

Group Investigation

1. Identifying the Topic and Organizing Groups

    Students scan sources, propose topics, categorize suggestions.

    Students join group to study subtopic of their choice.

    Teacher assists in information gathering.

2. Planning the Task in Groups

    Purpose and goals of investigation.

    Specifics of investigation. Division of labor. Timeline.

3. Carrying out the Investigation

    Students gather data, analyze data, reach conclusions.

    Each group member contributes a share to the group.

    Students exchange, discuss, clarify, and synthesize ideas.

4. Preparing the Report

    Group members decide the essential message of their report.

    They plan what they will report and how to make the presentation.

    Representatives of each group coordinate plans for the total presentation.

    Criteria for the presentation are determined.

5. Presenting the Report

    Presentation is made to the entire class in a variety of forms.

    Part of the presentation should actively involve the audience.

    Audience evaluates presentation according to predetermined criteria.

6. Evaluation

    Students share feedback about the topic, the work, and what they learned.

    Teacher and students collaborate to assess student learning.

    Assessment includes higher-level thinking.

FIGURE 5-2 Steps in a Group Investigation

Source: Adapted from S. Sharan and H. Shachar (1988), *Language and Learning in the Cooperative Classroom* (New York: Springer-Verlag).

Caesar did not seem to interest these students. After observing work groups in sixty-three elementary mathematics classrooms, Good and colleagues (1990) concluded that the value of collaborative learning "lies not in the method per se but in the quality of implementation."

To use collaborative learning effectively, teachers must enter into a collaboration with their students. When students enjoy a high degree of independence, they will not stay on task or persevere unless they are highly motivated to do so. Teachers can contribute only so much by the structure of the task and the system of rewards. Students must contribute their interest, curiosity, and integrity. Bringing all this together in a spirit of cooperation is not easy. Collaborative learning is not something that teachers should try once to see if it works. Teachers and students must become inveterate collaborators.

Modeling

The power of admiration is inestimable. Advertisers spend millions of dollars for endorsements of their products, courting the celebrities who are most likely to be admired by consumers. Educators employ the same strategy when we ask celebrities to talk to students about the dangers of drugs or the reasons to finish school. When we think about "good role models," we also think of young people who have much in common with the students yet possess some quality the students have not yet acquired. We hope that students will admire these role models and want to be like them. Because they have much in common already, emulation is not a great leap of imagination. Role models are not beyond reach.

We can bring role models to the students and take students out of school to meet role models in context. If they are not in positions that cause them to be overwhelmed with invitations, role models are usually delighted to visit a school. The third-grade teacher described earlier in this chapter has no difficulty finding physicians to come to her classroom to discuss anatomy with her students. If the teacher and students have enjoyed meeting a visitor, a second visit might be welcome, and a third, and so on. Alternatively, the students can be taken to visit the role model on his or her own turf. Public places like museums are not the only destinations for field trips. We can help students shape their aspirations in homes, offices, labs, studios, churches, and factories. We can plan curriculum around role models. We can plan collaborative projects in which role models serve as mentors in their fields of expertise.

Not all "modeling" is "role modeling," however. A math teacher demonstrates the method for solving a particular type of problem. A biology teacher demonstrates the techniques of dissection. An English teacher selects the best student essay and makes copies for everyone in the class to read. These lessons also employ models. It is very helpful when learning to do something to see it done properly. The teacher is not the only person who can give demonstrations. Sometimes, in fact, the teacher is not the best person to demonstrate. A student does not learn to try various strategies and to persevere by seeing a teacher do everything only once and always perfectly. Some teachers get around the problem by undertaking tasks they have not rehearsed, so that students can see the process of perseverance and discovery. Others invite advanced students into the classroom to help teach students at a slightly lower level of achievement. The Carnegie Council on Adolescent Development (1989) highly recommends cross-age modeling, especially because the older students seem to gain as much from the experience as the younger ones.

Modeling for the purpose of teaching is not a time for showing off. Models should reveal rather than hide everything going on "behind the scenes," the details they attend to, the judgments they make, the mistakes they catch and correct. Math teachers everywhere ask students to do problems "on the board" and then to tell what they have done. This is modeling if the students have been taught to *explain* what they have done. If they merely read what they have written on the board, the technique has limited value. Demonstrations should include the "process" and not just the "product."

Expert performance in context is different from demonstrations arranged specifically for the purposes of teaching. Shaquille O'Neal does not provide a commentary while taking a shot for the Orlando Magic. Yet boys and girls in the stands retain the memory of how he does it and return to their playgrounds to practice the same shot. This also is modeling. Students, however, do not often see a mathematician at work, a psychologist, an emergency medical technician, a chef, an electrical engineer, or a poet. Meeting and observing role models at work might help students envision a realistic future for themselves.

Drill

The various uses of the word "drill" have an interesting relationship. The origin of "drill" seems to be an archaic Dutch word for "hole." "To drill" a field means to bore row upon row of holes and put seeds in all of them. Drill is associated with order, uniformity, and repetition. Teachers who value individuality, originality, spontaneity, and independence tend to disparage drill. Yet drill has a purpose and produces results when used appropriately.

Repetition is useful. We repeat to remember. When we repeat something often enough, we learn to do it "automatically." Some things are best done uniformly and automatically. Traffic lights are most effective when everyone obeys them all the time. The product of two numbers is most useful if the same two numbers always have the same product, no matter who multiplies them. If we can make our verbs agree with our subjects without thinking much about them, we can pay more attention to what we are saying.

Drills may be organized for whole groups in the classroom, but time of involvement is increased when students are divided into small groups, led perhaps by capable student assistants. Computers have become worthy drill instructors. In a computer lab a whole classful of students can work simultaneously, but each student has an individual instructor controlling the pace and content of the drill. Computerized drill and practice is available in most subjects at levels appropriate for almost any age. However, teachers must make sure that computer-assisted drills, like all drills, are well coordinated with other methods of instruction. Students must be cooperative when engaged in a drill. If they are frustrated by the level of difficulty, they are not really engaged in a drill at all, because drill requires frequent successful repetition. Boredom, on the other hand, leads to rebellion.

The method of teaching foreign languages developed by John Rassias at Dartmouth University relies heavily on drill (Stansfield and Hornor 1980). Rassias's histrionic, emotional style of teaching is well known. That he is also a proponent of drill is not so well known. Two very different approaches integrated in a single course illustrate the need for different modes of instruction, each serving a specific purpose. In five hours a week of "master classes," students are engaged in skits and dialogues. These might be improvised entirely or might be adaptations of a text. In one technique known as a "micrologue," the teacher lectures for one minute to one student, who must then summarize what was said. All other students then answer questions about the lecture. These various exchanges, encompassing a broad emotional range, teach students to use the language for authentic communication. Drills, on the other hand, teach students to use the language automatically. For an additional five hours a week, students in groups of five to eight meet with a drill instructor. Rapid-fire questions produce approximately sixty-five responses per student per hour of class time. During the drill sessions, students are not allowed to consult books or notes. Games like "Jeopardy" and simulations of question-and-answer situations like press conferences add variety and fun to the drills. Instructors are encouraged to make the sessions exciting, and thus they use costumes, music, and visual aids to keep the students alert and wholly engaged. If a student delays in answering, the instructor calls quickly on another student, but always returns to the first. This combination of drill and authentic communication has helped foreign language students at Dartmouth achieve high levels of oral proficiency in relatively short periods of time.

The Rassias method exemplifies several important characteristics of effective drill. Drill is not an end in itself. Gains made through drill are integrated into the real task, in this case oral communication. The drill requires frequent repetition, with constant feedback to make sure that the right thing and not the wrong thing becomes automatic. And the format is frequently changed, with all sorts of clever variations, to offset boredom and to keep the students alert.

Simulations

Simulations engage students actively. To illustrate this effect of a simulation, we compare two classes taught by the same teacher (see Figs. 5-3 and 5-4). The first of the two classes was typical of this teacher's method of teaching history. A supervisor in the classroom noted all that was said and then classified the verbal interaction of the teacher and the students. The first few minutes of the class are represented in Figure 5-3. When the teacher examined this representation of the factual, question-and-answer, teacher-centered "discussion" he had led, he expressed his dissatisfaction.

This teacher said that he would prefer his students to talk to one another, to speculate about history, to question their opinions, to seek verification for their inferences. He felt that the students should have a goal for each class and come to class prepared, so that class time would be used productively. His intent in teaching had been to reinforce and explain the information in the textbook, but now he would

What the Teacher Does	What the Students Do
Provides information	
	CH asks about a procedure
Answers	
	CS comments on procedure
Provides information	
Asks a factual question	
	CZ answers
	JH answers
Accepts answers	
Provides information	
Asks factual question	
	JH answers
Criticizes answer	
Repeats question	
	BM answers
Accepts answer	
Asks factual question	
	JH answers
Accepts answer	
Asks factual question	
	JH answers
	CH answers
Accepts answers	
	CS asks interpretive question
Repeats CS's question	
	CS answers
Recognizes raised hand	
	LN answers
Asks interpretive question	
	BM answers
Provides information	
Asks interpretive question	
	CS asks for information
Provides information	
Asks factual question	
	JH answers
Accepts answer	
Recognizes raised hand	
	CF answers
Provides information	
Asks interpretive question	
	BM answers
Asks follow-up question	
	BM answers
Provides information	

FIGURE 5-3 An Excerpt from a History Class Showing Types of Verbal Interaction

prefer to help the students *use* the knowledge they found in the text and in other sources.

His first attempt at more active learning took the form of a simulation. He devised the simulation himself; it was nothing elaborate. On a Monday, he divided the students into two groups, the "Hamilton group" and the "Jefferson group." He told the Hamilton group to come to Friday's class prepared to advocate the formation of a national bank in 1791. He told the Jefferson group to come prepared to oppose the formation of such a bank. He would play the role of President Washington, and the students would be Washington's advisors. He began Friday's class by telling "his advisors" that he wanted to understand the advantages and disadvantages of forming a national bank so that he could decide on the best course of action for the country. The ensuing discussion shows the effect of this simple simulation on interaction among the students and the teacher. The first few minutes of the class are represented in Figure 5-4. Questions and answers are very different from those in previous classes. More students participate, and their contributions require thinking at a higher level than the factual recall of the first class. The students are doing the very things the teacher had hoped for, but never before achieved.

Simulations can be this simple, or they can be very elaborate. In the micro-society created at the Clement G. McDonough School in Lowell, Massachusetts, students elect representatives to their own government, refer discipline problems to their own court, manage and work for their own companies, and trade in "Mogans," their own currency, named for a former superintendent of schools. There are four strands to the curriculum at this magnet school: Publishing, Economy, Government, and High Technology. Students need what they learn in classes to fulfill their various responsibilities in the micro-society. They get jobs based on placement examinations and earn promotions based on performance. The micro-society school is as much reality as it is simulation. Rather than being "immature citizens of a larger society," they are "mature citizens of their own society" (Hayes, Hogan, and Malone 1991; Richmond 1973)

In simulations, students undertake life-like tasks with less risk and fewer complications than they would meet in equivalent real-life situations. Control and simplification increase the likelihood of success while limiting performance to specific skills. Practice tests, scrimmages, and rehearsals are actually simulations. Because simulations are con-

What the Teacher Does	What the Students Do
Gives directions	
	RS makes an assertion
	SEVERAL make a suggestion
	(ALL rearrange the seating)
	CS makes an assertion
Asks for elaboration	
	CF responds
	CS responds
	MR responds
Summarizes responses	
	CZ makes an assertion
	CS responds
	JH elaborates
	CF elaborates
	CZ responds
Asks speculative question	
	CS speculates
Asks for opinion	
	CZ offers opinion
	MR elaborates
	CS responds
	JH elaborates
Asks for clarification	
	LN clarifies
	CF elaborates
	SD questions
	CZ answers
Asks for clarification	
	CZ answers
	CS interrupts
Asks for opinion	
	CZ offers opinion
Asks for response	
	CZ responds
	CZ asks factual question
	MR answers
	CZ elaborates
	JH disagrees
	CF asks challenge question
	JH answers
	MR responds

FIGURE 5-4 Excerpt from History Class Showing Types of Verbal Interaction during a Simulation

trolled and simplified, and because they are further constrained by limitations of time and space, teachers must not assume that a simulation teaches students to do the task that it simulates. Simulations can only teach students to do what they do in the simulation. Teachers, therefore, must analyze the simulations they use and try to be precise about the behavior that students are required to practice. A simulation may exercise certain skills but may not be the best way to improve those skills. A simulation that takes huge amounts of class time may cause students to use a limited set of skills while neglecting other skills included in the objectives of the course. Carefully chosen and supervised, simulations are extremely valuable. No matter what students are learning to do, they must practice doing it. When "really" doing it is out of the question, or limits the teacher's opportunity to coach, a simulation might be the method of choice.

Real-Life Tasks

"Why do we have to learn this?"

"Is algebra useful in later life?"

"Do I have to know the difference between a restrictive and nonrestrictive modifier to get a job with a newspaper?"

In *A Place Called School,* John Goodlad (1984) reports that relatively few students expect their knowledge of academic subjects to be useful in their future. Only 57 percent of the high school students in the study expected *vocational* courses to be useful, and that was the *highest* figure for any subject. The next highest was 40 percent for mathematics. Even fewer of these students found anything they were learning in school to be useful to them in the present. Their estimate of the current relevance of their education appeared to decline the longer they stayed in school. Only English, mathematics, and vocational education were considered to be useful by more than 30 percent of middle school students, and only vocational education was considered to be useful by more than 30 percent of high school students.

We know from other research that students do not and sometimes cannot put their knowledge to use. The National Assessment of Educational Progress has shown that students who can calculate accurately cannot use mathematics to solve problems that require reasoning as well as calculating. Too many concluded that the number of buses needed to transport soldiers to an army base was "31 remainder 12." (Carpenter et al. 1983). Too many high school graduates rely on theories they formed in childhood to explain natural phenomena, rather than scientific principles they were "taught" in school (Bransford and Vye 1989). Students who have passed biology courses continue to think that plants receive energy from nutrients in the soil. Others who have passed physics courses think that a moving object retains the force that propelled it until the force wears down and the object comes to a halt. When students possess knowledge but do not use it for any purpose other than passing tests, the knowledge is said to be "inert."

Applications in the classroom—textbook problems, questions at the end of a chapter, typical science labs—are closely associated with specific bodies of knowledge. Math problems exercise knowledge of the algorithm that has just been taught. Answers to study questions are found in the pages of text immediately preceding the questions. Predictable science labs, if they "work," illustrate the topic of the week. In textbooks, clues to the solutions of problems are fairly obvious. One series of math texts was considered innovative simply because the type of problem associated with each chapter reappears in subsequent chapters (Saxon 1985). In real life, however, clues to the solution of problems are embedded in layer upon layer of detail, much of which is likely to be irrelevant. The very presence of a problem is not always certain. Experts discover problems in circumstances that appear perfectly normal to novices, or even to other experts. Whereas classroom problems are clearly defined and "decontextualized," real-life problems are poorly defined and inextricably connected to other problems that are also poorly defined.

Here are some textbook problems and some real-life tasks for comparison:

Find the area of a rectangular lot that has 250 feet of frontage along the road and extends 125 feet from the road.

The hallway is going to be carpeted. A representative from the carpet company will come to the classroom to show you samples of the types of carpet available. The class will estimate the advantages, disadvantages, and cost of using each type of carpet. You will present your estimates and recommendations in a written proposal to the Director of Buildings and Grounds.

Describe the members of the Martinez family whom you met in Chapter X. What did each one do on the first day of their vacation?

Interview an Hispanic immigrant. Ask this person to compare everyday experiences in his or her native country with experiences in the United States. What adjustments of lifestyle had to be made? Write a feature article that you might submit to a Spanish-language newspaper.

What is the relative humidity if the temperature is 72° F and the dew point is 24°F?

Keep a daily record of temperature, pressure, humidity, wind speed, precipitation, and any other data that might seem useful. Try to predict the weather. Evaluate and improve your method of prediction. Describe your methods, the improvements you made, and your results.

Why do you suppose Shakespeare used the poetic form of a sonnet when writing the first lines that Romeo and Juliet speak to one another (I, iv, 210–223)?

Is your dating restricted to people of a certain race, religion, or social class? Why? Have you ever dated anyone outside the accepted group? What might happen when you do? What advice do you get when you discuss dating someone "different" with your parents? Do your friends give you the same advice? Would the rules change if you were talking about marriage?

List six reasons for conserving water.

Make a recommendation for conserving water in your town. Using data gathered by reading and by experiment, compare current practice with recommended practice. Estimate the amount of water that might be saved per year if your recommendation achieved 100% compliance.

Textbook problems have a pedagogical purpose. They are solved quickly and easily by capable students. They permit repetition. They can be solved in any classroom or assigned for homework in any city in any state. Decontextualized problems facilitate a certain type of teaching and lead to a limited type of proficiency that is easily assessed.

Real-life problems, in contrast, are messy. They might cause people studying them to put on overalls or goggles or rubber boots. They differ from place to place. They stir up controversy. They attract the attention of people outside the school, who quite naturally have strong feelings about anything important in their lives. By decontextualizing education, schools escape all this bother. Classes can be scheduled in forty-five minute periods in relatively bare classrooms. Parents do not complain about their children getting wet or learning something controversial. The school does not have to worry about transportation, or special equipment, or anything unforeseen. And publishers can sell hundreds of thousands of books to schools in any community in any environment anywhere in the United States.

If, however, the exercise of proficiency is limited to textbook problems, students will continue to wonder if there is anything worth learning in school.

SUMMARY

Teaching teaches only if students learn. No one method of teaching will attain all the goals of learning, or even a single goal, because every school, every classroom, and every student is unique. Teachers therefore must have a repertoire of strategies and techniques that take advantage of all the necessary conditions and all the modes of teaching. Student achievement of learning objectives must be carefully assessed, and assessment must be used to evaluate the effectiveness of teaching. When students do not learn, the methods of teaching must be changed, re-evaluated, and changed again if necessary, until all the students learn. Even when all are learning everything that teachers intend to teach—the ideal to which we strive—conditions that no one had anticipated will cause schools to set new goals. Again teachers will be com- pelled to change the way they teach, and classrooms, schedules, materials, and equipment—the very fabric of the school—will also change.

REFERENCES

Bereiter, C. and M. Scardamalia. (1989). "Intentional Learning as a Goal of Instruction." In L. B. Resnick (Ed.), *Knowing, Learning, and Instruction: Essays in Honor of Robert Glaser.* Hillsdale, N.J.: Erlbaum.

Bransford J. V., and N. J. Vye. (1989). "A Perspective on Cognitive Research and Its Implications for Instruction." In L. B. Resnick and L. B. Klopfer (Eds.), *Toward the Thinking Curriculum: Current Cognitive Research.* Alexandria, Va.: Association for Supervision and Curriculum Development.

Carnegie Council on Adolescent Development. (1989). *Turning Points: Preparing American Youth for the 21st Century.* New York: The Carnegie Corporation.

Carpenter, T. P., M. M. Lindquist, W. Matthews, and E. A. Silver. (1983). "Results of the Third NAEPO Mathematics Assessment: Secondary School." *Mathematics Teacher 76,* 652–659.

Cliburn, J. W., Jr. (1986). "Using Concept Maps to Sequence Instructional Materials." *Journal of College Science Teaching 15:*4, 377–379.

Cliburn, J. W., Jr. (1990). "Concept Maps to Promote Meaningful Learning." *Journal of College Science Teaching 19:*4, 212–217.

Cooper, H. M., and D. Y. H. Tom. (1984). "Teacher Expectation Research: A Review with Implications for Classroom Instruction." *Elementary School Journal 85:*1, 77–89.

Fisher, C., N. Filby, R. Marliave, L. Cahen, M. Dishaw, J. Moore, and D. Berliner. (1978). *Teaching Behaviors, Academic Learning Time, and Student Achievement.* (Final Report of Phase III-B Beginning Teacher Evaluation Study). San Francisco: Far West Laboratory for Educational Research and Development.

Fogerty, J. L., M. C. Wang, and R. Creek. (1983). "A Descriptive Study of Experienced and Novice Teachers' Interactive Instructional Thoughts and Actions." *Journal of Educational Research 77:*1, 22–32.

Good. T. L., and J. E. Brophy. (1987). *Looking in Classrooms.* New York: Harper & Row.

Good, T. L., B. J. Reys, D. A. Grouws, and C. M. Mulryan. (1990). "Using Work-Groups in Mathematics Instruction." *Educational Leadership 47:*4, 56–62.

Goodlad, J. I. (1984). *A Place Called School.* New York: McGraw-Hill.

Hayes, D. P., S. E. Hogan, and T. F. Malone. (1991). "The Microsociety School." In *Interdisciplinary Curriculum in Middle Schools.* Reston, Va.: National Association of Secondary School Principals.

Holliday, W. G., P. E. Blosser, S. L. Helgeson, and B. L. S. McGuire. (1985). "A Summary of Research in Science Education." *Science Education 69:*3, 275–419.

Johnson, D. W., and R. T. Johnson. (1987a). *Learning Together and Alone: Cooperative, Competitive, and Individualistic Learning.* New York: Prentice-Hall.

Johnson, D. W., and R. T. Johnson. (1987b). *A Meta-Analysis of Cooperative, Competitive, and Individualistic Goal Structures.* Hillsdale, N.J.: Erlbaum.

Johnson, M. (1990). "The Science Skills Center, Brooklyn, New York: Assessing an Accelerated Science Program for African-American and Hispanic Elementary and Junior High School Students Through Advanced Science Examinations." In A. B. Champagne, B. E. Lovitts, and B. J Calinger (Eds.), *Assessment in the Service of Instruction.* Washington, D.C.: American Association for the Advancement of Science.

Joyce, B. R., and R. E. Hodges. (1981). "Flexibility as Repertoire." In B. R. Joyce, C. C. Brown, and L. Peck (Eds.), *Flexibility in Teaching: An Excursion into the Nature of Teaching and Training.* New York: Longman.

Marshak, D. (1986). *hm Study Skills Program, Level II.* Reston, Va.: National Association of Secondary School Principals.

McQuade, F. (1980). "Examining a Grammar Course: The Rationale and the Result." *English Journal* 69:7, 26–30.

McQuade, F. (1990). "Thinking and Learning." *Independent School* 50:1, 45–56.

Newman, F. M., and J. A. Thompson. (1987). "Effects of Cooperative Learning on Achievement in Secondary Schools: A Summary of Research." Madison: University of Wisconsin, National Center on Effective Secondary Schools.

Oakes, J. (1985). *Keeping Track: How Schools Structure Inequality.* New Haven, Conn.: Yale University Press.

Oakes, J. (1991). *Multiplying Inequalities: The Effects of Race, Social Class, and Tracking on Opportunities to Learn Mathematics and Science.* Santa Monica, Calif.: RAND.

Resnick, L. B. (1987). *Education and Learning to Think.* Washington, D.C.: National Academy Press.

Richmond, G. (1973). *The Micro-Society School: A Real World in Miniature.* New York: Harper & Row.

Rosenthal, R., and L. Jacobson. (1968). *Pygmalion in the Classroom.* New York: Holt, Rinehart & Winston.

Saxon, J. H., Jr. (1985). *Algebra I; Algebra II; Geometry; Trigonometry and Algebra III: An Incremental Development.* Norman, Okla.: Grassdale Publications.

Schmidt, W., and M. Buchman. (1983). "Six Teachers' Beliefs and Attitudes and Their Curricular Time Allocations." *Elementary School Journal* 84:2, 162–172.

Sharan, S., and H. Shachar. (1988). *Language and Learning in the Cooperative Classroom.* New York: Springer-Verlag.

Sharan, Y., and S. Sharan. (1990). "Group Investigation Expands Cooperative Learning." *Educational Leadership* 47:4, 17–21.

Shavelson, R. J. (1973). "What Is the Basic Teaching Skill?" *The Journal of Teacher Education* 24, 144–157.

Shavelson, R. J., and P. Stern. (1981). "Research on Teachers' Pedagogical

Thoughts, Judgments, Decisions, and Behavior." *Review of Educational Research 51*:4, 455–498.

Sizer, T. R. (1986). "Rebuilding: First Steps by the Coalition of Essential Schools." *Phi Delta Kappan 68*:1, 38–42.

Skon, L., D. Johnson, and R. Johnson. (1981). "Cooperative Peer Interaction Versus Individual Competition and Individualistic Efforts: Effects on the Acquisition of Cognitive Reasoning Strategies," *Journal of Educational Psychology 73*, 83–92.

Stansfield, C., and J. Hornor. (1980). *The Dartmouth/Rassias Model of Teaching Foreign Languages.* (ERIC Document ED197592).

Walberg, H. J. (1984). "Families as Partners in Educational Productivity." *Phi Delta Kappan 65*:6, 397–400.

Walberg, H. J. (1985). "Homework's Powerful Effects on Learning." *Educational Leadership 42*:7, 76–79.

Westerman, D. A. (1990). *A Study of Expert and Novice Teacher Decision Making: An Integrated Approach.* (ERIC Document ED322128).

White, R., and R. Gunstone. (1992). *Probing Understanding.* New York: Falmer Press.

6

ASSESSING STUDENT ACHIEVEMENT

TESTS AND GRADES

We educators have managed to forge a cast iron link between assessment and tests. Every student knows what tests are, but few would describe them as "the chance to express desired types of behavior," as Tyler (1949) described assessment in *Basic Principles of Curriculum and Instruction.* More likely, students would describe the common experience of being tested: There is a test at the end of each chapter or unit; the test is announced a few days in advance; students study for it by reviewing what they have learned; they know what the test will "cover," but they do not know what questions will be asked (to find out would be cheating); it is certain, however, that there *will* be questions on the test; the number of questions answered correctly will determine the grade; and all such grades will be averaged at the end of the term to provide the "test" grade. The "test" grade will be averaged with the "homework" grade, the "quiz" grade, and perhaps a few other grades, like the "essay" grade, the "oral report" grade, and the "class participation" grade to determine each student's "term" grade. Two, three, or four "term" grades will be averaged to produce the "final" grade. There will also be a "citizenship" grade and maybe an "effort" grade, but they usually "don't count."

Teachers often quantify their grades by telling students what percentage of the term grade is represented by tests, homework, class participation, oral reports, and so on. English and social studies teachers probably allot more weight to "essay" and "report" grades than do math and science teachers. Experienced students learn the ins and outs of rules adopted idiosyncratically by individual teachers: "Extra credit" may not raise the term grade by more than ten points; the lowest quiz grade of each term may be "dropped"; a poor test grade may be "made up," but the "make-up" grade will be no higher than a 70; grades are lowered ten points for every day that work is turned in late; any work outstanding on the last day of the term automatically gets a "0."

There is another type of test—another common experience of school. Students do not quickly forget being herded and hushed into the auditorium or gym to receive professionally printed test booklets, coordinated answer sheets, and #2 pencils. Although standardized tests have an enormous impact on education, students are largely unaware of any connection between these tests and their daily lives—until they take the SAT, that is. Schools have to be ingenious when explaining to students why they should take state-mandated standardized tests seriously and make an effort to do well. Yet many students, on the other hand, seek additional, out-of-school coaching for the SAT.

Tyler's model of assessment has been influential as a theory, even though it is only partially fulfilled in practice. Assessment of student performance, he argued, begins with objectives. Objectives for instruction describe the behavior one wants to teach, and assessment creates situations in which the desired behavior is likely to appear. One objective of a reading program, for example, might be that students will choose to read good literature. To assess achievement of this objective, students might be given a choice of reading any book in a library. If the books they choose are good literature, the objective is achieved. Clearly, good literature has to be defined and the behavior observed on several occasions, not just once, but these refinements are quite manageable. Characteristics of the behavior are recorded and measured—the amount of good literature read, for example, and maybe the percentage of good literature in a reader's diet. Information derived from assessment helps educators make decisions about the effectiveness of instruction, about each student's ability to learn, and about the program best suited for each student in the future.

Grades and scores are by-products—the measures and means of recording data—not the ends of assessment. Since educational decisions are indescribably complex and varied, it is a pity that a few highly generalized and abstract measures become attached to students like labels: a GPA, an IQ, a combined SAT. One would expect students to believe that the only form of assessment is tests and that the real purpose of tests is to select a few students for subsequent educational opportunities and to exclude the rest.

In addition to grading students, however, a comprehensive program of assessment will:

1. Provide information needed to evaluate the effectiveness of instruction
2. Suggest the next stage of learning for individuals and groups
3. Help teachers adjust their expectations of students
4. Embody the goals of teaching and learning
5. Set standards of achievement
6. Motivate students to achieve high standards
7. Communicate priorities
8. Reinforce the effort to learn
9. Teach students to evaluate their own work and set their own goals

ASSESSMENT IN RELATION TO GOALS AND OBJECTIVES

Teachers are frequently exhorted to "test what you teach and teach what you test." Since testing is seen primarily as a means of measuring how much a student has learned, it is considered both unfair and unwise to base this estimate on the performance of tasks that a student has had no chance to learn. Another reason for this good advice is that tests influence the motivation to learn. If something is taught and rarely tested, students are less likely to want to learn it.

Tests communicate to students what it is they are *really* expected to learn. "Will this be on the test?" is a question that teachers dread, yet students continue to ask the question in all sincerity, and they have every right to ask. The teacher makes the distinction between what a student is "required" to learn and what the student is merely "invited" to learn. The question "Will this be on the test?" is the student's way of making the same distinction. It is an important distinction to make, because most students cannot learn everything they are expected to learn. What will be on the test is a clear sign of priority, a chart for allocating time and energy. If a teacher finds in the question a student's reluctance to do anything extra for the sake of learning alone, then that is valuable information for the teacher who is interested in teaching students to be curious. Can curiosity be tested? Yes, and when curiosity is tested and rewarded, students will be more inclined to be curious. Tests are the "operational" objectives of the school.

How is curiosity tested? It must first be expressed as a desired behavior. Perhaps a science teacher sets out to teach students "to ask their own questions about science and seek the answers." A reading teacher might want to teach students "to gather information about the books studied, or about the authors, in addition to the information learned in class." These are behaviors. They may not express curiosity to the satisfaction of all readers, and no doubt a group of thoughtful readers could help us to refine these objectives—the chance to examine human qualities like curiosity is one of the pleasures of curriculum development. Once we have objectives, we have to expand the notion of a "test" to include other forms of assessment. We have to think of an opportunity to display the desired behavior. Perhaps the science teacher expects students to include a "Discussion" section in each lab report. In this section, students would have an opportunity to record the questions they had asked about each experiment and to describe what they had done to find answers to their questions. The teacher would record and measure the behavior—perhaps by counting and classifying the questions, perhaps by estimating the degree of effort displayed in the search for answers. The reading teacher, on the other hand, might ask students to keep a journal about their reading. In these journals they would have an opportunity to record, among other things, information about the books or the authors that they had gained independently. This information might also be quantified and classified. In any event, the assessment of curiosity would influence the assessment of the lab report or the journal, and curious students would be rewarded for their curiosity.

Understandably, students feel enormously betrayed when they believe that they have learned what was taught and then find that they were graded on something else. We can think of several reasons for this occurrence, none of them good.

Tests that do what they are supposed to do are sometimes hard to make. They take time that overburdened teachers might not have available. Tests are often constrained by institutional rules and conventions about grading, and teachers are not always encouraged to test what they purport to teach. Teachers also have a tendency to organize their work around methods of instruction rather than outcomes. Some will think of "creative" things to do in the classroom and "creative" questions to put on the test, without examining what the activites teach and what the questions test. If teachers were to analyze the time that students spend learning various types of information and skills throughout a term and the relative emphasis given to the same information and skills in the end-of-term test, they should find a high degree of congruence between the two.

Knowing the coercive power of tests and grades, and seeking to use that power to "raise standards" of student achievement, a determined department head, principal, or superintendent will sometimes institute new tests without prior approval or support from teachers. The hope is that teachers will modify their methods and outcomes so that their students will not be identified as failures. The practice is unfair to students and is probably also flawed as an implement of change. Almost all of the teachers we know teach what they believe the students should learn, and that usually coincides with what the teachers *can* teach. Teachers cannot suddenly start teaching something else with equal enthusiasm and success. Unless they understand and accept the new goals, know how to teach the new information and the new skills, and fully prepare their students to take the new tests, the students will suffer.

One can estimate the effectiveness of an assessment program by listing all the behaviors that are "tested" in a course, including assignments for "extra credit," and comparing the list with all the goals and objectives the course is expected to teach. If the exercise is to have any value, the list of goals and objectives will include the intellectual curiosity, problem solving, citizenship, love of learning, and so on that the school claims to be teaching. This comparison is appropriate for any level of assessment, for the course, department, or school. It will almost certainly reveal goals that are unassessed.

To build a comprehensive program of assessment, begin with the broadest goals of the school and ask what situations will give students an "opportunity to show the desired behavior." We have done that for the "Twelve Goals of Quality Education" required to be taught by all public schools in Pennsylvania (see note on page 185). Following each goal, we have listed situations in which students have an opportunity to display behavior that fulfills the goal. Our lists are not intended to be exhaustive or ideal; we intend only to illustrate the process. Anyone wishing to assess student achievement of a school's goals would go through a similar process, first listing situations that can be found or created in the school's environment. Later, any of these situations can be developed into a means of assessment. The opportunity to display the behavior is refined, and a means of recording and measuring the behavior is devised.

THE TWELVE GOALS OF QUALITY EDUCATION

Communication Skills

Quality education should help every student acquire communication skills of understanding, speaking, listening, reading, and writing.

Making a speech

Listening to speeches delivered by others

Discussing with peers and adults

Summarizing a speech, book, or article, orally or in writing

Evaluating oral and written communications

Writing an argument, editorial, story, play, or poem

Listening and responding to criticism

Managing in a society that speaks a foreign language

Mathematics

Quality education should help every student acquire knowledge, appreciation, and skills in mathematics.

Solving textbook problems

Collecting appropriate data and using the data to solve problems found in real life

Showing how knowledge of mathematical principles has influenced civilization

Extracting information from articles about mathematics

Programming a computer to solve types of mathematical problems

Describing various manifestations of a single mathematical principle

Showing how relationships of natural phenomena can be expressed mathematically

Science and Technology

Quality education should help every student acquire the knowledge, understanding, and appreciation of science and technology.

Designing and conducting an experiment to test a hypothesis

Telling the story of a scientific discovery

Summarizing the scientific knowledge about a single natural phenomenon

Collecting and analyzing the data needed to solve real-life problems

Designing and building a useful machine

Predicting the impact of a new product on society

Separating science from fiction in stories, advertising, and films

Citizenship

Quality education should help every student learn the history of the United States, understand its systems of government and economics, and acquire the values and attitudes necessary for responsible citizenship.

Knowing the history of racial and ethnic groups in the United States

Tracing the history of a current political or social issue

Showing through research that "history repeats itself"

Evaluating contributions of the United States to world peace and prosperity

Explaining the ethical implications of personal wealth

Planning and implementing a strategy to correct a social problem

Appraising one's own fulfillment of the responsibilities of citizenship

Acting to improve the quality of life in the school and community

Arts and the Humanities

Quality education should help every student acquire knowledge, appreciation, and skills in the arts and the humanities.

Becoming proficient in an art or craft

Developing a lifestyle that is interactive with visual and performing arts

Discovering and explaining the impact of arts on society

Making decisions influenced by aesthetic criteria

Enjoying and critiquing various styles of visual and performing arts

Learning about the values of a society from a study of its arts

Supporting the arts in one's own community

Analytical Thinking

Quality education should help every student develop analytical thinking.

Describing the structures found in oral and written communication

Organizing information according to the paradigms of a discipline or profession

Gathering, organizing, and retaining large quantities of information

Making decisions based on data and reasoned criteria

Implementing decisions and evaluating the results

Planning and meeting long-term goals through the achievement of subgoals

Using computer software to improve personal decision making and communication

Contributing to group planning and problem solving

Family Living

Quality education should help every student acquire the knowledge, skills, and attitudes necessary for successful personal and family living.

Identifying options and making plans for the future

Taking the first steps of the plan

Discussing personal and family life with a responsible confidant

Developing collaborative solutions to family problems presented in case studies

Contributing to the financial well-being of one's own family

Defining one's own responsibilities in personal life

Work

Quality education should help every student acquire the knowledge, skills, and attitudes necessary to become a self-supporting member of society.

Identifying the options and opportunities of various careers

Laying the academic foundation for future opportunities

Developing habits of integrity and perseverance

Learning to interact comfortably with people in various types of work

Agreeing to and fulfilling a contract for labor or services

Giving and receiving directions in a group project

Health

Quality education should help every student acquire knowledge and develop practices necessary to maintain physical and emotional well-being.

Maintaining physical fitness through exercise and diet

Choosing a lifestyle free of chemical abuse

Evaluating and selecting over-the-counter drugs and self-help treatments

Identifying appropriate and effective medical services

Coping with physical and emotional difficulties

Listening helpfully to friends in distress

Acting responsibly and constructively when accidents occur

Environment

Quality education should help every student acquire the knowledge and attitudes necessary to maintain the quality of life in a balanced environment.

Improving the immediate environment both ecologically and aesthetically

Knowing the options for waste disposal and choosing the best available

Advocating responsible management of the environment

Reading and thinking critically about environmental issues

Understanding the chemistry and ecology of energy sources

Predicting the effect of human behavior on the ecosystem

Self-Esteem

Quality education should help every student develop self-understanding and a feeling of self-worth.

Evaluating personal decisions

Anticipating and estimating risk when making plans

Preparing for challenge through practice and research

Examining, appraising, and forming personal values and beliefs

Persevering in times of hardship

Identifying conditions that one can and cannot influence

Aspiring to goals that challenge one's abilities and resources

Understanding Others

Quality education should help every student acquire knowledge of different cultures and an appreciation of the worth of all people.

Knowing the history, culture, and values of American racial and ethnic groups

Applying the laws of human equality and freedom to personal judgments

Living and working harmoniously in a multicultural environment

Learning the language and customs of another culture in preparation for travel

Enjoying the friendship of people whose appearance and beliefs differ from one's own

Listening to and respecting the points of view of people of either gender

Making ethical and moral decisions about one's influence on other people

This listing of situations helps one expand one's notion of assessment to embrace the full range of the school's goals. It also reveals the need for more instruments than paper-and-pencil tests. Often a school must participate in a testing program administered by a greater authority—the State Board of Education, for example. Pennsylvania has an Educational Quality Assessment, designed expressly to measure achievement of the "Twelve Goals" cited above. In urging schools to develop their own programs of assessment, we are not questioning the need for district, state, or even national organizations to set and monitor levels of achievement. We do believe, however, that the testing of large numbers of students by instruments designed for machine scoring severely limits the scope of any assessment, and schools must not let such testing supplant their own need to assess achievement of their own students. Each school must also resist the powerful pressure exerted by these limited tests to exaggerate certain parts of a larger and richer curriculum.

SCHOOLWIDE ASSESSMENT

After listing situations in which students have an opportunity to display goal-fulfilling behavior, teachers, administrators, and assessment consultants may select those in which they will observe, record, and measure student behavior. Assessment takes place at different levels. Some behavior is learned in specific classes and is therefore assessed at the level of the classroom. Some is learned through a sequence of classes in one subject and is best assessed by the academic department responsible for that subject. Some is learned through many experiences in and out of class, and that behavior is subject to assessment by the school as a whole. A certain amount of overlap will occur. The school may have some means of assessing achievement of citizenship goals, and some components of citizenship are assessed in history and government classes. The English department may conduct a periodic assessment of writing skills, but each English teacher is probably assessing the writing of some students in some form every day. Overlap is appropriate and useful. There are various purposes for assessing the achievement of students, and instruments designed primarily for one purpose may not suit the others.

What instruments will assess achievement of the overarching, schoolwide goals? One has first to determine the purposes of the assessment. Is the assessment meant to improve student attitudes and motivation? Will data derived from the assessment be used to improve, eliminate, or justify a program? What sorts of data are required? What decisions will the data inform? Will relevant data come from records of individual performance, or performance of a class of students, or a random sample? The student subjects of the assessment should also know the answers to these questions well before the assessment begins, especially if the results become a part of their individual records.

Frequently used instruments in the social sciences are the questionnaire and the interview. Both can be very useful, but both can also lead to disappointing results. Because questionnaires are widely used, almost everyone will have experienced the common problems: few responses, irrelevant responses, unquantifiable responses, unbelievable responses—and sometimes unprintable responses. In general, questionnaires are best when the population asked to complete and return them is highly motivated to provide accurate information. Yet even the most cooperative population can be irritated by too many questionnaires. In schools, teachers can distribute questionnaires to class-size groups, provide class time while students answer the questions, and ensure a high proportion of returns by collecting them personally. Even so, teachers and students have to believe that the data collected are useful and that time taken from class is well spent; otherwise the project is a prime candidate for sabotage.

One problem with interviews is that interviewees are influenced by interviewers. A teacher is not likely to get any information that might be considered discreditable to the student being interviewed. Another student might elicit such information—especially if the confidentiality of the interviewee is protected—but student interviewers would have to be trained for the task. (The training, however, might serve another educational goal.) Trained interviewers from outside the school might also be used to good purpose, and local universities doing research in schools can sometimes be interested in evaluative studies. While interviews are time-consuming, and expensive if conducted by paid consultants, they can elicit information normally omitted from questionnaires, which do not have the interviewer's capacity to interpret responses and ask follow-up questions.

Interviews with students graduating from a program present excellent opportunities for assessment. It is quite in the spirit of graduation and commencement to help students review what they have learned and identify their resources in light of plans and expectations for the future. In most high schools, exit interviews would be easy to arrange, since each senior has an established relationship with a college or vocational counselor. In a standard interview, modified each year as appropriate, we would ask questions related to our "Twelve Goals," particularly those of "Citizenship," "Work," "Self-Esteem," and "Understanding Others." The interviews would examine each graduate's awareness of social responsibilities, work attitudes, aspirations, self-confidence, and orientation to multicultural American society. Administrators, counselors, and teachers would each year determine the content of the interview and examine the results for signs of strengths and weaknesses in the educational program.

Schools concerned about citizenship and self-esteem might well consider the degree to which students can influence matters of school governance and curriculum. The degree of student involvement in decision making would certainly be an indicator of achievement in citizenship, and the opportunity to influence important decisions is likely to have an effect on self-esteem. If the school already has an active student government, there will be excellent opportunities for student-staffed assessment. Information requested by student committees might be more forthcoming and more candid than information requested by the school's administration and faculty.

Opportunities for schoolwide assessment are one of the by-products of an advisory system. If all the students in the school have a teacher-advisor and there are regular advisory meetings that encourage candid and respectful teacher-student relationships, these meetings can sometimes be used for data collection. Under these circumstances a combination questionnaire-interview is useful. The teacher listens to students as they discuss the questions, either individually or in small groups, and helps them formulate honest, helpful responses.

Through carefully planned questionnaires and interviews, one can find out how students define their responsibilities as citizens, how they feel about people of a different race, or how they evaluate their own actions. Questionnaires and interviews, in other words, can help one discover the degree to which students behave as one is trying to teach them to behave. Questionnaires and interviews, however, rely on how students report their behavior. Can behavior be assessed more directly?

In *Unobtrusive Measures: Nonreactive Research in the Social Sciences,*

Webb and colleagues (1966) describe methods of assessment that might seem unconventional to educators but must appeal to common sense. We recommend these methods for gathering data not otherwise available. They draw on sources that might easily go unnoticed or, if noticed, receive only anecdotal attention. If taken seriously, however, unobtrusive measures can provide compelling evidence concerning student achievement of school goals. They include physical traces in the environment, existing archives, and simple observation.

Physical traces related to the "Twelve Goals" would include the quantity and content of grafitti; the amount of litter; the books, notes, and other student writing found on the floor and in wastebaskets; damage to facilities; books defaced, lost, or stolen; injuries to students caused by other students; locked or unlocked lockers; decoration of lockers; decoration of classrooms and hallways; the amount and type of art displayed; the number and content of notices on bulletin boards; the defacement of notices on bulletin boards; food selected and consumed in the cafeteria; and so on.

Archival data would include the number and types of materials borrowed from the library; the number and types of infractions of school rules; the sign-ups for voluntary trips to concerts and museums; the number of students attending voluntary meetings; sales from the school bookstore and from vending machines; enrollment in elective courses, clubs, and other activities; issues raised in the school newspaper; voter turnout for school elections; formally lodged complaints and grievances; reports of theft; requests for letters of recommendation; drop-out rate and re-enrollment rates; the minutes of committee meetings; sign-ups for counseling services; written materials produced for students and parents; amounts of money raised for charity; the financial records of school clubs and other extracurricular activities. Records available in the larger community might also be relevant—the police blotter, voter registration, or membership in the scouting groups. Examination of these and similar archival sources will reveal much about the concerns, beliefs, and behavior of students.

Observation, like interviewing, influences behavior, but the influence can be minimized by simple precautions. Useful information can be collected by observing students arriving and leaving school, interacting in the cafeteria, occupying time when they are not in class, attending athletic events, or attending school assemblies. Observers with clipboards and notebooks are usually conspicuous, of course, and will sometimes be accused of spying. Inconspicuous observers are less likely to affect the behavior being observed but, when discovered, are more likely to be accused of spying. Nevertheless, there may be times when inconspicuous observation is acceptable. Tallying with a pocket counter is less conspicuous than using pencil and paper, and students in many situations will be less conspicuous observers than will teachers. The authors of *Unobtrusive Measures* discuss cases when situations are contrived for the purpose of observing and evaluating behavior. If simple observation can be irritating to those observed, contrived observation will seem more like entrapment. Is it justifiable for a teacher to leave the room in the middle of an exam for the purpose of checking student honesty? Is it justifiable to "plant" envelopes containing money or personal letters as in "Candid Camera"?

There is an abundance of data relevant to student achievement of school goals. It would be an impossible task to assess behavior related to all the goals all the time by all available means. Sometimes a growing concern about student behavior prompts an assessment. An outbreak of bullying might cause a school to assess student achievement of citizenship goals, or the number of students who seem to be smoking might cause a school to assess achievement of its health goals. Systematic assessment is preferable to hasty conclusions, exaggeration, and sounds of alarm, yet schoolwide assessment should be proactive as well as reactive. One or two goals might be chosen for assessment each year. In Chapter 2 we describe a cycle of curriculum evaluation and curriculum development. Information derived from assessment one year suggests improvements to be made the following year.

DEPARTMENTAL ASSESSMENT

Teachers working in isolation monitor student achievement only in their own courses. Teachers develop their own style of test, and the questions they ask are influenced by the materials they have chosen for their courses. Organization and collaboration are needed to plan and administer an assessment program that reveals how students have learned general knowledge, skills, and attitudes that are not dependent upon a specific text or a teacher's syllabus. Teachers collaborating in a program of assessment will help their students make connections between courses and meet standards set by the department. If teachers collaborate in assessment, they are likely to collaborate in other ways and to produce a more coherent educational experience for the students.

In Chapter 1 we showed how school goals are present in departmental goals. Continuing our analysis of the "Twelve Goals of Quality Education," we shall now look at methods for assessing achievement at the departmental level.

Each department will have created a sequence of subgoals that help students achieve the overarching, interdisciplinary school goals. If the school has decided that persevering in times of hardship is a component of self-esteem, each department will teach students to persevere. If the school has decided that agreeing to and fulfilling a contract for labor or services is a component of work, each department will teach students to know and fulfill their obligations. If the school has decided that solving problems is a component of the "Mathematics" goal, must all departments therefore teach math? Obviously not. Yet other departments *can* help students achieve *some* of the behavior needed to fulfill the "Mathematics" goal. Reading classes can help students read math texts. English, science, and social studies classes can help students integrate mathematical skills in argumentation, research, and interpretation of numerical data. Computer classes can teach students to program mathematical algorithms. And so on. Planning and coordinating departmental responsibilities is an important job for the school's Curriculum Committee. The amount contributed by each department to each goal will differ, and some departments will assume the principal responsibility for student achievement of some of the goals. Whatever the permutation, each department monitors its contributions through departmental assessment.

Teachers select the goals to assess at the departmental level and those to assess at the classroom level, with some overlap, of course, because teachers will want to know that their students are able to meet the departmental standards. Departmental assessment might include the final project or exam of a multisection course. A noteworthy feature of departmental assessment is that it temporarily removes the teacher from the role of evaluator and pushes the criteria of evaluation beyond the classroom. In this larger context, students find it easier to see the teacher as an ally helping them meet standards expected in the discipline. Teachers and students participate in the formative evaluation that guides a student's learning throughout the course, but when the time comes for a final evaluation, achievement may be assessed by a group of teachers who have agreed to common criteria. Departmental assessment of class projects will probably conserve a teacher's time. Teachers often feel compelled to write detailed comments about student work, but these comments have limited value at the end of a course. Departmental assessment relieves teachers of that temptation. Departmental assessment also helps preserve uniform and reasonable standards in large schools with many sections of each course.

A distinction should be made between departmental grading of the final project or exam in one course and assessment of the knowledge, skills, and values accumulated throughout several courses. To assess this accumulation of learning, each department must first describe the behavior needed to fulfill the departmental goals. Assessment at the classroom level addresses specific objectives, but departmental goals are broader. Like "curiosity," they have to be expressed as behaviors before they can be assessed. In Pennsylvania schools, departments might want to assess some of the following behaviors, all of which contribute to achievement to one of the "Twelve Goals." Again our list of examples is not intended to be ideal or complete, merely to illustrate the process of departmental assessment.

Language Arts

Writing an argument, editorial, story, play, or poem
The feeling of confidence when writing about a familiar subject
Frequent voluntary reading of age-appropriate literature
Comprehension of a variety of texts

Mathematics

The ability to use math textbooks for independent learning
Using accumulated knowledge and skill to solve a variety of
   problems
Persevering when a problem is difficult
Programming a mathematical algorithm for variable data

Foreign Language

Fluency of conversations with a native speaker
Knowledge of and respect for the culture being studied

Ability to cope when speaking a foreign language in unrehearsed situations

Explaining a country's national priorities in international relations

Science

Ability to design and conduct an experiment to test a hypothesis

Ability to synthesize knowledge from the various sciences

Applying scientific knowledge to health and environmental safety

Designing and making a safe and effective apparatus

Social Studies

Ability to gather and evaluate information

Ability to synthesize the history, geography, culture, and economics of a world region

Basing opinions and actions on reliable information and ethical reasoning

Presenting a clear and persuasive argument in writing or in speech

Arts

Using aesthetic criteria when appraising

Expressing feelings and ideas through the media of the arts

Becoming a knowledgeable and discriminating audience or viewer

Explaining the relationship between art forms and the feelings they evoke

Physical Education and Health

Setting goals for personal well-being and planning programs for exercise and diet

Developing a philosophy of competition and cooperation

Avoiding chemical abuse

Helping others physically and emotionally

The next step is to imagine situations in which student performance can be observed, measured, and recorded. The language arts department, for example, can find out how frequently students are reading age-appropriate literature from library records. The reading record of each individual student is confidential, but the reading patterns of whole classes may be examined. Another way to assess voluntary reading habits is to ask students to keep a written record of their reading. This record may be a card for each book or article, appropriately filed in an indexed box kept in each classroom. Levels of sophistication can be assigned to books and articles, so that teachers can make judgments about the quality as well as the quantity of the reading. If this assessment influences grades in class, however, students are more likely to falsify the record by omitting their "low"-quality reading and exaggerating their "high"-quality reading. If ungraded, the records will yield valuable information about the reading habits of individual students, groups of tudents, and the effectiveness of reading instruction.

If the mathematics department wanted to assess the students' ability to learn independently from mathematics textbooks, the teachers of one course might give an "open-book" test. Questions on the test might ask students to summarize selected passages from the textbook or solve problems using information found through reading. If a similar test were given at about the same time each year, teachers in the math department would be able to monitor their success in teaching students how to read the textbook.

A number of the behaviors would be assessed by asking students to write essays. A useful way to assess writing is to use the method of "holistic scoring" developed by Educational Testing Service for national examinations and now widely used in schools and colleges (Elliot, Plata, and Zelhart 1990). Teachers agree on the major criteria of a scoring guide and then read the student responses quickly, basing a single score on overall effect rather than detailed analysis. Scores can be grouped by grade level and by class to reveal information about the achievement and growth of large groups of students. If more detailed analysis of the writing is required, each student's work can go to the student's teacher after scoring, where it can be considered in the context of the student's current class in the subject. This methodology has been extended to the scoring of portfolios. However, because portfolios contain a variety of student work developed over a period of time, it is virtually impossible to arrive at a single score that can be used to compare the achievement of different students or groups of students.

Camp (1992) describes a process of developing evaluative criteria from the language of teachers as they read, discussed, and compared a sample set of portfolios. The vocabulary they used revealed the dimensions along which they were able to compare the various types of writing contained in the portfolios. Using this vocabulary, a rough scale was developed along each of these dimensions: the accomplishment represented by the writing, the student's awareness and use of strategies for writing, and the student's development as a writer.

"Holistic" assessment requires experts to form an opinion about the general qualities and characteristics of each performance, similar to the scoring of ice skaters in competition. In some cases, however, the purpose of assessment requires evaluators to record specific characteristics or behaviors. These specific judgments can be recorded in the form of a code. If, for example, one were looking for the synthesis of biological, physical, chemical, and ecological information in essays about a natural phenomenon like "rain," one could tally each occurrence with a *B, P, C,* or *E.* One could also distinguish among levels of sophistication by using a numerical scale. The statement "You sometimes see a rainbow when it rains," might be coded *1P* (physics at level 1), whereas "A combination of refraction and internal reflection separates sunlight passing through raindrops into two rainbows, one brighter than the other" would receive a higher numerical score. In this way one could measure the frequency and sophistication of references to the various disciplines of science. Readers scoring essays usually have to be trained before they can arrive at an acceptable level of interreader reliability. Training the members of a department in holistic scoring might be a simple matter of comparing and discussing scores for a few sample essays, but training readers to do a coded analysis is likely to be more complicated.

Interviews as a means of assessment are underused in schools. Interviews take time, and their results are often difficult to interpret. Nevertheless, interviews get at information about a student's ideas and attitudes that is not available any other way. This is why they are commonly used in college admissions and job placement. Everyone has to "pass" an interview at various important times in one's life. Interviews used for assessment in schools would reinforce the importance of proficiency in this form of oral communication. Yet schools neglect the interview, even when selecting students for academic honors. How else can one assess ability to converse in a foreign language? Foreign language interviews do not have to take place at the teacher's desk. They can take the form of simulations: Can the student purchase theater tickets, place an ad in a local newspaper, interview for a job? If an art department arranges an exhibition of student or professional work, on-the-spot interviews will reveal valuable information about the attitudes and knowledge of students who come to see it. Even brief interviews of students selected at random will tell a social studies department how well students use their knowledge of history to understand current events or what they know about the positions of candidates in an imminent election. In science, interviews are the recommended way to probe students' depth of understanding (Raizen et al. 1989). The interview can be combined with a test of lab skills in which students are asked to formulate and test a hypothesis using equipment available in the lab.

What students think they are doing and why they are doing it is sometimes more revealing than what they actually do. We are reminded of a driving instructor whose student quite correctly drove through an intersection just as the light changed from green to yellow, and on impulse the instructor asked what had gone through the student's mind when the light changed. "What light?" the student asked.

CLASSROOM ASSESSMENT

Bereiter and Scardamalia (1989) draw a distinction between learning and schoolwork. We expect students to achieve the complex goals for learning by doing the daily schoolwork we assign. Since success in schoolwork is assumed to be progress toward the goals, it is understandable that teachers and students focus their energies on schoolwork. Truly wishing to help students do their best, teachers assume responsibility for planning classes, arranging the sequence of activities, asking the questions, making the tests, setting the standards, evaluating the answers, and, when necessary, devising new strategies. Students, meanwhile, follow directions. They do each assignment, answer each question, unaware of the long-term goals and their progress in relation to the goals. Thus, learning degenerates into schoolwork.

It is crucial to the effectiveness of schools that students know the goals for learning, adopt them as their own, and see assessment as a measure of progress. What we want the students to learn and how we ask them to show that they have learned, if not identical, must at least be congruent. If we want them to write, we assess their writing. If we want them to remember, we asssess their memorization. If we want them to understand, we assess their understanding. If we want them to apply their knowledge, we assess their applications. If we want them to be curious, we assess their curiosity. If we want them to learn for the sake of learning, we assess their motivation.

A body of research in cognitive science has compared novice and expert performances in various disciplines (Chi, Glaser, and Farr 1990), and teachers are beginning to align the goals of instruction with the characteristics of expert performance. One result of this shift is the development of "authentic" classroom activities. When writers write, they write to communicate something they know to an audience that does not know it. They conceive the ideas for their work, they write drafts, they discuss their work with others, they revise, they publish. Authentic tasks in the writing classroom parallel the tasks of the writer, and English teachers have begun to find ingenious and satisfying ways in which their students can write and publish for real audiences. Historians gather information from primary and secondary sources, they evaluate the reliability of their sources, they draw conclusions based on evidence, they discuss their conclusions with other historians, and they write essays to show that their conclusions are valid. If young historians do likewise, they learn history as history is practiced and not merely facts "about" history. This trend in teaching leads to "cognitive apprenticeships," in which students learn the fundamentals of a discipline through work experiences in the classroom (Collins, Brown, and Newman 1989).

If assessment is congruent with methods and goals, assessment will also be authentic. While authentic tests might seem new to the classroom, they are not new to education. Wiggins (1989) has pointed out that student athletes, musicians, actors, and dancers are evaluated in the performance of tasks that are very similar to the work of experts in their fields. Athletic competitions and artistic performances justify the drill, the memorization, the labor, and the pain that are part of the learning process. Authentic tests, Wiggins argues, can be equally rewarding and place students in the same arena as the experts they aspire to be. The characteristics of an authentic test, according to Wiggins, include:

Structure and Logistics: Authentic tests are public, involving an audience or panel of judges. Evaluation entails multiple criteria. Success often requires collaboration. Assessment is recurring, so that lessons learned from one test are applied to the next.

Intellectual Design: Authentic tests have a context that has meaning and purpose other than testing the students. They are comprehensive, a culmination of practice and preparation, not fragmentary. They allow broad latitude for individual style and judgment.

Standards: Criteria are complex and are derived from expertise in the discipline. Because assessment is public, students can compare themselves to other students and recognized experts. Self-assessment is encouraged.

Fairness and Equity: Students can build on their strengths and interests. Not all students are required to do the same thing in the same way. Authentic tests are fair because they do not favor one learning style or aptitude.

The following discussion of assessment in each of the academic disciplines will help teachers design their own authentic tests.

Language Arts

An interesting trend in assessment in language arts is an adaptation of the artist's portfolio. A portfolio is a representative sample of the artist's work, used primarily when artists want to demonstrate their capabilities to galleries, agents, academies, or prospective employers. Used for assessment in language arts, a portfolio is a representative sample of student writing (Wolf 1989; Yancey 1992).

A teacher may specify what the portfolio should contain, recognizing that much of an artist's production is not fit for publication. Early drafts are abandoned or extensively revised. If students have some freedom to select and opportunity to polish work for their portfolios, they are more likely to experiment, to take risks, and to learn about their strengths and limitations. Self-evaluation is encouraged, because the student must make decisions about what to select and what to leave out. If the portfolios in a classroom are open to scrutiny, students can compare their own work to the work of classmates and develop a realistic sense of standards.

An authentic test of writing requires students to communicate with an actual audience. Teachers are learning to replicate the conditions of publication using the resources available in a school. We know of first-graders who write, illustrate, and bind stories into "books" that are then shelved in the school library for other young students to borrow. Bulletin boards in the corridors of some schools are the "broadsides" of school society, where students write about public issues. Writing produced for class projects—"newspapers" produced in foreign language and history classes, for example—can be posted on the walls outside the classroom. Debates can be conducted in a public forum or in another class studying the topic. Many such projects entail reading, naturally, but also other kinds of research—questionnaires, observations, interviews, or laboratory experiments. Projects can be judged by a teacher, a committee, or, for added excitement, a distinguished guest, who can also tell students about the work of experts in the same field.

Mathematics

Curriculum and Evaluation Standards of the National Council of Teachers of Mathematics (1989) emphasize that mathematics is an activity that all sorts of people "do." Students should not only "learn" math; they should "do" math. As usually taught and tested in schools, mathematics is a seemingly endless set of rules that apply to precisely defined numerical situations. Students learn to recognize a type of situation, learn the rules that apply to it, and show that they can apply the proper rules in cases that fit the type. Then they move on to another type of situation, another set of rules, and so on. Most of the situations are represented in numbers, so that students can immediately apply the rules of calculation, but some are "word" problems, in which students must translate verbal statements into a numerical situation about which they know the rules. If students learn slowly, however, many teachers save time by omitting the word problems.

The students' experience of mathematics is like "drill" in athletics. They drill, drill, drill, but, unlike young athletes, young mathematicians never get to play the game.

As mathematics instruction moves beyond drill to include mathematical reasoning and problem solving, assessment must keep abreast of the changes. Tests would emphasize problem solving rather than calculating. Students would learn to solve various types of problems, including "mixed" problems, which require the integration of algorithms taught at different times, and "ill-defined" problems, in which the algorithms to be used are not at all clear in the presentation of the problem. Ill-defined problems, in fact, might offer more data than are needed, or insufficient data. Not all problems are easily solved, and therefore assessment of problem-solving skills cannot always be accomplished in a forty-minute period. As students learn to persevere and to collaborate with classmates when solving difficult problems, assessment will entail group problem solving over longer periods of time, a week or more for older students.

We tell students that mathematics is useful. Its usefulness would be more apparent if mathematics sometimes appeared in other subjects. Students learn, for example, that the research in "research papers" is conducted in a library. If this is their only experience of research, they will not learn how to collect numerical data and use mathematical models for understanding and manipulating the data. Quantitative investigations require students to draw conclusions based on calculations and to communicate their conclusions using various forms of representation—verbal, graphic, and numerical. If students are learning to conduct quantitative investigations, which are relevant in English and social studies classes as well as science and math classes, the research project is the appropriate form of assessment (Countryman 1992).

Greenes (1989) describes one such project undertaken by a group of ninth-grade students. They wondered about the white stripes in the middle of the roadway. How long are they? What makes them reflective at night? What is the relationship between the speed of a car and the frequency at which the stripes appear to flicker? The students gathered data, set up mathematical models, and calculated the rate of flickering caused by cars driven at different speeds. Library research turned up information about strobe lights and epilepsy. Cars, they discovered, could not travel so fast that epileptics need worry about looking at the stripes.

Foreign Languages

The American Council on the Teaching of Foreign Languages (1986) has produced a series of guidelines for assessing proficiency in speaking, listening, reading, writing, and culture. Proficiency in each area is classified as Novice, Intermediate, or Advanced. Each level is further divided into three categories: Low, Mid, and High. Specifications for the nine levels of proficiency in each of the five areas are fairly detailed. Anyone assessing student achievement in foreign languages can use both the generic guidelines and those available for specific target languages.

Foreign language teachers, like mathematics teachers, have tended to use tests that are closely linked with recent instruction. After studying a chapter in the textbook, for example, students take a test on the vocabulary and grammar presented in the chapter. The chapter might include a story about a family on vacation, and hence the test items might all be related to the story and the students' general knowledge of vacations. If all tests are of this type, students can succeed in the course by memorizing vocabulary and sample phrases but without advancing their general ability to use the target language in less structured situations, when communicating with a native speaker, for example. Assessment, therefore, must put students into situations they have learned to manage but cannot rehearse, so that general levels of proficiency can be observed. As described earlier, these situations can be interviews, simulations, and real-life tasks that require the use of the target language. Advanced students, faculty, and native speakers may be recruited to conduct the interviews or take roles in the simulations, freeing the teacher to assess the students' performance. If performance can be recorded on audio- or videotape, so much the better. The recordings will help students to arrive at a self-assessment, and the opportunity to hear and see excellent performances in similar situations will help each student envision success.

Science

Raizen and colleagues (1989) have identified three areas for assessment in science: knowledge, skills, and the disposition to act appropriately when no action has been prescribed. Paper-and-pencil testing is appropriate for assessment of knowledge, and consequently most of the assessment that is currently conducted in schools assesses knowledge. Assessments of skills and dispositions are not so easy to arrange, although testing for lab skills is certainly within the reach of teachers who teach lab courses. Testing the disposition to think scientifically is most difficult, because the disposition is most evident when students are not required to think scientifically. Even if one arranges a task in which students are not *required* to but *may* think scientifically, one cannot safely infer that those who think scientifically in that one instance are disposed to think scientifically all the time. The behavior has to appear frequently over a period of time to justify the inference of a disposition. Yet the disposition seems to be an important component of science learning. Perhaps the best that teachers can do is to keep anecdotal records and reinforce voluntary scientific thinking when it appears.

Although science teachers everywhere are testing knowledge, not all teachers attempt to discover how students have organized their knowledge. Familiar formats like matching, fill-in-the-blanks, word definitions, labeling, multiple-choice, and even problems requiring mathematical calculations based on scientific formulas ask for discrete bits of information. Students who answer 20 or 30 percent of the questions incorrectly (and probably pass the test) might be led astray by basic misconceptions. Even students who answer every item correctly might harbor misconceptions about fundamental principles. For example, a student who mistakenly believes that evolution is guided by purposeful adaptations to environmental pressures might also be quite capable of describing the cause of mutations and citing examples of organisms that have adapted successfully to their respective niches. To discover basic misconceptions, teachers must require students to summarize knowledge in coherent chunks in addition to remembering discrete bits of information.

Assessment of laboratory skills might also be fragmentary unless teachers ask students to incorporate specific skills into larger scientific tasks. A basic routine in a lab, for example, entails finding the mass of a liquid in a container. That skill might be tested as one item in a series of disconnected items. Or students might be given a larger task that resembles a scientific experiment (Raizen et al. 1989):

> Predict the relative quantities of heat required to raise the temperature of 100g of ice from $-10°C$ to $15°C$; from $-4°C$ to $1°C$; and 100g of water from $5°C$ to $10°C$.
>
> Design an experiment to test your prediction.
>
> Perform the experiment.
>
> Compare your results with your prediction.
>
> Develop an explanation for any differences.

Design an experiment to test your hypothesis.

While tasks of this type are common enough in lab exercises, students usually follow the step-by-step directions of a lab manual. Their ability to design and conduct an experiment using the proper lab skills is rarely assessed. Assessments like the one above are conducted in a lab while the teacher observes and records student behavior on a checklist prepared for the purpose.

Social Studies

The social studies are a loosely defined conglomeration of subjects. The National Commission on Social Studies in the Schools (1989) recommended that geography and history be the matrix into which concepts from political science, economics, anthropology, sociology, and psychology be integrated. The Bradley Commission (1989) advocated history throughout the elementary grades and for four more years, at least, after sixth grade. Common to all social studies are the skills of gathering and evaluating information, drawing reasonable inferences, and communicating those inferences persuasively in speech and writing. While there is no national consensus concerning whose history and whose culture should be studied, there are powerful reasons to take a global approach, emphasizing the multicultural history of the United States.

Since the social studies do not comprise a tightly organized discipline of knowledge and skills, teamwork in curriculum and assessment is especially important. If teachers participate fully in the process of curriculum development, they will know how the outcomes of the courses they teach accumulate to produce the outcomes of the department and the school. A social studies teacher in a school that aims to achieve the "Twelve Goals of Quality Education," listed earlier in this chapter, will have a complex set of responsibilities, since social studies contribute richly to achievement of these goals.

Assessment will provide students with opportunities to collect quantifiable data and to use the statistical procedures they have learned in mathematics classes. Students will read and draw inferences from numerical and graphic data as well as from verbal data. They will also present data in various forms and incorporate these forms into coherent arguments presented orally and in writing to audiences they have some need to persuade. If these procedures of data gathering, presentation, and argument are to be authentic, the students will become involved in issues and arguments that have meaning in their lives. They will want to influence public opinion in some way, in the classroom, the school, or the larger community.

According to the Bradley Commission, history contributes both to the personal and the public aims of education. Ethnic and racial history will help students achieve the "Self-Esteem" and "Understanding Others" goals. Students of any age can collect, edit, and transcribe oral histories. They might employ the methodology of the historian by checking the recollections of people they interview against available public records. While studying personal histories, they may read and write biographies. To assess understanding of the interrelationship between national and personal histories, students might be asked to explain the combination of social, economic, and personal reasons why their families moved to their present location. Projects of this type are likely to be highly motivating, and it is relatively easy for a teacher to formulate criteria for judging the products, both oral and written.

History also contributes to the "Citizenship" goal. If good citizenship is a matter of choosing well when choice influences the well-being of others, assessment in history must ask students to choose. They should know about similar choices made in the past, contexts in which they were made, and the consequences. They should also be able to describe the similarities and differences between then and now and to predict the likely consequences of choices made today. If we want students to make connections between the past and the present, they should be asked to make those connections—not as an occasional diversion, but consistently, especially when it "counts" on a test.

When historians write books and articles, they make assertions about the past and cite evidence that justifies their assertions. They ask questions that interest them and construct answers to their questions from data they find in documents and other artifacts. They also cite the work of other historians, sometimes to enlist support for their own opinions and sometimes to refute contradictory opinions. Students learning history should be expected to do likewise. Their research cannot be as time consuming or ambitious as the research conducted by professionals, but almost any town library, museum, or historical society contains sources that will challenge the capabilities of the student historian. Assessment of writing in history classes should certainly provide students with opportunities to ask and answer interesting historical questions. History teachers must be prepared to teach their students the criteria of good research and sound argument (Holt 1990).

Arts

Significant changes are taking place in art education as art teachers, wishing to demonstrate that what is learned in art is as valuable as anything learned in any other subject, begin to plan their courses in terms of outcomes, assessment, and accountability. What is now considered traditional art education was heavily influenced by Viktor Lowenfield (1952), for whom the justification of art in schools was the growth of the children and not the development of their artistic capabilities. For Lowenfield, it was a mistake to assess the achievement of children by their creative products. What mattered was their emotional, intellectual, and motor development. Since art teachers have not had the means, other than intuition, of evaluating child development, traditional art teaching has neglected assessment. Now, according to Michael Day (1985), methods of assessment most clearly distinguish the traditional in art education from the contemporary.

As the arts occupy increasing prominence in the general curriculum, they provide more than a "creative recess" in the elementary school and more than vocational training in the high school. Gardner and Grunbaum (1986) recognize that study in any of the arts can lead to knowledge as well as the production of art works. They describe the PROPER study of the arts as a combination of production, perception, and reflection—hence the use of "proper" as an acronym. Assessment of knowledge may be similar to assessment of knowledge in other fields, the usual paper-and-pencil tests. However, they recommend the use of artistic media to assess knowledge that is unique to each of the arts. The ability to perceive concepts, for example, is revealed if students can select works or pieces of works in which certain concepts are present. A student who can identify the start and finish of a fugue while listening to music possesses a different type of knowledge from that of the student who can merely define the word. Furthermore, a student who can use metaphor, or color, or counterpoint, or tone of voice to produce a desired effect possesses a different type of knowledge from that of the student who can merely identify these concepts.

Arts teachers, it is claimed, typically employ more instructional techniques than teachers of any other subject (Goodlad 1984). Day (1985) suggests that they need more methods of assessment. He lists eleven methods for studio use:

1. *Observation:* The teacher observes students at work, noting how students use the medium, how active they are, how flexible, how much they collaborate, etc.
2. *Interview:* Students answer questions about their own work, their intentions, plans for revision and completion, perceived relationship of current and previous work, etc.
3. *Discussion:* The teacher listens as students discuss a topic, noting the examples they cite, their vocabulary, their use of concepts, etc.
4. *Checklist:* The teacher keeps a checklist or matrix of skills, noting each student's demonstration of competence.
5. *Performance:* The students produce sketches, drafts, or notes, which may serve to develop their own work or to analyze existing work of masters.
6. *Questionnaire:* Students provide information about their work or themselves. The questionnaire might reveal acquisition of an attitude or readiness to use new equipment.
7. *Test:* Students show that they know certain facts.
8. *Essay:* Students show that their inferences are valid.
9. *Identification:* Students identify examples and nonexamples of concepts.
10. *Attitude measurement:* How students rank preferred works might provide some insight into their attitudes.
11. *Aesthetic judgment:* Students select works that fulfill criteria taught in the course.

Teachers and researchers in ARTS PROPEL—a collaboration of Harvard University's Project Zero, Educational Testing Service, and the Pittsburgh Public Schools—have focused on three types of assessment in the arts: projects, portfolios, and reflective interviews (Wolf 1988, 1989). When working on projects, students are expected to save sketches, drafts, outlines, revisions, and notes at each phase of their work. Reviewing these as well as the finished project, a teacher can assess the student's creative process. Information derived from the "biography" of a project enables the teacher to make and the student to understand recommendations for future growth. Portfolios record growth over a period of time. They contain examples of finished projects, journals, sketches, revisions, and exercises. Portfolios in the performing arts include recordings in addition to written and graphic materials. Because they contain a range of works they reveal a student's strengths and weaknesses.

A student artist might also be asked to include an analysis and self-evaluation of the portfolio, which will reveal much about the student's independence. Alternatively, the self-evaluation may be recorded in the form of an interview. The interview may be conducted by a practicing artist, an art student, another teacher in the school, the current art teacher, or a classmate. By asking the right questions, the interviewer brings the student close to aspects of the work that the student might not otherwise have noticed. Similarly, information provided by the student can help the interviewer make a more accurate assessment of the product and the creative process. If an interview is a part of the assessment, students should have a chance to practice being interviewed. Learning to represent themselves well while talking about their work might be one of the goals of the arts program. Projects, portfolios, and reflective interviews all encourage students to think of themselves as artists, with their own styles, themes, and plans for future work.

SUMMARY

Assessment is inextricably connected to the goals and objectives of instruction. What schools claim to teach, in other words, should be taught, and what is taught should be tested. Assessment takes many forms other than paper-and-pencil tests, however, and serves many puposes other than grading individual students. Assessment motivates students to achieve the goals and objectives of instruction, for example. For that reason, assessment should address all the goals and objectives of the curriculum, not just some of them. A comprehensive plan to assess student achievement consists of three levels. Achievement of school goals is assessed through schoolwide assessment, departmental goals through departmental assessment, and course objectives through classroom assessment. At each level, assessment provides students with opportunities to display various behaviors that embody the goals and objectives. What students do when given these opportunities is recorded and measured. When a goal is general, anyone wishing to make an assessment must first express the goal in terms of behavior and then devise a situation in which students have an opportunity to display the behavior. As a new understanding of expert behavior influences teaching and learning, new forms of assessment are appearing in all subjects—portfolios, interviews, projects, investigations, questionnaires, and "authentic" tests, all of which engage students in tasks that resemble the tasks performed by experts.

NOTE

While this book was in production, Pennsylvania adopted a set of fifty-three outcomes to replace the Twelve Goals of Quality Education. We could have chosen almost any set of goals, standards, or outcomes to illustrate the development of school-based assessment. The Twelve Goals gave us a satisfactory example of systemwide standards supported by systemwide assessment, and although they are no longer used in Pennsylvania, we see no need to choose another example.

REFERENCES

American Council on the Teaching of Foreign Languages. (1986). ACTFL *Proficiency Guidelines.* Hastings-on-Hudson, N.Y.: American Council on the Teaching of Foreign Languages.

Bereiter, C., and M. Scardamalia. (1989). "Intentional Learning as a Goal of Instruction." In L. B. Resnick (Ed.), *Knowing, Learning, and Instruction: Essays in Honor of Robert Glaser.* Hillsdale, N.J.: Erlbaum.

The Bradley Commission on History in Schools. (1988). *Building a History Curriculum.* Washington, D.C.: Educational Excellence Network.

Camp, R. (1992). "The Place of Portfolios in Our Changing Views of Writing Assessment." In R. Bennett and W. Ward (Eds.), *Construction Versus Choice in Cognitive Measurement.* Hillsdale, N.J.: Erlbaum.

Chi, M. T. H., R. Glaser, and M. Farr. (1989). *The Nature of Expertise.* Hillsdale, N.J.: Erlbaum.

Collins, A., J. S. Brown, and S. E. Newman. (1989). "Cognitive Apprenticeship: Teaching the Craft of Reading, Writing, and Mathematics." In L. B. Resnick (Ed.), *Knowing, Learning, and Instruction: Essays in Honor of Robert Glaser.* Hillsdale, N.J.: Erlbaum.

Countryman, J. (1992). *Writing to Learn Mathematics: Strategies That Work, K–12.* Portsmouth, N. H.: Heinemann.

Day, M. D. (1985). "Evaluating Student Achievement in Discipline-Based Art Programs." *Studies in Art Education 26,* 232–240.

Elliot, N., M. Plata, and P. Zelhart. (1990). *A Program Development Handbook for the Holistic Assessment of Writing.* Lanham, Md.: University Press of America.

Gardner, H., and J. Grunbaum. (1986). "The Assessment of Artistic Thinking: Comments on the National Assessment of Educational Progress in the Arts." Washington, D.C.: Paper commissioned by The Study Group on the National Assessment of Student Achievement, Office of Educational Research and Improvement.

Goodlad, J. I. (1984). *A Place Called School.* New York: McGraw-Hill.

Greenes, C. (Summer 1989). "Math Education Reform: The Time is Now." *Academic Connections,* 6–8.

Holt, T. (1990). *Thinking Historically: Narrative, Imagination, and Understanding.* New York: The College Board.

Lowenfield, V. (1952). *Creative and Mental Growth* (2nd ed.). New York: Macmillan.

National Commission on Social Studies in the Schools. (1989). *Charting a Course: Social Studies for the 21st Century.* Washington, D.C.: American Historical Association.

National Council of Teachers of Mathematics. (1989). *Curriculum and Evaluation Standards for School Mathematics.* Reston, Va.: National Council of Teachers of Mathematics.

Raizen, S. A., J. B. Baron, A. B. Champagne, E. Haertl, I. V. S. Mullen, and J. Oakes. (1989). *Assessment in Elementary School Science Education.* Washington, D.C.: Office of Educational Research and Improvement.

Tyler, R. T. (1949). *Basic Principles of Curriculum and Instruction.* Chicago: University of Chicago.

Webb, E. J., D. T. Campbell, R. D. Schwartz, and L. Sechrist. (1966). *Unobtrusive Measures: Nonreactive Research in the Social Sciences.* Chicago: Rand McNally.

Wiggins, G. (1989). "A True Test: Toward More Authentic and Equitable Assessment." *Phi Delta Kappan 70:9,* 703–713.

Wolf, D. P. (1988). "Opening up Assessment." *Educational Leadership 45:4,* 24–29.

Wolf, D. P. (1989). "Portfolio Assessment: Sampling Student Work." *Educational Leadership 46:7,* 35–39.

Yancey, K. B. (Ed.). (1992). *Portfolios in the Classroom: An Introduction.* Urbana, Ill.: The National Council of Teachers of English.

7

HIRING EXCELLENT TEACHERS

AN OVERVIEW (BEFORE)

Anyone responsible for the education of children must be prepared to move heaven and earth if necessary to get the best teachers for those children. Nothing will contribute more to the quality of their education—and perhaps to the quality of their lives. Some lucky children live in charming communities, their parents can afford to pay stiff taxes on choice real estate, and their schools are just the sort of schools in which excellent teachers want to work. Children of low- and middle-income families living in cities and towns with few attractions need more help.

The first step is to record and examine all the steps, procedures, and policies comprised in the current hiring process. Hiring is subject to the influence of various individuals in various positions of authority, all of whom believe that they contribute something useful and necessary, but it is likely that they have never planned the process from start to finish for the express purpose of bringing the best possible teachers to specific children in specific classrooms. An overview (see Fig. 7-1) helps everyone involved see the whole picture.

The hiring process described in Figure 7-1 illustrates some of the problems that might occur.

1. Teachers are hired for a general list of jobs and then assigned to specific schools. The personnel office cannot know what the job in any one school consists of unless teachers and principal define it. The goal of hiring is to find a teacher who is able to

Hiring Stage	Individual or Office	Role in Hiring
Defining the position	Personnel Office	Develops a list of positions to be filled
	Principal	May suggest desirable qualifications for specific positions
Recruiting	State Office of Education	Certification process discourages out-of-state applicants
	School Board	Salary and benefits are not competitive
	Personnel Office	Announces position first within the district and outside when necessary
Screening	Personnel Office	Screens all applicants
	Principal	May ask to see applications
Interviewing and Placement	Personnel Office	Conducts interviews. Selects candidates and assigns them to positions pending a school visit
	Superintendent	Reviews applications of interviewed candidates, approves proposed assignment
	Principal	May confer with superintendent before assignments are made. Interviews candidates assigned to positions in the school
Selecting	Personnel Office	Offers contract and completes paperwork
Inducting	Principal	Invites new teachers to "drop in" before the start of school
	Mentor	Provides support for teachers new to the school

FIGURE 7-1 Chart Summarizing the Hiring Process (Before)

meet the needs of specific students while working cooperatively with colleagues and making good use of available resources. Only those who know a school very well can describe
the qualities required for each position and then recognize a
candidate who epitomizes them to a T.

2. The State Office of Education does not encourage out-of-state
   applicants, and the personnel office recruits locally before looking further afield. Unless recruiting efforts are aggressive, local
   schools will not attract applications from minority candidates.
   Recruiting problems in this district are further compounded by
   lower-than-average salaries. Local teachers will prefer neigh-
   boring districts where they can earn more.

3. Finally, near the end of this hiring process, a persevering applicant who has not already accepted a job elsewhere is allowed
   to visit the school where he or she might work, to see the
   classroom, meet the principal, and discuss the specifics of the
   job. The timing of this visit is bound to produce some last-
   minute withdrawals, because only then does a candidate learn
   exactly what the job entails.

Because we believe that each school must create its own identity
and shape its own program, we also believe that the responsibility for
hiring teachers should be given to each school principal. Even if the
hiring process must be uniform throughout the district, it should allow
principals to make the final choice of teachers who will work in their
schools. To make a wise choice, principals should be guided by teachers
within their schools. For that purpose we recommend the formation of
a school-based search committee. However, an effective hiring process
in one school might not work in another school, and the same is true at
the district level. A process used in one district might be impossible
even to implement in another district. Districts committed to site-based
management will want each school to have greater independence in
hiring than will districts where the management is centralized. Small
schools in remote rural areas must develop recruitment strategies that
are more aggressive and directed than the strategies of schools in
popular suburbs near large cities. In yet another category, independent
schools have access to teacher employment agencies that collect applications from all over the country, even from other countries. These
schools also have a national association and a national conference to

facilitate the screening of teacher candidates. Each school or school district must devise a process that brings excellent teachers to children by whatever means seems most effective. Any tradition of self-interest or negligence that frustrates that central purpose must be questioned and, if possible, changed.

Revising the hiring process is work for a task force. If the process must be uniform throughout the district, a task force of teachers, principals, and superintendent might be appropriate. If the process is school-based, a committee of teachers, principal, and a personnel officer is probably sufficient. In either case, a regional conference on the subject of recruiting and hiring would introduce new ideas and suggest new standards. Proposals to revise the process, needless to say, will have to meet the approval of the School Board, and some might be subject to negotiation with the teachers' union.

We suggest that a task force undertaking to improve the hiring process begin with a chart like the one we have created in Figure 7-1, describing the current hiring process as completely and accurately as possible. This is the *before* chart. It will serve as a focus for discussion. Suggestions for improving the process may be written into successive drafts. An *after* chart will represent the finished product (see Fig. 7-3).

TIMING

Hiring is competitive, and timing is critical. Schools cannot announce openings until they know that teachers are leaving, and teachers who apply for jobs elsewhere do not resign their present jobs until a new job is virtually ensured. The longer the delay, the greater the problem. Excellent teachers know their worth. They tend to apply for specific positions, and they receive attractive offers. Schools faced with the need to hire teachers in August cannot be very selective. They may be lucky in some instances, but excellent schools do not depend upon luck.

The practice and privilege of teachers transferring from one school to another in the same district is one of the causes of delay. It is quite understandable that teachers would want to move to a more desirable job for any of a number of reasons that need no justification. It is also understandable that teachers already employed in a district would expect an advantage when applying for another job in the same district. It does not seem conducive to quality education, however, to delay all hiring of new teachers for an extended period of time while district teachers rearrange themselves. If principals have no control over these transfers, the problem is even greater, because schools are not mass-produced and teachers are not interchangeable parts. A teacher who was hired for one position is not necessarily the best choice for another, entirely different position. At any rate, it is safe to assume that when the dust finally settles, the pool of teacher candidates has been picked over by other districts that managed to move more quickly.

Some large districts advance the hiring calendar by inviting applications in the fall. By interviewing early, they stock the pool of qualified teachers. Then, later in the year, teachers are drawn from the pool and placed in district schools. This system helps alleviate the problem of delay, but nothing guarantees that teachers selected for the pool will still be there when they are needed. Also, any system that depends upon centralized hiring inhibits the development of each school's identity and culture. In contrast to public schools, independent schools offer annual contracts. Although teachers may terminate a contract on relatively short notice, few teachers continue a job search after they have signed their contract for another year. As a result, independent schools recruit widely and hire outstanding teachers before contracts come due in March or April. The head of an independent school expects to have all positions filled by the end of May. Public school teachers, used to collective bargaining and the protection of tenure, would not want to change places with teachers in independent schools. Surely, however, some of the advantages given to children in independent schools can be made available to children in public schools. If the principal, teachers, and students in one school manage to develop a spirit of cooperation, loyalty, and pride, surely they should have the support of the School Board and the teachers' union in keeping that spirit alive. If teachers planning to leave the school give early notice, the children deserve every possible advantage when the principal goes looking for replacement teachers. This principal should not have to wait hopefully for a surprise package to come from the personnel office.

DEFINING THE POSITION

The teacher to be hired need not be a clone of the teacher who is leaving. Operationally, the job was defined by the teacher who did it. By the same token, the qualifications, experience, capabilities, and style of the new teacher will redefine it. In the meantime, there is an opportunity to envision what the job *should* become, and then to look for the teacher most likely to realize that potential. Perhaps the priorities of the school are changing. It may be very important at this time to hire a sixth-grade teacher who can get students interested in reading. It may be time to hire a high school teacher who can teach an interdisciplinary course in calculus and physics. Perhaps the teacher leaving has been the drama coach, and another teacher in the school has been waiting patiently for an opportunity to coach drama. After some reshuffling of responsibilities, the new position might make it possible to bring in a teacher who is able to start another, much needed activity.

Innovations in schools are often piloted by a few enthusiastic teachers. Every opening on the faculty is an opportunity to strengthen and extend a new program. Sometimes the success of a new program is hindered by personality conflicts or disagreements about methods. A new teacher might open communications and permit unprecedented progress. If the job entails teamwork, a compatible educational philosophy and the ability to get along with colleagues are important qualifications.

Finding the right teacher for every job should not be left to chance. Therefore, the job should be carefully defined before anyone is encouraged to apply for it. Some schools form a search committee for every opening (Wise, Darling-Hammond, and Berry 1987), and the search committee writes a description of the job as it should be done.

We suggest three parts to a job description: the job, the qualifications, and the context in which the job will be done. The first section is a list of the responsibilities expected of anyone taking the job. It must be carefully conceived and clearly written. Since it becomes one of the documents that define the conditions of employment, it must be approved by a responsible officer of the School Board. The list of qualifications should include necessary qualifications and desired qualifications, with a clear distinction between the two. A brief description of the context contains the priorities and prominent features of the academic program.

The whole point of defining the job and listing the qualifications needed to do it well is to find and hire precisely the right teacher. If the school district has blanket criteria for hiring teachers—a structured interview, for example, or a ranking system based on standardized tests—then the search committee must question the relevance of these criteria. The personnel office of a school district can do many things that teachers and principals cannot do. The office is staffed and equipped to manage a torrent of inquiries and applications. It has a staff to answer the phone, sort applications, set up files, keep accurate and up-to-the-minute records, and send out a steady stream of letters. There are trained personnel officers who know the laws, the ins and outs of contracts, the danger signals, the questions to ask in an interview. Schools need that expertise, but principals and teachers should not have to yield their own expertise in order to get help in the process of hiring. Personnel officers, teachers, and principals have to work together. The criteria for hiring new teachers have one clear and compelling priority, the real needs of real children who come to school every day.

Because teachers already employed in the school or the district tend to move into less demanding and more satisfying positions, the most difficult jobs are left for newly hired teachers. Sometimes they are filled by experienced teachers moving from other districts, but often they are thrust upon inexperienced teachers whose first year in teaching becomes a trial by ordeal. This is not the best way to introduce novices into a profession. Too many leave after one or two years, and it is a sad fact that those who leave are more academically able than those who stay (Vance and Schlechty 1982). By defining the job and the qualifications needed to do it, the search committee can virtually eliminate this problem—if, that is, the school budget permits the hiring of veteran teachers to do the difficult jobs. Novices, on the other hand, might be brought along gradually, with lighter workloads and opportunities for professional development.

Once the job is announced and the job description made public, it is unfair to change it during the process of hiring. That would be akin to bait and switch advertising. If a candidate being interviewed proposes any modifications to the job description, the proposal and how it is made must be taken as information about the candidate's expertise and ability to work with others. If the proposal is ever accepted, it should be accepted only if that candidate is hired and only after general agreement among all the parties involved, including the committee who wrote the original job description. An example of this sequence of events occurred when a computer specialist was hired to work in an elementary school. Instead of teaching children exclusively, as the original description had specified, the specialist also undertook a training program for fellow teachers. This instruction enabled classroom teachers to support the work of the computer specialist in a collaboration of great benefit to the students.

RECRUITING

Announcements of a job opening are advertisements. Like all advertisements, they should be right for the market. If a personnel office in a large school district is responsible for recruitment, then a personnel officer should meet with the search committee. Together, they should develop a strategy for recruiting and screening applicants. In times of teacher shortages a small rural school looking for a mathematics or science teacher might have to sweep with a wide net. Instead of finding the perfect candidate, the school might have to beat the bushes to find any candidate. Then the job description and the corresponding announcement would have to be general and inclusive. If the pool of candidates is plentiful, however, the announcement may describe the job in more detail. The difference between this announcement: *"Fourth-Grade Teacher for a literature-based, whole-language curriculum"* and this: *"Flexible Fourth-Grade Teacher with phonics background to work with children of mixed abilities and learning styles"* will be noted by elementary teachers, some of whom would pass up one opportunity and apply for the other.

Like everyone else, teachers looking for work are concerned about personal as well as professional needs. They have preferences for small towns or large towns, life on the coast or life in the mountains, proximity to family or a complete change of scene. Teachers who have families probably want nice homes, good schools for their children, and opportunities to save and invest for the future. When they choose the profession, teachers are not highly motivated by visions of wealth. Nevertheless, most will tolerate a degree of inconvenience for a higher salary. When the people in a community make decisions about taxes, and school boards negotiate contracts, they are competing with other communities and other schools that offer teachers a comparable lifestyle. There is no doubt that higher salaries help to attract qualified teachers. By the same token, higher salaries also encourage more college graduates to enter the teaching profession, since teaching is in competition with other professions just as schools are in competition with other schools.

Salary is not the only attraction, however. The salaries of teachers in independent schools tend to be lower than those of teachers in public schools, yet independent schools manage to attract well-qualified teachers. To teach in a public school, a parochial school, or an independent school seems to be a choice of values as well as income. To attract the best teachers, a school has to do more than offer a competitive salary; it has to offer something else. What is the something else?

The answers seem fairly obvious: a happy school, cooperative students, encouraging colleagues, an appreciative and supportive principal, opportunities for professional development, a manageable workload, a challenging curriculum, and the strong likelihood of success. In other words, principals, superintendents, and personnel officers who want to recruit excellent teachers must strive to have excellent schools. If they do not have excellent schools already, they must try to convince teacher candidates that everything possible is being done to make the schools better. A recruiting brochure sent to every candidate who makes an inquiry is one way to spread the word.

When teacher candidates read job announcements, they are looking for clues that this is a job they should apply for. Where the announcement appears is one clue: a local newspaper, a big city newspaper, a college career office, an employment agency, or a professional publication. The recruiting school, like any advertiser, must consider the type of candidate who buys the newspaper, attends the college, signs up with the agent, or reads the professional publication. The candidate who finds the announcement where he or she has chosen to look is likely to think, "This school wants people like me to apply." There are other clues. If an excellent school is looking for excellent teachers, the message will find its way into the announcement, either in the description of the job, the list of qualifications, or both. "Buzzwords" are perfectly appropriate, and well-informed teachers will recognize them: "whole-language," "phonics," "authentic assessment," "basic instruction," "gifted and talented," "NCTM standards," "hands-on science." The right calls attract the right teachers.

Our own experience of hiring teachers suggests that college career offices are an under-exploited resource for schools interested in hiring young teachers. Here, newly credentialed graduates find long lists of schools and school districts with the names and addresses of people to whom to write. Many choose the region where they want to live and then write to all the districts in that region. Although these offices usually keep files of current openings in education, the files tend to be sparse. A school making good use of this resource would keep the file meticulously updated with announcements describing excellent jobs in well-managed educational programs. Surprisingly few schools and school districts make themselves known to the staff in these offices. With little effort, a school could develop a reputation among the counselors in a dozen feeder colleges. Teacher candidates at these colleges would soon learn that such-and-such a school is an excellent place to work.

Laissez-faire recruitment limits the chance of finding a perfect candidate for each position. It raises the chance of hiring a homogeneous faculty, because most candidates will come by the same path and enter through the same door. Social, racial, and ethnic homogeneity is not even roughly equivalent to a diverse faculty working as a team to achieve school goals. The student body of any school, even a selective independent school, is likely to be diverse, and the world that the students will enter is certainly diverse. Some schools tend to hire teachers whom other teachers know and recommend. Many are content to hire local residents who have earned degrees at local colleges. If the teacher pool is racially and ethnically diverse, the problem of homogeneity might be avoided. Otherwise, a passive approach to recruiting is likely to favor one race, one gender, and one view of the diverse world. Active recruiting requires teachers and administrators to think about diversity. Homogeneity or diversity becomes a matter of choice instead of chance. Then the recruiting challenge is to overcome the odds.

It is illegal to hire or reject applicants for reasons that are unrelated to the job—for reasons of race, gender, marital status, or age, for example. One can target certain minorities for recruitment but not for selection, unless the very characteristic found in the minority is needed to do the job. It is permissible to prefer a mathematics major for a mathematics position, but not to prefer a Jewish African-American young single female. Recruitment for diversity, ideally, will bring a steady stream of applications from all sorts of qualified candidates. To achieve this, the school must extend its recruiting network beyond the immediate community to colleges with large enrollments of minority students, professional associations with statewide or national membership, organizations that help and encourage minorities to join the teaching profession, and international associations that bring teachers to the United States for temporary teaching positions.

Special bonuses and incentives are one way to gain an advantage in the competition for teachers. A sign-up bonus, so common in professional athletics, is not out of the question in education. Young teachers especially might appreciate extra cash to furnish an apartment or make a down payment on a car. Other suggestions (Van Meter 1984) include paid professional days taken at a teacher's discretion, a longer contract period that adds a week or a month to the annual salary, tuition grants for advanced study, and various forms of salary supplement. Teachers in King William County, Virginia, schools earn additional income if they agree to certain conditions concerning attendance and professional development (Winbourne and Stainback 1984). Sabbaticals are also an attractive feature. In spite of the term "sabbatical," a year for study or travel might come due after any number of years, with full pay or half pay. A sabbatical offered after four years and again after an additional ten years might encourage teachers to stay at the same school for as long as fifteen years—(unless, of course, they can earn another four-year sabbatical by moving to another school). Some schools that find the cost of sabbaticals prohibitive have developed salary deduction plans instead. A monthly investment of $500 earning 8-percent interest will accumulate $46,000 in six years. If a school contributed half of that, the sabbatical plan would cost the school board and the participating teacher only $250 per month.

Aggressive recruiting costs money, but not a lot compared to the cost of a teacher. One teacher over the course of a thirty-year career will cost the Board at least a million dollars. A teacher whose work is barely satisfactory will cost just as much, if not more, than an excellent teacher. It is not unreasonable to add an up-front cost that helps to protect a million-dollar investment.

THE APPLICATION

The application form, the documents requested, the wording and appearance of all communications to the candidate convey information as surely as they request information. Every detail of the application process will influence a prospective candidate to apply or not to apply.

When designing the application package, the personnel office must seek the advice of teachers and principals. The procedure must elicit useful information, but not so much information that candidates are daunted by the task of assembling it all. We offer the following suggestions, but each school must consider its specific needs in the competition for qualified teachers.

1. An application form requesting relevant information about the candidate and the candidate's work experience
2. A résumé of additional information volunteered by the candidate
3. A written statement of professional values and aspirations
4. The candidate's personal estimate of strengths and weaknesses
5. Instructions concerning letters of reference: whom to ask, questions to be answered, name and address of the person to whom they should be addressed
6. Official copies of college transcripts and relevant certificates

Later in the process, selected candidates will be asked to provide additional information in the form of:

7. A videotape and self-analysis of a lesson the candidate has taught
8. Interviews with members of the search committee

All secretaries and members of the search committee who will be reading and handling applications must be familiar with the whole application process and know precisely what is expected of them personally. It is very important work, requiring high standards of confidentiality, courtesy, punctuality, and attention to detail.

COMMUNICATIONS

A stack of applications from qualified candidates is only an interim objective. If, when an offer is made, the best candidate accepts, the recruiting effort has been successful—although some principals will say that it takes at least another year before they can be certain.

Communications are of vital importance. The process of screening, interviewing, and selecting takes time, even when well planned. Unless tight, carefully monitored procedures are followed, time expands to delay because teachers transferring within the district cannot make up their minds, because someone sits on a stack of applications for a week, because candidates call to reschedule interviews, because the search committee cannot meet until after the school play, and so on. Floods of applications come in. They are carried from office to office. Piles accumulate. Letters have to be printed and mailed. The overwhelmed secretary has too many other things to do. Meanwhile, applicants are checking their mailboxes every day, anxious for news. They call with questions, some of which are difficult to answer. Messages are left in mailboxes: "Please call back." If anything goes wrong, if a secretary is discourteous, if a message is lost, if an application is lost (yes, it happens!), if the process seems to take forever, the best candidates will take the offers they receive from other schools.

A set of form letters should be written well in advance and stored in the computer, ready for names and addresses (see Fig. 7-2). (Note that form letters are used only if perfectly appropriate. If a form letter is not exactly right for the purpose, a special letter should be written.) Every applicant should receive a prompt reply. A letter of inquiry should bring back an invitation to submit an application, an application form, a list of requested documents, a recruiting brochure, and a description of the hiring process—if, of course, there is a suitable job available. If there is not, a pleasant note of regret will accompany the recruiting brochure, which might encourage the candidate to try again. Applications are logged as soon as they arrive. The format for the log is carefully prepared, so that dates, decisions, and a record of communications can be entered with relative ease. This log should always be available in the appropriate office, in a notebook or on the computer, so that anyone answering the phone does not have to ask, "What is your name again? Would you spell it please? What job are you applying for?" Instead, the candidate will hear, "Oh, yes, Ms. Willoughby, we received your application for the music position the day before yesterday. At present it is being reviewed by the selection committee. How may I help you?" If the screening decision is made promptly, no acknowledgment of receipt is needed. Instead, each applicant will receive a note of rejection or an invitation for an interview. If, however, the screening decision on each application takes more than a week, then cards acknowledging receipt of the application should be preprinted and mailed as applications arrive.

A second letter informs candidates about the screening decision. Employers should remember that anyone applying for a job is probably feeling anxious and vulnerable. The future is uncertain. Self-esteem is on the line. Rejection notices should be respectful and encouraging as well as decisive: "Yours was one of many applications from excellent candidates. . . . I'm sorry to say that your qualifications do not match our needs. . . . We wish you well. . . ." An invitation to come to the school for an interview should be warm and congratulatory. Some schools send interviewees more detailed information about the school and the program in which they might work. Independent schools send attractive "lookbooks" and course catalogues. Interviewees should know what to expect, who will greet them when they first arrive, whom they will meet, what they will see, and the length of time the interview will take. If the interview process is complex and time-consuming, candidates should be greeted by the search coordinator, who supplies them

Stage of Hiring	Response
Inquiry	Letter inviting application with all necessary forms and a recruiting brochure
	Or a letter of regret with a recruiting brochure
Application	A letter or card acknowledging receipt of application. May confirm completeness of application or list missing documents
Screening	Letter extending invitation to come for an interview and requesting a telephone conference to arrange the interview. Additional information about the program enclosed
	Or a letter of regret
Interview	A letter offering the position and requesting a reply

FIGURE 7-2 Form Letters Prepared for the Hiring Process

with a schedule of events, an orientation to the building, and the names of interviewers.

The search coordinator is responsible for keeping in touch with each candidate after the interview. A sensitive coordinator will try to arrive at a mutual understanding with promising candidates. It goes something like this: "We are interested in you, and we hope that you are interested in us. We have other candidates, however, and our commitment to quality education requires that we consider every application carefully. If you have any questions at any time, feel free to call me. If there is any unexpected delay in the process, I will call you. If for any reason you wish to withdraw your application, please let me know. If you are offered another job before we have made our decision, please check with me before you accept. Who knows, our decision might be in the mail."

SCREENING

A common problem of screening in large school districts is the lack of coordination among various individuals and groups who are operating on different assumptions about what makes "a good teacher" (Wise, Darling-Hammond, and Berry 1987). All sorts of candidates are invited to come for an interview, and then the people responsible for making a decision find themselves embroiled in a power struggle over educational philosophies and teaching methods. If a committee agrees on everything from defining the job to selecting the best candidate, the problem is greatly reduced. Screening by committee is difficult to manage, however. It requires a capable administrator to serve as the search coordinator. This coordinator, secretaries, aides, and members of the search committee must devise a system for moving, sorting, and keeping track of files. Time is one problem. It might take a busy teacher two weeks to read a stack of applications that could be read in two hours if he or she had nothing else to do. Communications are another problem. Unless the committee meets constantly, how can it come to a decision about every applicant? Each search committee must solve the problems, which arise when large numbers of applications have to be processed in a short period of time. They are good problems to have, in other words.

It might be convenient to store and examine applications in one central location, where a secretary keeps them organized and serves as a liaison between the various members of the committee. They would come to this location as often as necessary to read applications and note their responses. In most cases they make the basic screening decision: to interview or not to interview. A "review sheet" attached to each file, with space for comments, serves as a record of readers and decisions. When discussing the system, the committee must agree on how many votes are needed to authorize an interview. One other vote in addition to the search coordinator's might be sufficient.

When an application is approved, it goes into the "interview" basket. Before the applicant is invited to the school, however, the search coordinator must check the candidate's references. This is more than a formality to confirm the authenticity of an application. In some states the laws requiring background checks are very explicit. Schools must protect children from possible abuse and at the same time protect themselves from any conceivable interpretation of negligence. Also, the decision to interview might have been made contingent upon certain conditions that have to be verified by telephone. These conditions would be noted on the "review sheet" as a reminder for the search coordinator when he or she is making a call. Checking includes calls to college professors, principals, and supervisors who have written letters of reference. Fallacious claims and forged documents are relatively rare, but all candidates want to create a favorable impression and tend to omit anything discreditable from a job application. Sometimes letters of reference are written by principals and school heads who are only too eager to help a problem teacher find work elsewhere. Checking might also entail a telephone interview with an applicant. A search coordinator should be reluctant to reject an applicant because of insufficient information, especially when qualified candidates are scarce. Then, especially, every phone call is made in the spirit of a quest.

INTERVIEWING

An interview has two explicit purposes, and it is not impolite to acknowledge them during the interview. The interviewer gathers information to help make a decision about the candidate, and the candidate gathers information to help make a decision about the school. There is also a web of unspoken purposes. While giving and requesting information, both the interviewer and interviewee try to make a favorable impression on the other. And if more than one interviewer is present, one may try to send signals to the other by asking a certain question or expressing a certain opinion about the school. Personnel officers are likely to know more about the techniques and pitfalls of interviewing than do teachers on a search committee. But teachers are likely to know more about the students, the curriculum, and the qualifications needed for the job. Before the first candidate arrives, the interviewing team should assemble, compare notes, and develop a strategy. It is practically impossible in most schools to reassemble the team before every interview, but members who see one another in the course of work usually manage to discuss individual candidates before and after the candidates arrive.

Interviewers should know the questions that the law forbids them to ask, questions about marital status, age, religion, indebtedness, national origin, and medical history, for example, all of which violate a candidate's right to privacy. They should also know the questions that other members of the team are counting on them to ask. There is no point in four or five different people all conducting the same interview and making the candidate repeat the same information four or five times. An interview strategy will assign specific areas of inquiry to different members of the committee. It will also recognize the candidate's need to gather information about the school and the job. Hence, a schedule of interviews might allow for a classroom visit, a discussion with students, a tour of the school, a meeting with the teacher who is leaving, or time for examining curricular materials.

Since teachers have limited time for interviewing, there is likely to be a different search committee for each position to be filled. A principal, however, would meet with all the committees in the school, and a personnel officer would meet with committees in several schools. Therefore, the interviewing strategy for any one position would combine districtwide procedures with special procedures devised for each position. The search committee must review the job description and list of desired qualifications. These now serve as the basis for standard questions to be asked of all candidates. Answers to these questions will be noted on an interview form, which ultimately will help the committee compare candidates and make a decision. Interviews should not be confined to a list of standard questions, however, because the experiences and capabilities of teachers are wondrously diverse. Before each candidate arrives, interviewers should review the application and then, during the interview, ask specific questions that give the candidate an opportunity to talk about work experience. If the questions are clear and forthright, the candidate will know where the interview is going and will want to answer completely. Nevertheless, to elicit specific examples in sufficient detail, interviewers must be curious, interested, and responsive. Inexperienced interviewers may talk too much or talk too little. They may try too hard to impress the candidate or ask curt, impersonal questions that elicit curt, impersonal answers. Although candidates should do most of the talking, they should also have a chance to ask questions of the interviewers. The questions they ask, of course, are revealing.

One ability we would look for in all candidates is the ability to grow professionally. We would ask candidates what they think they might need to learn if they get the job they have applied for. We would also ask them to talk about a mistake they have made, or a failure, or something they find very difficult to teach. Some candidates will admit to tiny, insignificant problems. Some will admit to feeling inadequate when what they claim to have done is only a shade less than perfect. Others will describe a real enough problem but intimate that someone or something beyond their control—the principal, the parents, or the size of the classroom—was the true cause. We tend to favor candidates who have learned to do some things very well but do not claim to do everything very well. If in the course of a job interview they can identify and take responsibility for something that did not work, that might even have left them looking a little foolish, they are not likely to become defensive and hostile when their work is evaluated.

Demonstration lessons serve a similar purpose. Some schools require candidates to prepare a lesson and teach a class while members of the search committee observe. In spite of its artificiality, a demonstration lesson of this type might reveal valuable information about a candidate's teaching style and manner of interacting with students. A postconference with a prospective colleague or supervisor would certainly reveal the candidate's willingness to be self-analytical. Nevertheless, the practice is not widely employed. It deprives students of class time they might have spent with their own teacher, and it puts candidates into an artificial, anxiety-provoking situation that probably distorts this one glimpse of their teaching. An alternative is to send members of the search committee to the school where the candidate currently works. There they would see the candidate teaching familiar students in the course of a normal or nearly normal day. This practice, however, is expensive and raises the problem of exceptions—candidates who are not now teaching and those whose present job is so different from the one they hope to acquire that its relevance is questionable. As a compromise, we suggest a videotape of a lesson accompanied by a written self-analysis. Any one of these three options might satisfy the committee's need to see a candidate at work.

Sooner or later, the members of the search committee will meet to compare candidates and make a decision. Some will be astonished to discover that they cannot remember anything about one of the candidates or that their recollection of one candidate has inexplicably become attached to another candidate's name. Notes made immediately after each interview are absolutely essential. Interviewers should retain their personal notes for reference during the selection process, but standard interview forms are collected by the search coordinator. The coordinator abstracts and tabulates comparative data from these forms and reports the results to the search committee.

SELECTION

The criteria for selecting teachers were established when the search committee defined the job and listed the qualifications needed to do it well. If conditions are favorable and recruiting was effective, there will be at least one candidate who meets all the criteria. One fully qualified candidate about whom the committee is enthusiastic is quite sufficient—provided that the candidate signs a contract. If there are several excellent candidates, the task of selection might be more difficult, but the chances that one of them will sign are somewhat improved. If the committee has reservations about all the candidates, then the decision is most difficult: to choose the best available candidate or to continue the search.

Even when the choice is obvious and all the members of the committee have made it clear whom they prefer, the search coordinator should follow an established procedure of elimination in which every candidate is given a fair chance. Every member of the committee should have a chance to speak about every candidate. The committee is composed of people who will work with the new teacher when he or she is hired, and their feelings about the candidates are relevant. When the choice is between candidates who are well qualified, the feelings of prospective colleagues will probably determine the outcome. When all the candidates have been discussed, the committee votes, and votes again until there is a clear majority for one candidate. Then the committee must decide what to do if the chosen candidate declines the offer. The others are listed in order of preference, and the search coordinator is authorized to offer the job to each in succession, until one accepts.

INDUCTION

A rite of initiation recognizes the importance of new members. Initiations foster pride and a sense of community. If the hiring process is rigorous, the survivors feel privileged. Before hiring a candidate for the East Williston, New York, schools, the entire search committee travels to the candidate's present school to observe a class and to meet the candidate's present colleagues (Wise, Darling-Hammond, and Berry 1987). This visit is as much ceremony as appraisal, since by that time the candidate is virtually hired. Then the job is officially offered in a meeting with the superintendent. One East Williston teacher said, "I was flying high when they selected me." Another said, "I felt a tremendous boost. . . . The process made me feel like I was wanted there." When the school year starts, a ceremony in which the returning teachers welcome the new teachers is in order. Anything the teachers value is appropriate: a breakfast, a dinner, a party, a dance. These occasions are then embroidered with tradition: flowers, toasts, songs, pledges of excellence.

After the ceremony, there are good practical reasons for a period of orientation. The school is developing a culture with history, values, archives, vocabulary, procedures, rules, standards, bureaucracy, and very special people. New teachers have been chosen because they are likely to appreciate this culture and contribute to it. They have learned something about it from the interviews, but now they must learn to love it and "own" it.

Integrating the orientation of new teachers into the first faculty meeting of the school year results in a long series of introductions, reports, procedures, and exhortations that bores everyone to tears. Much of the information crammed into one meeting is already known by most of the teachers present and is soon forgotten by the others.

Many schools have a faculty handbook of rules and procedures for just about everything. Almost all of it is new to new teachers, but returning teachers need only to learn about changes, which can be summarized quickly in a general meeting. A leisurely tour of the school, during which new teachers meet janitors, office staff, kitchen staff, athletic director, counselors, nurse, colleagues, student body president, newspaper editor; have their pictures taken; learn how to use the photocopier; and so on is probably a better way to convey a lot of information to new teachers than making them sit through long and confusing speeches. Meanwhile the returning teachers can get on with the business of decorating bulletin boards, entering names in grade books, and preparing materials for the first week of school.

Novice teachers rarely have materials to put on their bulletin boards, and they might never have had to keep a grade book of their own. Their plans for the first week are often sketchy and often change radically after the first day of classes. A mentor is very helpful to young teachers in their first teaching jobs. We have conducted orientation sessions in which a mixed group of novice teachers, newly hired experienced teachers, and mentor teachers all planned their first week of classes. During this time, mentors helped novices develop realistic plans incorporating the goals and objectives of the curriculum. They also showed them how to lay out a grade book and offered to lend them materials for their bulletin boards. Then, in role-playing sessions, all the teachers demonstrated what they had planned for the first day of school. Later, when we asked for evaluations of the orientation, novice teachers said that these practice teaching sessions were most useful. The demonstrations took place in a mutually supportive environment, and they helped the inexperienced teachers form attainable images of excellent teaching. Not everything they had planned for the first week worked out as they had hoped, but they had felt ready, and they had learned to turn to their mentors for advice. More experienced teachers starting new jobs at the school also found these exercises to be beneficial. In their estimate, planning for the first week of school had led to a better start than they would have enjoyed if they had been left to their own devices.

SUMMARY

Hiring the best possible teachers is a major responsibility of the School Board. It requires planning and a smooth operation, because hiring is competitive. Even at times when jobs are scarce and teachers are plentiful, a passive approach to hiring will not bring the right teachers to the children who need them. Each school, each classroom has a population of students for whom some teachers are exactly right, others are not exactly right, and some are quite wrong. The challenge of hiring is a perfect teacher for every classroom.

In order to do so, hiring must be school-based. The teachers and principal in any one school know the children and know the community. They also know the academic program and its stage of development. A vacancy gives them the opportunity to redesign the position according to current and future needs and then to look for the teacher best suited to fill that position. We suggest that teachers, principal, and personnel office collaborate to define the job and list the qualifications needed to do it well.

Aggressive recruiting extends the search beyond the local district in order to attract a diverse faculty. The School Board must consider the incentives that will cause teachers to want to come to teach in local schools. Apart from salary and other financial incentives, each school can offer a supportive environment in which to work.

A volume of applications from highly qualified candidates is only an interim goal of recruiting. When the hiring process runs its course, one applicant is offered one position. At the outset, however, no one knows who that applicant will be. Communications must be thoughtful, courteous, and prompt. Candidates invited for interviews should have a chance to meet colleagues, students, and the principal. Thus, when the right candidate is offered the job, the right candidate is ready to accept.

New teachers are most effective when they become team players. An orientation helps them learn the rules and strategies and values of the team. Schools should consider the symbolic and emotional value of opening ceremonies in which new teachers are made to feel welcome by returning teachers. A mentor system is invaluable for novice teachers especially, but even experienced teachers need help learning the ropes in a new job. An appropriate focus for an orientation is the first week of school. If new teachers incorporate school goals, school climate, and specific learning objectives into their opening classes, they are off to a good start.

Improving the hiring process is the work of a task force. We suggest that this group begin by summarizing current procedures and policies

Hiring Stage	Individual or Office	Role in Hiring
Defining the position	Search Committee Principal Personnel Office	Work together to define position, write job description, list qualifications
Recruiting	State Office of Education School Board Personnel Office	Encourages minority and out-of-state candidates Reimburses expenses for interviews and relocation Announces position in press and professional publications. Maintains recruitment file at selected colleges. Publishes recruitment brochure
Screening	Personnel Office Search Committee Principal	Personnel officer reads all applications, checks references before inviting candidates to interview Members read applications and advise search coordinator Reviews selected files and approves interviews
Interviewing	Personnel Office Search Committee Principal	Work together to interview candidates and view videotapes of teaching
Selecting	Principal Search Committee Personnel Office Superintendent Personnel Office	Work together to rank-order candidates for the job Reviews files, approves choice Prepares contract package and invites candidate for meeting with superintendent
Inducting	Principal Mentor	Organizes orientation for new teachers Supervises and supports new teachers

FIGURE 7-3 Chart Summarizing the Hiring Process (After)

in the form of a chart like the one in Figure 7-1. When the problems have been identified and various changes have been tried and evaluated, a revised chart will help everyone involved understand the new process and each person's place in it (see Fig. 7-3).

REFERENCES

Vance, V. S., and P. C. Schlechty. (1982). "The Structure of the Teaching Occupation—the Characteristics of Teachers: A Sociological Interpretation." Paper presented at the National Institute of Education Conference at Airlie House, Va.

Van Meter, E. J. (1984). "Eight Ways to Recruit the Teachers You Want for the Jobs You've Got." *American School Board Journal 171*:2, 27–28.

Winbourne, C. R. and G. H. Stainback. (1984). "Our Salary Supplement Program Gives Teacher an Incentive They Can Bank On." *American School Board Journal 171*:2, 29–30.

Wise, A. E., L. Darling-Hammond, and B. Berry. (1987). *Effective Teacher Selection: From Recruitment to Selection.* Santa Monica, Calif.: RAND Corporation.

8

EVALUATING AND
SUPERVISING TEACHERS

WHY EVALUATE TEACHERS?

Teachers are evaluated in response to various needs perceived at
various times by influential groups and individuals, including legisla-
tors, boards, administrators, students, parents, interested bystanders,
and teachers themselves.

The right to evaluate is an assumption of power—thumbs up or
thumbs down. Anyone can feel aggrandized simply by holding an
opinion that someone else is inferior. When one's opinion becomes the
official verdict of an institution, power and its potential for abuse are
enormously increased. Those who are evaluated, on the other hand,
are vulnerable and quite understandably want to protect themselves,
not only from unfair treatment, but also from unpleasant feelings like
inadequacy, embarrassment, or fear. Teaching, furthermore, is not
easily evaluated by counting seconds, or centimeters, or repetitions of
something. Evaluation of complex human behavior requires judgment.
Even judges in a court of law follow clearly established rules that are
well known to the prosecution and the defense, yet there are no clearly
established rules for evaluating teachers.

Who has the power? Is it hoarded or shared? With whom is it
shared? From whom is it withheld? How do various parties in the
power structure feel about one another? Are they amicable, hostile, or
helpful? To what end is the power directed? Political, economic, or

educational? Depending upon the distribution and purpose of power, teacher evaluation takes many forms:

Protecting students: When just about everyone associated with the school or the school system is content, evaluation is little more than a precaution. Evaluative criteria are easily met. Teacher evaluation is a screening device to protect students from incompetence or abuse.

Fair trade: Schools trade their services for a price. There is an understandable need to evaluate the transaction. Those who pay, whether they pay through taxes or through tuition, want to know that their money is well spent. Their need is met partly by appraisal of student behavior and partly by appraisal of the school. When the consumers of education become dissatisfied, they want to know if teachers are doing their jobs properly. Teacher evaluation is strongly influenced by common beliefs about "good teaching."

Showing who's boss: An administrator or governing board claims the sole right to decide who is and who is not doing a satisfactory job. Invariably, there are public and private reasons why some teachers are discouraged or discharged.

Protecting teachers: Teachers want to defend themselves against arbitrary judgments, especially when reputations or salaries are at stake. They favor rules that limit the power of the evaluator. Terms negotiated by teachers in a defensive mode, while self-protective, might compromise the effectiveness of teacher evaluation.

Improvement: When schools feel pressed to improve, the emphasis of evaluation is on teacher improvement. Evaluative criteria become more specific, sometimes requiring teachers to adopt a recommended instructional model. Teachers might be asked to set goals for their own professional development, and a satisfactory evaluation depends upon achievement of these goals. Ideally, the school provides inservice education and rewards teachers for taking postgraduate courses.

Incentives: "Tough" evaluation identifies weak teachers who must improve their performance or lose their jobs. Evaluation at a higher level of performance identifies teachers who deserve to earn more than their colleagues. It is hoped that these incentives will eliminate incompetent teachers and raise the aspirations of mediocre teachers. Schools will improve, and highly qualified candidates will seek the higher rewards of a teaching career.

Curriculum implementation: When a change in curriculum requires teachers to acquire more knowledge or learn new methods, evaluative criteria might embody these new expectations. Depending upon the sanctions employed, teachers are encouraged or forced to implement the change.

Effectiveness: Evaluation, theoretically, might help teachers learn more about effective teaching practices. Although lessons gained from experience are told and retold in teachers' rooms, few schools gather information about teaching, as distinct from teachers, and use the information when making educational decisions.

Generic checklists for "rating" teachers, once the predominant method of evaluation, have been discontinued by schools seeking a method of evaluation that will have a beneficial impact on performance. Rating systems protected students by getting a supervisor into every classroom at least once a year. However, few teachers or administrators had much faith in these ratings, even as a means of weeding out incompetence. In the interest of fairness, the same checklist was used to evaluate teachers of different subjects and levels. How well teachers actually fulfilled the items on the checklist was subject to the interpretation of each evaluator. Disputes between teachers and evaluators, likely to occur any time a teacher received a low rating, were hard to reconcile. Consequently, most teachers received satisfactory ratings, because ill-will between teachers and administrators—and not much else—was the usual result of less-than-satisfactory ratings. Although rating scales rarely had the substance on which to base a decision to dismiss a teacher, a community without cause to complain about its schools was none the wiser.

As the move to improve schools has gained momentum, teacher evaluation has become more closely identified with faculty development. Since a system that finds most teachers excellent is not likely to produce improvement, new forms of evaluation must help teachers analyze their performance objectively and rigorously. Virtue in teaching becomes incremental and adaptive, not a state of perfection. If in response to evaluation teachers are expected to attend workshops, invest in postgraduate courses, or even indulge in serious soul searching, then teachers must find some reason to respect the conclusions of their evaluators. It is emphatically important, therefore, that teachers "buy into" the system.

MERIT PAY

The argument for sanctions is argument by analogy, and perhaps that is why it is more appealing to people outside schools than it is to teachers. Many industrial workers are paid in proportion to their productivity. The more you make or sell, the more you earn. Those who do not produce do not thrive, and hence, it is hoped, they will learn to do better or go to another job for which they are better suited. When this logic is applied to teaching, it leads invariably to merit pay. The more the students learn, the more the teacher earns.

Critics of merit pay point out that relative achievement of the goals of teaching is not as easily measured as productivity in manufacturing or sales (Hoko 1988). The contribution that a teacher makes to the achievement of a group of students cannot be isolated from all other influences. A fourth-grade teacher, for example, contributes enormously to the success of fifth-graders. An Algebra I teacher contributes to the success of students in Algebra II. Students contribute to their own success, and good students can learn from poor teachers. Teachers may not take all the credit when their students succeed, and they must not take all the blame when their students fail. Many of the problems of education are beyond the capability of teachers acting in isolation to solve. Even one student in a class can frustrate a teacher's efforts to teach the whole class, yet solving the problem posed by one student can challenge the resources of the administration, the counseling system, the student's other teachers, the student's family, and the student's friends. Actual problems encountered in teaching are more pervasive than one student per classroom, of course. It is virtually impossible to make reliable comparisons from one classroom to another, never mind one school to another. Class groups are not created and classes are not assigned so that all teachers have an equal challenge. Some teachers are assigned consistently to teach highly motivated students, and other teachers are assigned consistently to do the best they can for students who have no wish to be in school.

The state of Tennessee after controversial debate initiated a Master Teacher Plan in 1984. As teachers accumulate years of experience, they may apply successively to five stages in a Career Ladder: Probationary, Apprentice, and Career Levels I, II, and III. Promotion to each stage requires a satisfactory evaluation and is rewarded with higher pay. After one year, Tennessee teachers were overwhelmingly critical of the Career Ladder Program (Johns 1988). Only 11 percent believed that the program would improve the quality of teaching and administration; only 4 percent believed that the program had a positive effect on the morale of teachers; only 10 percent believed that merit pay provided a strong incentive for improvement; and only 11 percent believed that teachers at Level II and III were considered superior by their colleagues. Almost half the teachers sampled said that the program had caused them to consider leaving teaching. After six years and much revision, most teachers still preferred to remain at Level I rather than submit themselves to an evaluation that seemed incongruent with their own professional goals (Martin 1990).

If merit pay does not work as an incentive, it does not work. We do not believe that merit pay for teachers can ever work, for several reasons:

1. The conditions of teaching and the methodology of teacher evaluation make fine distinctions impossible.
2. The gross distinctions made possible by teacher evaluation, like "Unsatisfactory," "Satisfactory," and "Excellent," exclude huge numbers of teachers from the highest levels of accomplishment.
3. Gross methods of evaluation cannot detect incremental progress toward excellence. Some measure of progress is critically important, if not essential, in a system that is supposed to provide incentives.
4. Excluding a majority of teachers, who have no clear path to higher achievement and higher rewards, produces resentment, not improvement.
5. The criteria used to determine merit, to be fair, tend to be uniform. However, the needs of students are far from uniform. General standards of "merit" are likely to distract teachers from the needs of their current students.

6. Because merit tends to be exclusionary rather than inclusionary and categorical rather than incremental, it fosters competition among teachers. The needs of students are better served by teachers working cooperatively in teams.

If a merit pay system could be modified and made to work, what would help? First, a method of evaluation based on the needs of actual students currently in each teacher's classroom. Second, a support system to help teachers solve the problems they face in the classroom. Third, formative evaluation to help teachers measure progress and learn from mistakes. Fourth, incentives to encourage teachers to collaborate with other teachers and professionals serving the same students. Fifth, a budget that permits a majority of teachers to receive merit pay. In short, were we to tinker with a merit pay system, it would lose its identity as a merit pay system.

EVALUATION AND SUPERVISION

We believe that teacher evaluation can contribute to school improvement, but only in a school that is making every effort to address the needs of its students. We do not believe that a system of teacher evaluation in isolation will accomplish much. In the literature about teacher evaluation there is plenty of advice about how to do it, but not much evidence to show that any form of teacher evaluation has any effect on student learning. Meanwhile, a substantial body of research shows that a combination of features as diverse as leadership style and homework contribute to student learning (Squires, Huitt, and Segars 1984). It seems clear that teacher evaluation should contribute to—and certainly not detract from—a climate of growth and accomplishment. Evaluation must be fair and be perceived by teachers to be fair. Evaluative criteria that teachers are expected to meet must address the conditions teachers face daily in their work. Evaluators must respect the teachers they evaluate—and be respected by those teachers, showing and earning their respect through practical knowledge of students, classrooms, and teachers. Teachers who meet or surpass expectations should feel proud. Those who are judged to be less than satisfactory should feel respected, supported, and motivated to improve.

Defined broadly, the task of supervising teachers in a school includes evaluation. While this evaluation is absolutely essential, it is only a part of the whole program for quality control and improvement of instruction. Evaluation falls into two categories, formative and summative. "Teacher evaluation," as we use the term, is summative. It is the responsibility of administrators. It sets a deadline and makes a judgment. Summative evaluation is not intended primarily to improve performance, although it may have that effect. Summative evaluation informs other decisions made outside the realm of evaluated performance. Summative evaluation of a teacher's performance informs the decision to retain the teacher, dismiss the teacher, or put the teacher on probation. Formative evaluation, on the other hand, is intended to improve performance and may be conducted by teachers themselves. Formative evaluation informs decisions within the realm of evaluated performance. Formative evaluation informs the decision to purchase new equipment, or change multiple-choice tests to essay tests, or introduce a unit on world religions. Teacher evaluation is summative. The evaluative component of supervision is formative. We recommend that these two processes, teacher evaluation and teacher supervision, be used where they are best suited: evaluation for evaluation, supervision for improvement.

Criteria for Evaluation

To evaluate the work of teachers, two sets of criteria are needed, one provided by the school's administration and the other by teachers themselves. We call these two sets contractual criteria and instructional criteria. Criteria of both types must be acceptable to both parties and to the community of parents and students served by the school.

Contractual criteria are related to the performance of the teacher as an employee rather than a teacher. If there is a job description for teachers, fulfilling the duties specified in the job description is included in contractual criteria. They specify when a teacher must come to school, write reports, give grades, and so on. They probably also contain less precise but generally understood guidelines about courtesy and respect for the students. All teachers joining the school must accept these criteria as conditions of employment.

Although teacher evaluations invariably include periodic conferences between teachers and administrators, an administrator should not wait until the next scheduled conference to discuss a teacher's failure to meet contractual criteria. A teacher who has not shown up for work, for example, must be confronted as soon as possible. A teacher who ignores the dress code should not have to wait until the end of the year to find out that he or she has been dressing improperly. The responsibility for overseeing the school and maintaining standards of conduct is continual. If there is any suspicion that a teacher is negligent, the teacher must be informed without delay and given a chance to explain. If a teacher has been warned and given a chance to improve, yet negligence is persistent and severe, the administrator in charge must initiate procedures for dismissal. In most public schools these procedures will be carefully prescribed in the collective agreement teachers have made with the School Board. In independent schools the procedure to dismiss a teacher is usually an unwritten agreement between the head of the school and the faculty. In either case, the procedure must include sufficient evidence and sufficient cause.

Instructional criteria are related to the performance of the teacher as a teacher. They are an attempt to characterize the type and quality of teaching required to keep a certain job in a certain school. The source for instructional criteria, therefore, is not in general recommendations that apply to all teachers everywhere. Each teacher in each school has to teach students to achieve the objectives of each course and must collaborate with fellow teachers to help all the students in the school achieve the goals of the school. Goals and objectives are the best source of instructional criteria for teacher evaluation. If we could isolate the effect of each teacher on a group of students, assessment of student achievement would provide all the data we need for teacher evaluation. Since we cannot control the many variables that this evaluation would entail, all we can expect of teachers is that they try conscientiously to help their students achieve the goals and objectives. Trying conscientiously is doing the sort of teaching that is likely to lead to success.

Teachers, in departmental teams, grade-level committees, or representative faculty committees, are best able to write the guidelines for teaching in their school. If, for example, a goal for language arts in an elementary school is that students will use writing as a means of communicating with others, then the elementary school teachers must devise a strategy for teaching students to do that. Were we evaluating a teacher in that school, we would expect the teacher to explain how he or she employs the strategy. When visiting the classroom, we would expect to see the teacher implementing the strategy as described. If the strategy and its implementation seem reasonable, we would conclude that the teacher is doing a satisfactory job. If subsequent assessment reveals that students are not successful when they attempt to communicate in writing, the language arts teachers would have to address the problem and modify the recommended method of teaching writing. We would not change our opinion of the teacher we had observed. However, we would expect the teacher to discuss the problem with colleagues, to understand his or her role in the proposed solution, and to make the appropriate changes.

Criteria for teacher evaluation that have been developed in this way will be unique to each school and each subject taught. When teachers analyze goals and objectives and write their own guidelines for teaching, they are, in fact, writing the criteria for teacher evaluation.

A team of teachers in one elementary school agreed that their students should learn:

1. To write clearly and honestly
2. To use and value writing as a means of learning
3. To use and value writing as a means of communicating with others
4. To generate ideas for writing, to select and arrange them, to develop them, and to find appropriate modes for expressing them
5. To evaluate their own writing
6. To revise their writing
7. To write for various audiences
8. To appeal to and persuade various audiences
9. To use correct spelling, grammar, punctuation, and other elements of manuscript form

The same team developed a set of criteria for evaluating themselves and their colleagues as teachers of writing. They would provide opportunities for students:

1. To share ideas and experiences with real audiences
2. To develop and clarify ideas and experiences through revision
3. To learn and practice correct spelling, grammar, and punctuation

4. To write for self-understanding
5. To write about ideas in all subjects of the curriculum
6. To read (or hear) and respond to other students' writing
7. To evaluate their own writing
8. To use the card catalogue and reference materials in the library

All the teachers in the school examined and agreed to these criteria before the document was handed over to the principal for use in evaluations. Meanwhile, other teams created similar criteria for teaching mathematics, reading, science, and social studies. The elementary principal then had a comprehensive description of the type of teaching recommended in the school. Criteria for middle and high school teachers may be developed by interdisciplinary teams or subject-specific departments, as appropriate in each school. The specialists who teach high school students must meet only one set of criteria, while elementary school teachers face the multiple challenge of competence in several subjects.

One of the responsibilities of academic leadership is to understand the academic program provided for students in the school. Administrators need not attend all the team meetings at which instructional criteria are developed, but they should expect, and receive, an explanation of the finished products. Principal, school head, director, or dean should understand how the criteria in each subject are related to school and subject goals, to educational theory, and to the recommendations of professional organizations. Team leaders and department heads may serve as advisors when administrators need help interpreting what they see in certain classrooms.

Evaluation for minimal competence ensures that the methods employed by each teacher are known to the school administration and have been found acceptable. Once instructional criteria have been established, teachers are held to them. When assessment of student achievement reveals the need to change the methods of teaching, instructional criteria change too.

Results of Evaluation

Although shortcomings in teaching may be less evident than failure to meet contractual criteria, teachers should learn about perceived deficiencies immediately. At a conference following each observation, or after a series of observations within a fairly brief period of time, the evaluating administrator and evaluated teacher discuss the progress of the evaluation. The teacher is fully informed about data recorded during the observation and any judgments the evaluator has made. When the evaluator files a written report following such a conference, the teacher should receive a copy. The teacher may file a dissenting report. In a written evaluation, prepared on a prearranged schedule of faculty evaluations, the teacher's performance in relation to the contractual and instructional criteria is summarized. If this report is unfavorable, the teacher should have an opportunity both to appeal and to improve. Since it is unfair to burden students with a teacher of questionable competence, any probationary period must be clearly defined, the teacher must work under close supervision, and continued failure to meet the criteria of minimum competence must result in dismissal.

The whole procedure of documentation, supervision, and ultimate dismissal of a teacher is likely to be unpleasant for everyone involved, certainly for the teacher and evaluator, and probably also for all the students and teachers in the school. Behavior that causes a teacher to be dismissed is not usually secret. Typically, the same behavior has caused students and parents to complain, and the whole community waits to see what will happen. With careful preparation the school might be able to avoid outright conflict—yet conflict has a way of taking people by surprise, no matter how reasonable they think they have been. In times of relative peace, it is best to build huge stockpiles of goodwill, so that various factions in the community are at least slow to declare war on one another. If teachers and administrators work together to produce the criteria and define the procedures for evaluation, trust and mutual respect are likely to grow. These will prove to be more valuable than the system of evaluation over which many conscientious people have labored. No matter how well conceived, the system will not eliminate the need for judgment. The principal or head of the school will sometimes have to make difficult decisions. Clear evaluative criteria will guide and support these decisions but will not relieve administrators from the need to make them. Attempts to anticipate every manifestation of incompetence with rules and regulations and sanctions will only exchange goodwill for cynicism.

Goals for Professional Development

When a teacher's performance has been thoroughly evaluated and the teacher meets or surpasses minimal expectations, what then? When and how is the teacher evaluated again? Because the ability to teach does not usually desert a teacher without warning, teachers do not have to be evaluated continuously. A significant change in responsibility, on the other hand, might present a teacher with new challenges that he or she is not wholly prepared to meet. Each teacher in the school might be evaluated every three years, with an understanding that anyone who has undertaken a new teaching assignment or whose effectiveness is questioned might be evaluated before the three years are up. Teachers whose competence has been established may be evaluated subsequently by the same method and similar criteria, even if periodic evaluations become a formality. Since instructional criteria are based on curriculum, and the curriculum is in constant evolution, regular evaluation ensures that all teachers are teaching the curriculum as planned.

It should be evident that periodic evaluation of the type described does not have the primary purpose of professional development. It is meant to establish a basic level of competence and a commitment to methods that are right for the students and the curriculum of a single school. For professional development, supervision rather than evaluation is preferred. To avoid periodic re-evaluation of teachers according to criteria they repeatedly surpass, some schools have turned to a practice that combines evaluation and supervision. The teacher to be evaluated is observed in various circumstances that offer an overview of the teacher's work. To prepare for a conference, both teacher and the evaluator-supervisor consider the teacher's performance in relation to the minimum expectations of teachers, the curriculum, specific challenges presented by the current students, the teacher's experience, the teacher's aspirations, and so on. They share their reflections when they meet, and then they discuss developmental goals that the teacher might aim to achieve in the coming year. The evaluator-supervisor helps the teacher appraise these goals in the light of school and district priorities. Available resources for professional development will be used most effectively if teachers are working toward similar goals and if the students in the community feel the result of funds allocated for inservice education of teachers. On the other hand, the teacher's strategy for improvement is likely also to have some unique features that will benefit the teacher's students and perhaps be of interest to colleagues. Out of these possibilities, the teacher and the evaluator-supervisor agree to specific goals, and the evaluator—more supervisor at this point—helps the teacher muster the resources to achieve them. Since progress toward achievement of these goals now becomes a condition to be met in subsequent evaluations, the teacher and the evaluator-supervisor must carefully specify the criteria of success and the data to be used as evidence of success.

Done well, this practice ensures that teachers in the school continue to grow professionally. Improvement goals emerge from cooperative analysis of the teacher's strengths and weaknesses. If achieved, they have an impact on what the students learn. If expected changes do not occur, the teacher is not therefore considered inadequate. This is evaluation above and beyond the level of competence. It is formative rather than summative. The teacher and the evaluator-supervisor confer to revise the goals or to plan a better strategy for achieving them. In any case, an evaluator—more evaluator than supervisor in this capacity—continues to monitor the teacher's work, and if at any time the teacher's competence is called into question, the more basic criteria of competence still apply.

Some schools prefer to split the responsibilities for evaluation and supervision. Evaluation of novice teachers (or experienced teachers in new positions) may be conducted by an evaluator who has no supervisory responsibilities. If a teacher is found to be deficient in any of the contractual or instructional criteria, the evaluator may refer the teacher to someone else for help, to a mentor teacher or department head who has been trained as a supervisor. In all likelihood, the probationary teacher would also receive help from colleagues, because the evaluation criteria would be standard operating procedures in the context of a given school. Evaluation that entails individual goal-setting, on the other hand, is probably best conducted by one person who is both evaluator and supervisor. This form of evaluation is more formative than summative, with an emphasis on professional development. While the role of evaluator-supervisor might at times prove to be uncomfortable for one person to fulfill, the coordination of two people, an evaluator and a supervisor, with a third person, the teacher, also proves to be uncomfortable. Teachers are evaluator-supervisors for their students. One person can fulfill both roles very well.

Eclectic Supervision

In the professional literature of the past twenty years, "teacher supervision" has been used for almost any activity related to the management of teaching personnel in a school. Various theorists have recommended certain types of management, and hence we have subsets of supervision, like "Clinical Supervision" (Cogan 1973), "Consultant Supervision" (Champagne and Hogan 1987), "Peer Supervision" (Alfonso and Goldsberry 1982), and "Developmental Supervision" (Glickman 1985). The recognition that a school might choose any combination of methods to suit its purposes and circumstances has led to "Differentiated Supervision" (Glatthorn 1984). We recommend eclectic supervision (no capital letters), because supervision, like teaching, is only a means and never an end. One method of supervision, like one method of teaching, is not enough.

Accordingly, we have developed a broadly inclusive concept of supervision. We recognize, from the outset, that supervision is necessary. Many teachers do not like the idea of supervision, but there is no escaping it in one form or other. When an institution has purpose, design, and management, it has supervision. Supervisors in other walks of life take many shapes to fulfill many functions: captain, conductor, coach, cheerleader, host, pastor, speaker, whip, steward, stroke, nurse, warden, mayor, foreman, chef, valet, moderator, father, mother, buddy, and baby-sitter, to name just a few. In schools, as elsewhere, supervisors watch others to see how they are doing. Sometimes they merely watch; sometimes they help; sometimes they direct; sometimes they applaud. A contract is one result of supervision. Vacations are another.

Supervisors are there to help teachers teach and students learn. Problems arise when the help is not wanted or the help is not helpful. Contracts and vacations are not always received with gratitude, but they are generally preferable to no contracts and no vacations. When help invades the classroom, however, it implies that the teacher has not been doing well enough alone. The resentment stirred in teachers by visiting supervisors has been characterized by Blumberg in *Supervisors and Teachers: A Private Cold War* (1974). Clinical supervision, first developed as a method for supervising the teaching of MAT candidates at Harvard (Cogan 1973), was meant to minimize the resentment and maximize the help. Cogan made a distinction between general supervision and clinical supervision. General supervision "denotes activities like the writing of and revision of curriculums, the preparations of units and materials of instruction, the development of processes and instruments for reporting to parents, and such broad concerns as the evaluation of the total educational program." Clinical supervision "is focused upon the improvement of the teacher's classroom instruction. The principal data of clinical supervision include records of classroom events: what the teacher and students do in the classroom during the teaching-learning process." In a footnote, Cogan explained, "As used in this book, the term supervision refers to clinical supervision unless the context makes clear a reference to supervision in general." We, on the other hand, use the word in its broadest sense. Much can be done to help teachers teach without stepping into their classrooms. Much can be done outside the classroom to create a climate favorable to professional growth. In such a climate, the supervisor who comes to watch in the classroom will be welcome.

Who does the supervising? Principals are supervisors, whether or not they spend time in the classroom—and research in effective schools offers strong evidence to show that principals become instructional leaders by visiting classrooms (Ellis 1986). Heads of independent schools are supervisors. No one is in a better position than the principal or school head to emphasize the academic mission of a school or to support the efforts of teachers. Vice-principals and academic deans are supervisors who act in a supervisory capacity when they produce a master schedule, chair a committee, or call meetings of teachers to discuss a particular student. Department heads are supervisors responsible for curriculum and instruction in their departments. Teachers are supervisors when they share materials and methods or help a new teacher learn the ropes. And "supervisors" are supervisors, the subject specialists appointed in many school districts to help teachers individually and in groups to improve curriculum and instruction.

Supervision might consist of any of the following activities:

- The principal of an elementary school has created a schedule that permits groups of teachers to meet regularly in the computer room. With the help of a computer teacher, they experiment with software and share ideas about its use.
- The head of an independent school invites interested teachers and

parents to join a discussion group that meets regularly at her house to discuss books and articles on topics of professional interest.

- A pair of high school science teachers who teach the same course meet regularly to plan and set up laboratory experiences for their students.
- An interdisciplinary team of middle school teachers agree that each will attend a day of classes, following the schedule of a student.
- The English department meets to read student essays and review the criteria used for grading essays.
- A high school principal forms a committee to work out a code of professional conduct for all administrators, teachers, and staff in the school.
- The dean of studies, head of the math department, and head of the science department together attend a conference on teaching math and science to girls.
- An elementary school principal joins with first-grade teachers once a week in a team-taught writing workshop.
- A first-year teacher is locked out of her classroom by a mischievous class. She asks the vice-principal for help.
- Students in an elementary school have a class in the science lab once a week. The science coordinator teaches the weekly lab and helps teachers prepare related classroom activities. Science teachers in the secondary school make themselves available for consultation and guest teaching.
- A special education teacher and a group of secondary teachers want to try cooperative learning techniques in mainstream class-rooms with special-needs students. The director of staff devel-opment for the district arranges release time and a series of work-shops.
- Students and parents complain that a veteran history teacher "does not teach." The principal asks the teacher and the head of the history department to discover likely causes of these complaints.

While anyone in the school may assume the role of supervisor for a period of time, a climate favorable to professional growth does not materialize spontaneously. Climate is an accumulation of effects set in motion by acts of leadership (see Chapter 9). While learning illuminates a school like sunshine, it is not a source of energy. Learning consumes energy. All the school's resources are thrown into the effort every day.

The flame engendered in each child is coddled and fueled every day. The accomplishments of students light up hallways, classrooms, and auditoriums, burning on the energy of teachers. This energy is replenished through appreciation, admiration, and respect. Teachers should not have to use a pay phone in the hallway or ask permission to use the telephone in the office. When they photocopy materials for their students, they should not have to pay out of their own pockets. They should not have to pay their own expenses to attend a conference. And sometimes they should be urged to attend a conference for the benefit of their students and colleagues; they should not always have to beg. Sometimes a teacher should have a substitute in order to attend a meeting held during school hours. There should be computers made available in a faculty work room, and free instruction in the use of educational software. Teachers should be consulted when furniture is chosen for their classrooms, when a new schedule of classes is created, when their parking spaces are changed. When they need a slide projector, a working slide projector should be delivered to the classroom on time, with a spare bulb. Teachers should expect administrators to take an interest in their teaching, to ask how they teach students to be independent, how they were able to motivate a problem student, or how they teach division of fractions. They should have a say in what they teach, and if coordination of curriculum is desired, they should have time provided in the working day in which to meet with their colleagues.

Teachers will want to work in a school that treats them this way. Administrators in this school—advised by teachers, of course—will have the luxury of being selective when new teachers are hired. To get a job in this school, candidates will have to be intrinsically motivated, first to join a profession with limited opportunities for fame and fortune, and then to succeed as a teacher, not just to settle for a regular paycheck and long vacations. Hiring teachers who want to grow professionally is an essential component in a supervisory plan. If their expectations are disappointed, of course, they will leave, but if fulfilled, these teachers will pass up chances to earn more because they prefer to teach in a school where they can feel good about themselves even as they aspire to be better. And the wonderful bonus in such a scheme is that teachers who are learning and growing themselves are more likely to teach their students to do the same thing (Aspy and Roebuck 1977).

Clinical Supervision

There is nothing in the methodology of clinical supervision (Champagne and Hogan 1981; Cogan 1973; Goldhammer 1969) that ensures that teachers will like it. Each observation entails a pre- and a post-conference, which occupy time a teacher might otherwise use for read- ing student work, preparing materials for an upcoming class, meeting with colleagues, tutoring a student, or taking a much needed breather. If in the teacher's opinion the time is not well spent, the teacher will resent it. While the pre-conference does permit the teacher and the supervisor to cooperate in planning the observation, it is relatively easy for an inexperienced or insensitive supervisor to collect irrelevant data in the classroom and then in the post-conference to draw the teacher into a detailed analysis of them. The process is much enhanced if the supervisor, or observing colleague, has a shared understanding about teaching and common goals to pursue. It is indeed possible for a good supervisor and a receptive teacher to strike up a useful relationship wholly within the confines of the supervisory cycle of pre-conference, observation, and post-conference, but there is no need to confine professional exchanges between teachers and supervisors to this fairly formal, episodic mode of discourse. Limiting teacher supervision to clinical supervision is a bit like limiting a religion to its liturgy.

Clinical supervision is probably the best way to engage a single teacher in analysis of his or her own teaching. However, a rich regimen of clinical supervision for all the teachers in a school seems virtually impossible to maintain in the helter-skelter context of schools as we know them. We have helped train supervisors in various schools, large and small, public and private, and a year later, invariably, the story is the same: Supervisors cannot find enough time for classroom observation. District-level supervisors might have hundreds of teachers to observe, yet spend most of their time in meetings at the district office. Principals are forced to attend to business thrust on them daily by students, parents, and the superintendent. Heads of independent schools do not have a superintendent to respond to, but they have a Board, and they have a huge job of fiscal management. Principals and heads delegate academic leadership to vice-principals and deans, whose first priority is usually student rather than faculty affairs. Administrators who value classroom observation tend to drop in on teachers whenever an opportunity arises, thereby appearing in classrooms as often as possible, rather than planning the cumbersome cycle of clinical supervision. Department heads find little time for observation. Usually they teach one class period less per day than teachers in their departments. If there are ten teachers in a department, and clinical supervision is at the very acme of a department head's priorities, then it is conceivable that each teacher in the department will be observed once every ten weeks, maybe three times a year. Team leaders in elementary schools, freed from their own classrooms during PE and music, subjects taught by "specialty" teachers, have even less time for supervision than department heads in secondary schools. In actuality, almost all the teachers and administrators we meet in schools would like to spend more time observing classes, but almost all do something else in the time they have available.

As things now stand, clinical supervision is a luxury. Each school should try to get as much of it as possible and then to portion it out wherever it does the most good. Novice teachers will benefit from clinical supervision. The student teaching required for certification in public schools is not nearly adequate to prepare beginning teachers for their first full-time jobs. Independent schools recruit teachers directly out of college, in many cases with no experience of teaching whatsoever. A weekly cycle of supervision will help a novice teacher develop classroom routines, lessons, and methods of assessment appropriate for the students who come to that particular school. Since this supervision takes time and preparation is always harder for a novice than it is for a veteran, novice teachers should enjoy some exemption from duties outside the classroom, like proctoring study halls or monitoring behavior in the lunchroom. Teachers in pilot programs deserve the coaching and encouragement that clinical supervision can provide. In a study of teachers learning new skills, Joyce and Showers (1982; Brant 1987) discovered that coaching in the classroom significantly increases the likelihood that what is learned outside the classroom will be implemented in the classroom. And teachers of marginal competence are helped through clinical supervision. When evaluation reveals that a teacher is less than satisfactory, the school has an obligation to the students, the teacher, and the teaching profession to minister help. A weekly cycle of clinical supervision might be enough to safeguard the students while the teacher learns to overcome the problem.

If administrators, department heads, and team leaders are expected to observe in classrooms, then all the administrators and teachers in the school should have an introductory workshop in clinical supervision. Providing teachers with knowledge of the methodology and values of their supervisors is one way to foster independence and respect in the supervisory relationship. The supervisors will need more than an introduction, however. It is not easy to be helpful to a variety of teachers, who have different expectations, abilities, personalities, and aspirations. The presumption of supervision is that coaching will help teachers continue to grow, no matter how long they have been in the profession. Might the same presumption extend to coaching supervisors? Educators fall too easily into the trap of wanting to know everything. After observing a class, educational administrators seem compelled to make a pithy comment that diagnoses the teacher's problem, remediates it, and establishes their own expertise all in the same breath. The methodology of clinical supervision asks supervisors to resist that tendency and instead to help teachers become independently analytical of events in their classrooms. If supervisors allow themselves to be learners too, they will benefit from supervision of their supervision.

If, however, the climate of professionalism has fomented various forms of peer supervision, then everyone on the faculty is a potential supervisor, and all will benefit from follow-up training aimed at practical skills beyond the level of understanding gained in an introduction. These skills might include:

Pre-Conference

- Helping teachers articulate objectives, plans, hopes, concerns, etc.
- Assessing the appropriateness of objectives in relation to curriculum and the needs of students
- Appraising methods of assessment in relation to objectives and current student achievement
- Communicating respect for each teacher observed
- Seeing issues from each teacher's point of view
- Selecting or designing a data-gathering instrument appropriate for each observation

Observation

- Sensitivity to a broad range of issues as perceived and construed in different classrooms
- Perceiving and recording details of teacher and student behavior

- Perceiving patterns of behavior related to various instructional issues

Post-Conference

- Communicating interest in each teacher's work
- Analyzing classroom data in collaboration with each teacher observed
- Using data when appraising progress toward instructional goals
- Helping teachers set or modify instructional goals
- Planning instruction in collaboration with each teacher observed

Although these are skills required of a supervisor observing teachers, they are obviously also skills that a teacher can apply to his or her own teaching. Providing teachers with training in clinical supervision, therefore, is not only helpful when they observe their colleagues at work but also helpful when they think about their own work. It should also be obvious that the attitudes of objectivity, mutual respect, and professionalism that permeate clinical supervision as it is usually represented in training programs are attitudes that most schools will want to embrace.

AN INTEGRATED PROGRAM

Everything in the school serves the purpose of learning. Helping teachers is one way to promote learning. Evaluating teachers is another way. Those who help and those who evaluate need to know precisely what the teachers are supposed to teach and the students are supposed to learn. Helping teachers be clear about goals is the first step toward effectiveness. Teamwork when writing goals and objectives (Chapter 1), making connections across the disciplines (Chapter 3), planning instruction (Chapter 5), and devising methods of assessment (Chapter 6) is central to a program of teacher supervision. Until this teamwork has produced a curriculum that is right for the students, the school, and the community, teacher evaluation must be seen as transitional. When the curriculum has achieved a degree of stability and compatible methods of instruction are beginning to show results, then the program of teacher evaluation and supervision is brought up to date.

Participation

The program must meet the needs of teachers, administrators, Board, and—indirectly, through the quality of service provided by the school—students and their parents. All constituencies, therefore, should be represented in its development and revision. Boards invariably give the highest school administrator, the superintendent or the head of the school, responsibility for evaluating teachers. Wise administrators seek the counsel of principals, division heads, deans, and teachers—actual participants in teacher evaluation. Although work groups need not include students and parents, now is a good time to ask them what they expect from competent teachers and administrators. The constitution of work groups will change as development proceeds. One group, for example, might investigate alternative approaches to supervision and evaluation and make recommendations to administration and faculty. Another group, when the time is right, will seek advanced training in clinical supervision. Instructional criteria, on the other hand, are best written by groups of teachers in each discipline at each level.

Trust

Supervision and evaluation work best in an atmosphere of trust. Teachers must believe that the stated purposes of supervision and evaluation are the real purposes. They must believe that supervisors and evaluators have a respectful and sympathetic understanding of the job of teaching. Communication must be genuine. What evaluators tell teachers in conference must coincide with what is written and filed. When teachers tell their supervisors that they understand and agree, they must not feel pressured to pretend. Board members making public statements about weeding out deadwood do not contribute to trust. Principals who use evaluations to discourage dissent do not contribute to trust. Supervisors and evaluators must concern themselves only with professional behavior related to widely accepted criteria. Administrators who use the power of evaluation to try to stifle criticism simply draw more criticism.

Timing

Climate is more important than systems, although systems might help produce the right climate. Adults in the school respect the students and make every attempt to understand them. Administrators and teachers are optimistic. When students do not live up to expectations, the adults respond, changing programs if necessary, because failure is not acceptable. A vision of success comes first, then goals and objectives that embody high expectations. The challenge of leadership is to muster enthusiasm, imagination, and trust. New goals mean experiment and change. Teachers and students are asked to take risks. This is a time for team building and peer support. Supervisors work closely with teachers to appraise early efforts and organize inservice as needed.

Change stresses the current method of teacher evaluation. Contractual criteria have to be revised as new roles and expectations challenge the conventional understanding of a teacher's duties. Checklists and rating scales must be abandoned as they become irrelevant. In times of transition, evaluating teachers and administrators according to goals for individual professional development helps coordinate evaluation with curricular and instructional change. As effective patterns of instruction develop, the most adept teachers help administrators hire and train new teachers coming into the school. Everyone at this point will benefit from an introduction to clinical supervision, and additional training will help administrators and mentors coach inexperienced teachers in classrooms and other locations where teaching and learning now occur. When new patterns of successful teaching are understood, teachers of each subject in each department, reflecting the current organization of the school, write differentiated instructional criteria required for competence.

Documentation and Records

The first task when developing or modifying a program of supervision and evaluation is a "manifesto" that summarizes the purposes and values of the program. Documents needed for a system of evaluation will specify the roles and responsibilities of everyone participating in evaluations and everyone with access to records of evaluations, decisions based on evaluations and how these decisions are made, the frequency of evaluation, the data collected, the substance and format of records, the procedure for appeal, and any assistance that is made available to teachers whose performance is considered unsatisfactory. To be fair to teachers and to guide their efforts to satisfy all requirements of the job, documents detailing evaluative criteria should be readily available and should be reviewed in the process of every evaluation. There will be contractual criteria, which are common to all teachers in the school, and instructional criteria, which specify the type of teaching required if students are to achieve the goals established in each subject. Documents needed for supervision will describe discrete methods of supervision made available to teachers or required of them; the roles and responsibilities of teachers and supervisors; and any constraints on the process of supervision, like time for meetings, frequency of observations, etiquette of teacher-supervisor relations, and confidentiality.

Records of summative evaluations will be kept in a personnel file and made available only to people specified in the documents just described. Records will consist of written reports prepared by evaluators and supplementary data to which the reports might refer. Teachers should have the option of writing and filing a response to each report. Portfolios, used increasingly to record student achievement, might also be used to record teacher achievement. In addition to evaluative reports, a teacher's portfolio might contain a course syllabus, curricular material prepared by the teacher, a teaching plan, an instrument and scale for student assessment, a report or recommendation written by the teacher about a student, a list of honors and awards, samples of student work with the teacher's comments, and the results of a questionnaire eliciting students' opinions about the teaching they have received. One advantage of portfolios is the opportunity for retrospective insight into work done over a period of time. Portfolios would be an invaluable resource in schools where teachers set developmental goals in the process of evaluation. They would also be a rich source of information for anyone evaluating the program of supervision and evaluation.

Issues of confidentiality must be settled carefully and expectations of confidentiality scrupulously fulfilled. When evaluation reveals that a teacher's performance is less than satisfactory and a supervisor is asked to help the teacher improve, will the records and observations of the supervisor remain confidential? Dividing the roles of evaluator and supervisor between two people makes confidentiality possible. If one person is both evaluator and supervisor, or if confidentiality has not been guaranteed to the teacher and the supervisor, then the supervisor should be advised to keep a record of the supervision and be prepared to surrender it to the process of evaluation. Records of nonevaluative supervision and of formative evaluations should not find their way into a teacher's personnel files, unless the teacher chooses to put them there.

Administration

The best laid schemes for supervising and evaluating teachers atrophy and fail if they demand inordinate amounts of time from teachers and administrators. The pay-off from teacher evaluation seems remote to school personnel who spend much of their time and energy responding promptly to the needs of children. Administrators must be taught how to initiate and conduct evaluations, how to distinguish and record useful data in the classroom, and how to relate to teachers in various types of conferences. Even so, many will neglect their supervisory responsibilities unless they, themselves, are supervised. Moreover, a sort of box-in-a-box principle of supervision and evaluation suggests that administrators will supervise and evaluate the way they themselves are supervised and evaluated. If school administrators are left to their own devices, teachers will be similarly abandoned (Aspy and Roebuck 1977).

Summative evaluations of novice teachers and teachers on probation are more focused and easier to sustain than annual evaluations of all the teachers in the school. If experienced and capable teachers are evaluated every three to five years, then more time and attention can be given to each evaluation. Sound judgments that seem relevant and useful to teachers take time—time for multiple observations and thoughtful conferences. Teachers are expensive investments who cost more every year that they teach. It makes sense to start them well and to help them become better and better as time goes on. Rigorous evaluation supported by skillful supervision is a sound investment. But time for supervision is even harder to find than time for evaluation. Administrators find it more motivating to deliver evaluation reports than to deliver a climate conducive to professional growth. School boards both public and private must pay attention to school climate and help administrators monitor and effect it. Committees, teams, and task forces, adequately funded, with time to meet, supported and coordinated by administrators whose highest priority is the exaltation of teaching and learning, all contribute to climate. To a great extent, climate is the result of general supervision. In that climate, clinical supervision helps some teachers one at a time learn how they and their students work.

Judgments

If teachers are hired carefully and given adequate support while learning to do their jobs, there will be few unsatisfactory evaluations. There will be—and probably should be—some, however. A novice teacher will suffer a disappointing start. An experienced teacher will face new challenges for which he or she is ill prepared. The process of evaluation must identify teachers who are doing satisfactory work and those who are not. A teacher who does not meet evaluative criteria (which fellow teachers have helped to develop) is given help and guidance. If the teacher's problems are pervasive and the help needed is more than a peer can provide, then close supervision by someone trained to work with marginally qualified teachers is required—for the students' sake as well as the teacher's. If improvement does not occur within a reasonable period of time, then the teacher must be transferred to a job that he or she can do well—or dismissed. Any teacher receiving an unsatisfactory evaluation, on the other hand, has a right to appeal. If the school has provided an appeals procedure and an appeals board (on which there is teacher representation), then the case might be resolved "in house." If there is no process for appeals, or if the process fails to redress a grievance, the teacher might go to court. Preparation for this unfortunate outcome is also the way to avoid it: clear criteria, adequate data, more data to be certain, coaching in the classroom, re-evaluation, more data, a written appeals process, all taking place in a climate of professionalism.

Confidentiality

If supervisors are to be of any help in the classroom, teachers have to be able to trust them. When someone comes to a classroom to observe, the teacher must know the purpose of the visit. Often the observer is not associated in any way with the system of evaluation. The observer might be a colleague, or a subject specialist from the district office, or a consultant from a university helping teachers learn a new method of instruction. It would be a disastrous breach of confidence if these observers contributed information to a teacher's evaluation. It is conceivable, of course, that an observer will see something awful and feel compelled to report it to someone in a position of authority. Even then, the teacher should be the first to hear the criticism. Usually, however, observations conducted by nonevaluative supervisors are confidential, and anyone responsible for evaluation will not pry by asking a supervisor for information.

When supervision is associated with evaluation, supervisor, teacher, and senior administrators should all clearly understand the limits of confidentiality. If a teacher's work is flawed and a supervisor has been assigned to help the teacher make a change, the supervisor's observations might be confidential, or they might be included in the process of evaluation. The issue of confidentiality, however it is decided, makes an enormous difference in the relationship between supervisor and teacher. Complete confidentiality might encourage a teacher to reveal and deal with problems the teacher has hidden from an evaluator. Nevertheless, confidentiality is not prerequisite to trust. Someone acting as both evaluator and supervisor can still be trusted. Clear communication becomes essential, of course, especially when a teacher's reputation and security are at stake. The distinction between formative evaluation and summative evaluation is useful under these circumstances. For a period of time, in the supervisory mode, all evaluation is formative, but later, when the teacher has had a reasonable chance to improve, the teaching is subject once again to a summative evaluation.

Program Evaluation

How can a school leader evaluate the program of supervision and evaluation? First, ask if the program is in operation as originally intended. One way to do this is through a questionnaire that asks teachers to check and appraise various events they should have experienced if implementation of the program has been thorough. If the questionnaire reveals problems, interviews of sample teachers will provide further insight and possible solutions. The files, of course, are a rich source of information. Obviously, they should be read; the system will require at least that much. Once all the teachers in the school have been evaluated, the files will yield a profile of the faculty. If there have been major changes in the curriculum or in the population of students, reflections of these changes will appear in evaluation reports. The recommendations of evaluators and the goals of teachers will address the changing needs of students. The files of teachers in the same department or at the same grade level might describe a collection of individuals with disparate goals and interests or a team with common understanding and common purpose. Files will tell stories of triumph and struggle. Because they are records of evaluation, they should contain evidence as well as conclusions. Teachers who are struggling should have help. Teachers who appear to make progress should not appear to fall back into old habits when they are evaluated a second time.

Teaching at the school will be respected. When students and parents complain about a teacher, something is done. The teacher is informed, the complaint investigated. If a complaint is justified it is followed by apology, change, redress if possible, and support for the teacher in question. If unjustified, a complaint is followed by an explanation, evidence, and support for the teacher in question. While individual teachers will make mistakes and sometimes have to suffer the indignity of being corrected, a system of evaluation will enable students to have confidence in their teachers and teachers to have confidence in their colleagues. If a teacher must be dismissed, there will be evidence to support the decision, and the teacher's colleagues, especially, will find the evidence persuasive.

If the supervisory system is working, every teacher in the school will be involved in some form of professional development, either individually or as part of a team effort. Teachers will belong to professional organizations, read and discuss articles from professional journals, and attend conferences. They will welcome colleagues into their classrooms. They will know what they teach and know how they measure their success. Young teachers will want to work in the school. The number of applicants, the willingness of applicants to take a job when it is offered, the rate of turnover of teachers, are all measures of climate. Teachers and administrators will leave, but few will leave because they are frustrated and ineffective. Most conclusively, the success of the teachers will be mirrored in the corresponding success of the students.

SUMMARY

Evaluation is an assumption of power, and people in a position to evaluate are usually in a position to determine the purpose and process of evaluation. Generic checklists and rating scales, once commonly used for teacher evaluation, are associated with a summative evaluation—a decision that does not much affect a teacher's future performance. If the checklist applies to all teachers in a school or a district, any one teacher is not likely to receive helpful information from an evaluation. Evaluations for merit pay scales tend to have the same problem. To be fair, the same criteria apply to all teachers in the system, but the conditions in each classroom vary so much that the relevance of common criteria is questionable. Teachers tend to be cynical about general criteria of good teaching, and hence the value of these criteria as an incentive for professional development is lost.

We recommend three types of evaluation, to be used in combination. Teachers may be evaluated according to "contractual criteria," which apply to their performance as employees; "instructional criteria," which apply to their performance as teachers; and "developmental goals," which apply to their professional development and continuing education. Instructional criteria are closely related to objectives of instruction and guidelines developed for each subject at each level. Hence, they differ from subject to subject and school to school. Evaluation according to contractual and instructional criteria is sufficient to determine a teacher's competence. Consistently competent teachers need not be evaluated continually according to the same criteria. These experienced teachers may set developmental goals in conjunction with their supervisors, and achievement of these goals then becomes the focus of their evaluations.

Supervision attends to the conditions that help teachers grow professionally, adapt to changing conditions, and stay abreast of recommended teaching practices. Supervisors of teachers, therefore, who need not hold any specific office in the school system, must contribute to a climate in which professional development is valued and rewarded. Observing teachers in order to understand and appreciate their work is one way to supervise, and supervisors who observe are then in a good position to discuss possible needs for professional development.

An integrated program of teacher evaluation and supervision depends upon certain conditions. These include:

- Broad participation of teachers and administrators in planning and implementation

- Careful timing of the transition from an existing program
- Development of necessary documents
- Record keeping consistent with the purposes of the program
- Administration to ensure continued support for the program
- Judgments based on data in a climate of trust
- Confidentiality of observations and records
- Evaluation of the program and modifications as needed

REFERENCES

Alfonso, R. L., and L. Goldsberry. (1982). "Colleagueship in Supervision." In T. J. Sergiovanni (Ed.), *Supervision of Teaching*. Alexandria, Va.: Association for Supervision and Curriculum Development.

Aspy, D. N., and F. N. Roebuck. (1977). *Kids Don't Learn from People They Don't Like*. Amherst, Mass.: Human Resources Development Press.

Blumberg, A. (1974). *Supervisors and Teachers: A Private Cold War*. Berkeley, Calif.: McCutchan.

Brant, R. S. (1987). "On Teachers Coaching Teachers: A Conversation with Bruce Joyce." *Educational Leadership* 45:5, 12–17.

Champagne, D. W., and R. C. Hogan. (1987). *Consultant Supervision: Theory and Skill Development*. Wheaton, Ill.: CH Publications.

Cogan, M. L. (1973). *Clinical Supervision*. Boston: Houghton Mifflin.

Ellis, T. I. (1986). "The Principal as Instructional Leader." *Research Roundup* 3:1, 3–6.

Glatthorn, A. A. (1984). *Differentiated Supervision*. Alexandria, Va.: Association for Supervision and Curriculum Development.

Glickman, C. D. (1985). *Supervision of Instruction: A Developmental Approach*. Boston: Allyn and Bacon.

Goldhammer, R. (1969). *Clinical Supervision*. New York: Holt, Rinehart & Winston.

Hoko, A. J. (1988). "Merit Pay—In Search of the Pedagogical Widget." *The Clearing House* 62, 29–31.

Johns, H. E. (1988). "Faculty Perceptions of a Teacher Career Ladder Program." *Contemporary Education* 59:4, 198–203.

Joyce, B., and B. Showers. (1982). "The Coaching of Teaching." *Educational Leadership* 40:2, 4–10.

Martin, O. L. (1990). "An Examination of Teachers' Attitudes of a Six-Year Career Ladder Program." Paper presented at the Annual Meeting of the Mid-South Educational Research Association, New Orleans, La.

Squires, D. A., W. G. Huitt, and J. K. Segars. (1984). *Effective Schools and Classrooms: A Research-Based Perspective*. Alexandria, Va.: Association for Supervision and Curriculum Development.

9

LEADING TO A BETTER SCHOOL

TWO SCHOOLS, TWO PRINCIPALS

Deer Run Regional High School and Hillsdale Elementary School are both fictitious. The two principals of these schools are also fictitious. If the schools and the principals have anything in common with actual schools and actual principals it is because we have hundreds of actual schools and hundreds of actual principals in mind. We have jumbled the jigsaw puzzles of schools we know and pulled out some pieces that when placed together help us illustrate two different types of leadership.

Deer Run Regional High School

Deer Run High is surrounded by small farms. Cows graze peacefully beyond the chain-link fence that surrounds the athletic fields. This is not a small-town high school, however. Fifteen hundred students from dozens of small towns up and down the valley are bused to Deer Run. The brick and glass maze of the main building looks like half a dozen separate buildings, each with a different roofline, built close together on a wooded lot. A quarter of a mile away, through the trees, is the junior high, almost as large.

In some ways, Deer Run is a typical high school. Classes meet in the same order every day. Students take English, history, math, science, and maybe a foreign language. There are three tracks in each subject: "basic," "college prep," and "honors." In addition, there are programs for students at both ends of the learning scale: mandated programs for "special-needs" students and AP for the "gifted and talented." An amnesiac attending classes at Deer Run would have to search diligently for clues to its location in the United States. On the other hand, the school has a spit-and-polished appearance that is far from typical. Instead of a large grey counter in the office, a handsome wooden rail with a gate—the sort seen in old-fashioned banks—separates the staff from the students. The office staff are friendly and approachable. Paintings of well-known scenes in the region adorn the walls. The corridors are clean, orderly, and color-coordinated. Attractive bulletin boards are integrated into the up-beat design, like display cases in an airport. As students troop from class to class, they are cheerful and courteous. They notice visitors, at any rate, and make way for someone going in the opposite direction.

Teachers say that they have "nice kids" in their classes. Discipline is not a problem. Most of the teachers have been at Deer Run for more than ten years. "We don't have the horror stories you hear about in other schools," they say. Teachers like and respect Stan Leaman, the principal. "He leaves us alone to get on with the job." They say he is fair, firm, and honest. "He treats everyone the same way. He doesn't play favorites. When *he* makes a mistake, he doesn't try to persuade you he did the right thing." Like many schools in the early nineties, Deer Run has been hit by recession. The budget has been trimmed, trimmed, and trimmed again. Class size is creeping upward—twenty, twenty-two, now twenty-five students in a class has become acceptable. So far, "only arts teachers" have been laid off, but no new teachers in any subject have joined the faculty in the past two years. This year, no new purchases of books were permitted. Although the teachers complain about the cutbacks, they understand the need for them. "The money just isn't there," they say. "We have to pay the bills. Deer Run has the highest gasoline bill in the state."

Everyone gives Stan credit for doing a good job in hard times. Teachers of AP classes voiced the only criticism we heard. They explained that their students are subject to high academic standards imposed by the Advanced Placement Examination of The College Board. On the basis of this examination, many colleges give entering students credit for courses taken in high school. AP teachers at Deer Run feel a discrepancy between "AP standards" and "Deer Run standards." They believe that their students can work harder and achieve at a higher level, but the principal consistently supports students and parents who complain about low grades and excessive homework. Now there is "open enrollment" in all AP classes. Moreover, students who elect to take AP classes are not required to take the AP examination. In addition, a "weighting system" effectively raises all the grades given by AP teachers. Even these teachers, however, concede that Stan is "smart." "He knows the community, and this community isn't Silverlake," they say regretfully. Silverlake is a well-heeled suburb of the state capital. The comparison implies that Deer Run students are not expected to work as hard or accomplish as much as Silverlake students.

Stan Leaman has achieved a state of peaceful resignation at Deer Run. After observing a "basic" English class, we asked the teacher why Charlene, a particularly alert and articulate ninth-grader, had not been placed in a "college prep" class. "She should be," the teacher said, "and she's not the only one." The teacher had not discussed Charlene with the counseling department, however. "It's the student's choice," he said. "If the student and her parents want 'basic,' 'basic' is what she gets. I can tell her counselor to move her to another class, but if she doesn't want to move, she doesn't move." He himself had not told Charlene that he considered her misplaced in his "basic" class. He had not consulted with any of her other teachers. And it had not occurred to him to take up the matter of placement with the principal, even though he firmly believed that other "basic" students, in addition to Charlene, were qualified for "college prep" classes. "Stan has too much on his plate," the teacher told us. "He doesn't get into this sort of thing." As a result of our prompting, however, the teacher did agree to discuss Charlene's placement with her academic counselor.

Seniors in the AP English class were not pleased with the counseling office. Several had asked for permission to go to a College Fair taking place the following day in a nearby town. All the juniors were given permission to go if they wished, but seniors were not given permission because "we're supposed to have made up our minds and sent in our applications." They appealed to one another. "Are you sure you've made the right choice? I'm not. I'm going anyway, what can they do? It's worth it to me, whatever they do."

"If we had more than five minutes with the college counselor. Five minutes, that's all you get, and you have to sign up a month in advance!"

"Seniors at Silverlake are going. I know, because I've a friend who said she'd see me there."

A history teacher told us that the biggest problem, from her point of view, was the students' "lack of background." "They don't know what 'Brown v. Board of Education' really means. They think the Supreme Court is a legislative body. They don't know how jobs and industries are distributed in various regions of the country. They don't know how interest rates and tax breaks affect the economy. They just don't seem to have any concept of 'collective good.' They think that people they don't like have to suffer so that they themselves can prosper. . . . " Her list went on. We asked her if she had raised the issue of "background" at a department meeting. Maybe something could be done . . . ? She told us that the social studies department met infrequently and never discussed anything like that. She was not sure what they did discuss "nuts-and-bolts sort of stuff," she reflected, "textbooks and how to fill out grade reports." We pressed the issue, hoping to suggest a course of action: What if you mapped out a common body of knowledge you want all students to have and maybe in addition helped students develop a habit of inquiry . . . ? The teacher thought that would be a wonderful occupation for her department, but she did not think it would ever happen.

This teacher meets with her colleagues in social studies only twice a year to discuss business. Informally, she meets them more often, but briefly. All she ever hears in the faculty room, she told us, is "constant complaining." In her only free period of the day, she goes for a walk. She is not a recluse, however. She is thrilled to have visitors come to her class. The previous year, she had won a teaching award for which she had to be nominated by three students and her principal. Subsequently, a newspaper reporter had spent a day observing her classes before writing an article about her. That visit and ours, she said, were more important to her than the award itself. "It's such a pleasure to talk about teaching with another adult," she said. Stan had written her a glowing letter of nomination, but Stan visits her classroom for about ten minutes once a year.

Hillsdale Elementary School

Hillsdale used to be a rural school, but now it occupies a prominent position in a newly developed community. Benches on the grass in front of the long low building overlook a vista of rooftops and small trees. This is the least expensive real estate between the school and the city center, only fifteen minutes down the Interstate. There are eight hundred students in the school, K–8. Some still come a long way from outlying farms, the littlest kids rubbing sleep from their eyes as they stumble off the bus. Many live within walking distance, but only those who come up the hill behind the school are allowed to walk. Traffic past the front of the school is too heavy and too fast. Evelyn Anders, the principal, wages a constant campaign to make the road safe for children.

Every morning and afternoon, Evelyn is at the front door to greet or say goodbye to the children. She conducts mini-conferences with parents on the sidewalk. When we visit Hillsdale, she seems to be waiting for us in the hallway outside the office, a blondish-grey grandmotherly looking woman who appears to be shy around people until she finds a good reason to give them a hug.

As she leads us from one classroom to another, Evelyn is torn between the quick tour that visitors expect and her desire to show off her teachers and students. "This is Mrs. James's third grade. If you want to see hands-on math, you must watch Mrs. James. She has a collection of shells, and buttons, and blocks, and rope, and nuts and bolts, and all sorts of beautiful stuff. Children and parents bring them in, and she uses them for everything you could possibly imagine." We yield to Evelyn's enthusiasm and enter Mrs. James's classroom. The children are working in pairs. Sure enough, each pair has a bin of something countable. They are making little piles of objects in "empty" equations that are printed on boards. For example:

$$\Box + X = \Box$$

$$X + \Box = \Box$$

$$\Box = X + \Box - \Box$$

When they exchange equations, the partner has to figure out the value of X and place the appropriate number of shells or nuts or whatever in the empty X box. The teacher has similar empty equations printed on transparencies, so that objects placed in the boxes are projected on a screen. As we leave, Evelyn is describing how Mrs. James will promote a mathematical discussion using the overhead projector.

The tour continues in this way. The real purpose of our visit, however, is to watch a goal-setting conference with a teacher. It is mid-October. A third of the Hillsdale teachers and all new teachers will be evaluated in the course of the year. Evelyn has been observing her evaluatees for the past six weeks. Now she is holding her "state of the teacher" conferences, as she calls them, referring both to the teacher's classroom and the teacher's well-being. Carol Nesbitt, a new sixth-grade teacher, has allowed us to watch. She has written her goals for the year and given Evelyn a copy in advance. They are "wonderful" goals, Evelyn tells Carol. They fit right in with the needs of the school and seem right for Carol, too. However, she is not so sure that "better discipline" should be a major concern.

"I think the behavior problems you're getting in work groups will go away if you give the groups different tasks they can do independently. Someone like Jennifer, for example, can read books and have a wonderful time. But George and Kevin and what's her name, the youngest McCready—Margie?—read so slowly they get lost and don't know what's going on." The teacher agrees with Evelyn's perceptions and asks what Evelyn recommends. "I'd like you to try differentiated reading groups," Evelyn tells her.

Carol, a first-year teacher, is hardly in a position to disagree. She looks anxious, however. "I've never done it that way," she says.

"Don't worry," Evelyn assures her, "you'll love it once you get the hang of it. You'll have more time for all the groups. Now, you have to go back to the same group over and over again just to keep them on task."

As the conference progresses, Carol modifies her goals. She would like to do more with calculators and computers in math classes. She hopes to take a math education course at State College. She would also like to introduce more word processing into language arts, but she thinks she can handle that on her own. In addition, she agrees to start the differentiated work groups.

Evelyn reminds Carol that the whole faculty will be learning more about technology as they make decisions about calculators and computers in math classes, but Carol wants to move ahead on her own. She worked in an office before starting to teach and enjoys using a computer. "It's just something I'm interested in."

Evelyn beams. "Wonderful! Everyone will be pestering you for help. We really need help."

She asks Carol to talk with the Sixth-Grade Team about differentiated reading groups. The sixth-grade teachers meet twice a week, when their classes are combined into large rotating groups for PE and chorus. "You'll get good ideas from the team meetings," Evelyn tells her.

The goal about "better discipline" is dropped. Carol says that she feels relieved. "I thought I had to be tougher," she said. "If this works, can I be a nice teacher? I've always wanted to be a nice teacher!"

They laugh. "Let's talk a bit about what to expect if this works," Evelyn said.

Later, Carol tells us that Evelyn has been very helpful in the first six weeks of school—with one difficult student in particular. Evelyn arranged a conference with the student and another with the student and his parents. Carol participated in both conferences. "The parents were very helpful. I thought they'd blame it on me, but they didn't. They said they were sorry that Brian was a bother. And Brian apologized, too. They all advised me to stop Brian sooner. Everyone agreed that he was worse when he really got going. Now I find that saying "Brian . . ." before he gets into trouble is usually enough."

We met Joan Hilton, the sixth-grade Team Leader. She had been teaching at Hillsdale for eight years, two years longer than Evelyn had been there. However, she began her teaching career at another school, where Evelyn had also been the principal. "I was thrilled when she was transferred to here," she said. "We were in trouble. Every year we had new kids from the development across the way. It was like they hadn't gone to school before. I know they had, but we had to teach them how to behave in our school. We were fighting with the kids and fighting with their parents and fighting with each other. Evelyn quieted things down. She opened up the school and got parents more involved. When their kids misbehaved, she said, 'Here's what your son or your daughter is doing. You know that we can't allow it. What do you think we should do and how can you help us?' What people soon learn about Evelyn," Joan told us, "is that she comes across as this grandmotherly type, but she has a bottom line. And it's rock solid."

Joan and Carol had been talking about reading groups. "I've offered to come to Carol's room during reading," Joan said. "Also, we'll talk about reading at team meetings. Carol's going to teach us about computers. She's putting our report forms on the computer so that we can fill them in and print them off." Joan made a wry face. "I suppose that's progress," she said. "Still, I can't teach the students unless I learn myself."

Integration of technology, we discovered, was a school goal. Evelyn brings the faculty together in the spring and again in the fall to review school goals and to set priorities for the year. The district encourages Evelyn to set her own agenda for inservice and, taking her cue from the teachers, she organizes inservice around priority goals. "It's the thing to do, now," Joan said, "but Evelyn was doing it back when I first started teaching. I swear, she's always one step ahead."

Stan and Evelyn Compared

Stan has been at Deer Run for twenty years. There has been no other principal since a number of local schools were consolidated and the Deer Run Region was created. There have been four superintendents in that time, but Stan remains. He was put in charge of a brand new building, a mixed faculty from local schools, and a student body who had never been to a big, modern high school. He has not given up his image of the simple country schoolteacher who knows no more than his own experience, but he took control of the new school and has managed it successfully all these years. He is a careful, almost obsessive manager. Meetings with the superintendent and the School Board make him nervous, and he prepares fastidiously. Although he has a vice-principal who helps with the business of the school (and another who handles discipline), Stan pores over sheets of paper on his desk and remembers everything. Off the top of his head he can cite details about property taxes in all the local towns, budgeted amounts for any item, bus routes, test scores, and the résumés of teachers. He knows the janitors and cafeteria staff and most of the vendors by their first names, and they call him, respectfully, Mr. Leaman. He regrets that he does not recognize all his students by sight, but once he knows a student's name, he can remember something about other members of the family: an older brother in college, a sister who opened a boutique, an uncle with whom he used to play softball. Conversation outside his office is almost all small talk. Only his job of managing Deer Run seems to engage his intellect.

Evelyn is more interested in education and children than in budgets and buildings. (Her vice-principal takes care of scheduling and book-keeping, and he responds to the daily problems of buildings and grounds.) When she takes a proposal to the superintendent and, at his request, to the Board, it is always a proposal for a new program. At the time of our visit, she had asked for funds for acquiring calculators and computers. A committee of teachers was preparing a presentation for the next Board meeting. Evelyn knows all the children in her school. When they talk to her, they tell her the latest news about themselves and their families—a new car, a new baby, a divorce, a pet turtle, a high grade, a good book. When teachers talk with her, they tell her what has been going on in their classrooms or what they have learned about a child. Everyone, regardless of age, recommends books she should read. Evelyn loves to read.

Rutherford (1985) and colleagues at the Research and Development Center for Teacher Education at the University of Texas have observed and interviewed principals over a period of five years. When they compared effective and less effective principals, they found that the more effective principals:

1. Have clear, informed visions of what they want their schools to become—visions that focus on students and their needs
2. Translate these visions into goals for their schools and expectations for the teachers, students, and administrators
3. Establish school climates that support progress toward these goals and expectations
4. Continuously monitor progress
5. Intervene in a supportive or corrective manner, when this seems necessary

Although Stan and Evelyn are both highly regarded in their districts, Stan fits the profile of a less effective principal, and Evelyn the profile of a more effective principal.

Vision
Stan's vision for Deer Run is a well-organized, orderly school, free of drugs, vandalism, teacher strikes, and major embarrassment. His vision for the future is a continuation of the past. The superintendent, School Board, and most of the parents in the Deer Run Region share and support his vision. Although there are problems of drugs, alcohol, and absenteeism in the community, no one would argue that these problems are school problems. Teenagers are more likely to misbehave during the evening and weekend hours than at school. Absenteeism is seen as a misdemeanor committed against the school, not a fault of the school. Among Stan's few critics are a handful of teachers whose plans

are thwarted and a few parents whose academic aspirations for their children are unfulfilled. Since few teachers, Board members, or parents attend educational conferences or read educational journals, Stan's vision for Deer Run is largely unchallenged.

Evelyn's vision for Hillsdale is also unchallenged. Children whose families have moved from the center of the city to its outskirts find a different kind of school. They are given more homework, which they cannot ignore. Their classmates, on the whole, cooperate with the teachers. Troublemakers are not widely admired. When children find themselves in trouble, their parents soon become involved. Summoned to the school, parents find an attractive, productive environment, where happy children are very much in evidence. Student work is displayed everywhere. Classroom doors are open. Children of all ages work independently at tables and desks in nooks and alcoves in hallways. Children parade from one location to another wearing costumes for a play or carrying gadgets they have made in the studio or the lab. Not many parents complain about a school that works.

Evelyn says that Hillsdale was an excellent school before she arrived. "But the population started to change, and they didn't know how to accommodate an influx of new students. The students hassled the teachers because the teachers asked them to do things they hadn't learned to do, and the teachers hassled the students because they were hassling the teachers. When I came, I knew that children were not all alike, but I didn't know how different they could be! Now we know. We welcome all kinds. But every child is expected to learn. No excuses."

Teachers share Evelyn's vision because they contribute to it. In faculty meetings and team meetings, they talk and Evelyn listens. If she does not like what she hears, she reiterates fundamental principles. "Every child can learn at Hillsdale. If this child is not learning, we have to try something different." "Let's not make a hell when one soul sins. What can we do for the sinner?" "Her parents only want what they think is best. Let's ask them what they think that is." When she arrives at school in the morning, she makes herself a cup of coffee and spends a half-hour reading professional journals. On her way to meet the first busload of arriving students, she delivers the day's stack to the librarian. She has marked the articles she wants photocopied and the names of the teachers she wants to receive them. She puts herself on each list. The librarian offers the same service to teachers. Each journal is circulated to teachers who have asked for it. If any teacher feels that colleagues will be interested in an article, the librarian will make and deliver the copies. Hillsdale has a budget for sending teachers to conferences. It is not generous, only as much as Evelyn can get from the superintendent. Its insufficiency might be advantageous, however. In order to receive funds, a teacher has to persuade Evelyn that something learned at the conference will benefit the students and has to agree that everything learned will be shared with other Hillsdale teachers. In August, when teachers review the school's goals and discuss priorities for the coming year, they consolidate the individual exploration taking place in their classrooms.

Translating the Vision
When teachers at Deer Run are asked to name the "real" leaders in the school, they hesitate. We imagine them mentally scanning the list of appointed leaders and asking themselves if these are "real" leaders. Before long, they admit to a lack of leadership. "It's hard to be a leader here. We all do our own thing." Or they raise autonomy to a virtue. "Teachers here can be counted on to pull their own weight. We don't need anyone looking over our shoulders." In contrast, teachers at Hillsdale say, "It depends on the situation. We have lots of leaders," or, "Evelyn is the glue that holds us together." One teacher explained, "We work in teams. On one team, one teacher might be the leader. On another team, another teacher might be the leader. But we're also one big team, and Evelyn is the leader."

Few teachers at Deer Run have taught at a better school. Many have started their careers at Deer Run, and some were transferred to Deer Run twenty years ago when high schools in the region were merged. Some younger teachers have moved from other rural schools, attracted by higher pay, better facilities, and Deer Run's reputation as a "good place to work." Teachers talk as if they have arrived and have nowhere else to go. Hillsdale teachers talk about other good schools where they have worked, and some have plans to move on. "I wish I could keep teachers forever," Evelyn says. "But the district always invites teachers to transfer before they hire anyone new. So teachers tend to move from one school to another. They move to a bigger house in another area, and then they look for a job that's closer to home. Or they want to teach kindergarten, or teach in middle school. Or they take courses at State and move into administration. We have two teachers right now who are getting principal's certificates. Maybe one of them will take my place when I retire."

There is a sense of privilege at Hillsdale, that teachers can get jobs in other schools just because they have taught at Hillsdale. There is always something "going on," and someone is always "moving on." Hillsdale loses excellent teachers, but other excellent teachers come to replace them. For children and adults alike, it is a place to learn. Because the local university likes to place student teachers at Hillsdale and because Hillsdale teachers like to coach beginners, there is a "JV faculty" of student teachers who add to the vitality and bridge the age gap between the oldest students and the oldest teachers.

Deer Run is a safe and orderly environment, but it lacks vitality. Because of its size, its athletic teams do very well, yet the editors of the newspaper mourn the loss of "school spirit," measured by the number of spectators at the games. Although Stan Leaman could not manage without imagination, his interests are managerial rather than academic. No one could be more conscientious in implementing "policy" than Stan. His agreeable compliance to higher authority is translated into compliance—not always agreeable—throughout the school. Hillsdale is also a safe and orderly environment. Evelyn also implements "policy." However, just as her teachers contribute to the "vision," Evelyn contributes to the "policy." She fights City Hall about safety on the road in front of the school. She takes the ideas of her teachers to the superintendent and the School Board. Leadership at Hillsdale is a two-way street.

A Supportive Environment
No one working with such limited resources could do as much to create a beautiful school as Stan Leaman has done. Deer Run is immaculate. The floors are washed and polished every day. Graffiti are painted over as quickly as they appear. Restrooms are repaired and repainted at the end of every term. All the bulletin boards in the hallways have glass doors. Notices to be posted are turned in to the office. One of the secretaries puts up new notices every day and removes old notices as soon as they are out of date. Since there are never enough notices to fill the available space, a committee consisting of the secretary and one interested teacher has a small budget for buying posters. Art classes also supply posters advertising school plays and other events. The most attractive of these are left in place, along with posters for French films, bullfights, and art museums. All the homeroom doors are decorated for Christmas, and Stan invites local dignitaries to help him select the

prizewinning doors—the "Most Creative," "Best Regional," "Best Traditional," and so on.

The walls at Hillsdale are covered with student work. Bulletin boards are borderless, fabric-covered expanses, some public and some staked out for certain teachers. Essays, poems, paintings, photographs, and math problems go on the bulletin boards. It would take all day to look at every picture and read every word from one end of the school to the other. Two elaborate frames are mounted on the wall near the front door. Each bear the legend "Masterpiece of the Month" and the name of the artist. In one is a portrait of a woman by Renoir; in the other is a portrait of "MOM" by one of the students.

A "supportive environment" means more than bulletin boards, of course. The University of Texas study (Rutherford 1985) found that less effective principals "were primarily concerned with not rocking the boat. If one of their teachers requested some kind of support that could be granted easily and without creating problems, they honored the request. But they offered this support without any real consideration of goals or expectations for school improvement or school effectiveness." Stan Leaman has earned his reputation for fairness by treating large numbers of people the same way. Teachers say that he is "firm, but fair." In various ways, students say, "Mr. Leaman sets the rules, and nobody gets away with anything." Fairness and uniformity, however, are easily confused. Different students need to acquire different skills and learn by different methods. Different teachers face different problems and need to solve them by different means, even when teaching the same subject. By being "fair" to everyone, Stan tends to neglect the needs of individuals and small groups. Some seniors need to go to the College Fair. Most do not need to go. However, if some seniors are permitted to go because they feel the need, many more will choose to go because they feel like taking a day off school. Extra buses, chaperones, substitutes, and half-filled classrooms are all administrative headaches, and Stan's sense of order, not to mention frugality, is offended when the need does not justify the trouble and expense. It is much simpler to rule that all juniors must go to the College Fair and all seniors come to school as usual. Seniors who have the need and the self-confidence will go to the fair anyway—and complain about the consequences.

Complaints at Hillsdale are not extinct. Teachers who never take their students on field trips complain that other teachers take too many field trips. Teachers who are not interested in computers complain that too much money is spent on computers. There is, however, a forum for airing these opinions. At a recent faculty meeting, a middle school math teacher complained that too many of his classes were disrupted by field trips. He explained that some subjects require regular classes, practice, and frequent tests, when everyone should be present. Field trips that take students out of class two or three times a week interrupt the routine for all the students and account for more disruption than teachers of other subjects might realize. A lengthy discussion ensued. Although teachers who favored field trips spoke to the advantages of field trips, teachers who had no need for field trips argued that an advantage in one class did not justify the disruption of another class. When Evelyn closed the discussion, she thanked the faculty for clarifying the problem. "Surely," she said, "there's some way to minimize the problems caused by field trips without sacrificing the learning that field trips make possible." She found it interesting that elementary teachers in self-contained classrooms did not have the problem that middle school teachers in specialized classrooms had described. "Maybe there's a way to retain some of the advantages of self-contained classrooms, even when students have several different teachers. If everyone in a math class left on a field trip once a month, that might not be as disruptive as an eighth of the class leaving eight times a month." There was a murmur of assent. "Would anyone like to work on the problem with me?" Several teachers volunteered, including the middle school math teacher who had brought up the subject. "But I think there's more to it than just field trips," he said. Evelyn grinned at him: "Isn't it always the case? But we can start there and see where we go."

Typically, Evelyn refers her decisions to learning first and convenience second. She allows for different needs and different interests. According to Rutherford, "Effective principals allocate funding and materials in ways that maximize teaching effectiveness and student achievement. In addition, they *selectively* and systematically apply such other support mechanisms as advantageous scheduling, careful assignment of teachers, and the dispensing of recognition to achieve these ends" (italics added). Joan Hilton, the Sixth-Grade Team Leader, will be free to observe Carol Nesbitt teach reading because Evelyn will arrange a substitute for Joan. In fact, Evelyn has agreed to be the substitute when Joan observes Carol. "I love to teach," she said, "but I have to ration myself or I'd do nothing else."

Monitoring

Stan Leaman observes each teacher at least once a year. Two observations and an evaluation are required by the teachers' contract, but the vice-principal does the second observation when Stan can manage only one. Stan stands inside the classroom door for ten to fifteen minutes. He carries a schedule of classes on which he marks the date and time of his visit. A teacher who happened to meet Stan on his way to her classroom asked him if he would sit through the whole class and maybe, for a few minutes before the period ended, chat with her students about how they were doing. He said that he would like to do that, but if he gave that sort of time to one teacher, he would have to give the same time to all teachers, and he just did not have enough time to go around. He has about eighty-five teachers to evaluate each year. Another teacher said that Stan appears to be uncomfortable in the classroom. Perhaps he conveys that impression because he has one eye on the class and the other on the clock.

Soon after the second observation, a teacher receives an evaluation. It is a list of twenty desirable qualities in a teacher, each followed by a checkmark indicating "Unsatisfactory," "Satisfactory," "Outstanding," or "Insufficient Evidence." Stapled to the evaluation is a note thanking the teacher for his or her service to the students at Deer Run High School. If the teacher wishes to discuss the evaluation in a conference with the principal, the note invites the teacher to make an appointment with the principal's secretary within five school days. A biology teacher described such a conference. It was her first evaluation at Deer Run. She had received two "Unsatisfactory" checks, one for "Employs a variety of questioning strategies" and another for "Fulfills all professional obligations." She wanted to know what she had done wrong. She was puzzled. "Students participate in the lesson" had been checked "Outstanding." "Overall performance" had been checked "Satisfactory."

During the conference, Stan referred to his own copy of her evaluation, to which he had added interlinear notes. Each time he had been in her classroom, he explained, all the questions she asked were factual questions. In order to receive an "Outstanding" check for "questioning strategies," she had to ask thought-provoking questions. She asked

Stan to give an example, hoping to reveal his ignorance of biology, but he pulled a sheet of paper from his files and handed it to her. It was a list of sample questions categorized and arranged according to "Bloom's taxonomy." He asked her to keep the sheet and practice asking questions at all the levels. Then he explained why he had given her an "Unsatisfactory" mark for "professional obligations." Each time he had passed her classroom in the transition time between classes, he had never once seen her out in the hallway. All the teachers were supposed to stand outside their classrooms to keep an eye on the passing students. "But," she protested, "I always have students asking questions after class, and things to clear away or set out for the next class coming in." Stan shrugged. "Every teacher can find a good excuse," he said. "Fortunately for you, you have two conscientious teachers on either side, who cover for you. So your absence hasn't been the problem it might be if all three of you stayed in your classrooms."

She threw up her arms as she finished the story. "He still gives me 'Unsatisfactory' for not standing in the hallway! So who cares? When he comes to my classroom, I throw in an 'Evaluation' question or a 'Synthesis' question. But kids in my class still know they've got to know their facts!"

At Hillsdale, all new teachers are evaluated during their first two years, and all other teachers are evaluated every three years. Evelyn evaluates about fifteen teachers each year, and her vice-principal evaluates about five. If Stan employed the same system, he and his two vice-principals would divide the labor of evaluating about thirty-five teachers per year.

Evelyn employs two types of observation. Any teacher can expect to see her at any time. "Drop-in" observations are brief, between five and fifteen minutes. After "dropping in," she will make an attempt to "get back" to a teacher with some sort of feedback. Sometimes this means writing a note. "But notes are awkward," she says, "unless we're in the middle of a dialogue. Then I can write, 'Yes, I see what you mean,' or 'Good work—I've never seen Eric so cooperative.' But it's usually easier to talk, and usually the teacher has something to tell me about what I saw." The other type of observation entails a pre-conference, one or more observations, and a post-conference. She observes at least six entire lessons during the process of evaluation, not counting drop-ins. She tries to see new teachers at least three times before the goal-setting conference in the fall.

Teacher evaluation is one form of monitoring. Curriculum evaluation is another form. Every year at Deer Run, all the students take standardized tests, and Stan receives stacks of computer printouts and individualized labels. He passes the data concerning individual students to the counseling department, where the labels are pasted into student files. Stan studies the summaries. He keeps a record of mean scores for every class in the twenty-year history of the school, and now they are all in his computer. He writes reports to the superintendent and tries to explain why certain scores have moved up or moved down. Fortunately, they have been relatively stable over the years. There has been a gradual downward trend, but since the national trend has also been downward, Stan believes that Deer Run is holding its own.

Evelyn considers herself responsible for curriculum implementation. She works in a district that provides principals with criterion-referenced tests keyed to districtwide curriculum, and at certain times throughout the year she and the other principals meet to compare the results. An evaluation specialist attends these meetings, interpreting scores and trends for the principals and asking how conditions in each of their schools might have influenced results. The specialist summarizes the scores and writes a report for the superintendent. These meetings often generate questions that Evelyn takes back to Hillsdale. The correlation between reading comprehension and spelling scores of the fourth-grade class is unusually low. Why should that be? Are they teaching poor readers to spell? Are they failing to teach good readers to spell? She asks for reading and spelling scores organized by class groups and gives them to the Fourth-Grade Team. In a group meeting, she discovers that every teacher does something different about spelling. She decides to map spelling in the curriculum as it is taught throughout the school. Although she was a language arts specialist herself, she confesses that she does not know the latest research on spelling. She will need a language arts consultant from the district office to help her with this one.

Intervening

Because Stan catches fleeting glimpses of teaching and learning, he is unaware of the details. Teachers do not volunteer additional information because they assume he is not interested. His attempts to intervene, therefore, tend to miss the mark. In conversations about teaching he invokes well-known principles of instruction remembered from graduate school, but they seem tangential to the central issues as seen by the teachers. Nevertheless, teachers smile and accept his advice about

"Bloom's taxonomy," "advance organizers," or "positive reinforcement." When they take the time to describe a problem in detail, Stan
somehow manages to misunderstand. He employs a variety of misun-
derstanding strategies, but the result is always the same: Teachers stop
trying to talk with him about teaching. "You tell him that you're having
a hard time working with Albert Einstein and Lou Costello in the same
classroom, and he tells you to do the best you can. He means well. He's
saying to you, 'You're a good teacher, the best that you can do is OK.
Don't worry about it.' But you know there's got to be a better way. Or
he says to you, 'It's Board policy. Our job is to make it work.' If you tell
him you don't know how to make it work, he acts as if you're standing
in the way of progress. Or he files away in his mind the idea 'This guy's
got a problem.' So you keep your mouth closed and say, 'Yes, Stan,'
'No, Stan.' And you do the best you can. He may be right. Let's face it,
the best we can do is pretty good. And next week there's a different
problem."

Evelyn says, "The trick is to solve a problem in such a way that it
stays solved. I wish I could do that better. Sometimes you stick a
band-aid on something and next thing you know you're running out
of band-aids. If you solved the problem in the first place, it might have
been a little problem. But next time it comes up, you still haven't
decided what to do about it, and you use another band-aid. Soon it's a
huge problem, and it consumes everybody's time and good sense for
weeks. I try to think: 'If we do this every time the situation arises, what
will happen?' One teacher got a Downs syndrome student in her class
and started meeting him off the bus and walking him to art and the
cafeteria and the gym. It was heart-warming and generous and lovable,
but I should have put my foot down and stopped it. I didn't say, 'If we
do this every time the situation arises, what will happen?' Well, you
can imagine what did happen. The teacher got tired of protecting the
darling little boy, and the darling little boy wasn't learning to cope by
himself. But the family accused us of taking away a service we had
agreed to provide and wanted me to assign an aide to do what the
teacher was doing. Believe me, there wasn't an aide who didn't want
to do it. I refused. There was nothing about an escort service in the IEP.
But now the sort of educational problem you want to solve was a big
problem you don't know how to solve. The parents got a lawyer, and
of course they went to the press. Instead of working together, we were
in a fight. How not to solve a problem!"

Evelyn blames herself for failing to intervene sooner. Nevertheless, the outcome in the long run was beneficial to students receiving special services at Hillsdale. A consultant respected by the parents and the School Board was asked to mediate. The teacher started a buddy system for all the students in her class. The buddies were taught to walk together and help one another in various ways. An aide was assigned to watch the Downs syndrome boy and his buddy for the first two weeks, and all went well. So everyone learned from the experience, and the school was strengthened. Now, parents of special-needs children are invited to meet with the special needs coordinator to discuss the best strategies for helping each child. The special-needs coordinator writes the IEP with the teachers involved, and then she arranges a conference with the teachers and the parents. There's a consultant available when differences of opinion seem to threaten the working relationship between home and school. The same outcome might have been achieved had Evelyn intervened sooner, yet it was achieved in the end because Evelyn acted in a child's interest, in spite of opposition from his parents.

X, Y, Z

In *The Human Side of Enterprise,* a book that has become famous in the management field, McGregor (1960) describes Theory X and Theory Y. Theory X was "the traditional view of direction and control." Although working conditions were much improved in the period between 1920 and 1960, McGregor maintained that the fundamental theory of management had not changed. Decisions were still made on the basic assumptions of Theory X:

1. The average human being has an inherent dislike of work and will avoid it [if possible].
2. Because of this human characteristic of dislike of work, most people must be coerced, controlled, directed, threatened with punishment to get them to put forth adequate efforts toward the achievement of organizational objectives.
3. The average human being prefers to be directed, wishes to avoid responsibility, has relatively little ambition, wants security above all.

McGregor concedes that managers of mills and factories might have found some justification for these assumptions. When people in certain circumstances seem to behave in certain ways, there is a temptation to generalize about human nature. However, when circumstances change and people behave in different ways, the generalizations have to change. McGregor looked for a new set of assumptions consistent with current understanding of human motivation. These are the Theory Y assumptions:

1. The expenditure of physical and mental effort in work is as natural as play or rest.
2. External control and the threat of punishment are not the only means for bringing about effort toward organizational objectives. [People] will exercise self-direction and self-control in the service of objectives to which [they] are committed.
3. Commitment to objectives is a function of the rewards associated with their achievement.
4. The average human being learns, under proper conditions, not only to accept but to seek responsibility.
5. The capacity to exercise a relatively high degree of imagination, ingenuity, and creativity in the solution of organizational problems is widely, not narrowly, distributed in the population.
6. Under the conditions of modern industrial life, the intellectual potentialities of the average human being are only partially utilized.

We have not met an educational leader anywhere who upholds the outmoded assumptions of Theory X. Theory X management was shaped by class structure, the Industrial Revolution, and miserable working conditions. It is wholly inappropriate for a school. In a school, teachers are managers. They are the colleagues of administrators. They are just as well educated as administrators. They have broad areas of responsibility within which they make decisions that define the school and set the standards of its service. Administrators do not know as much about the curriculum, the students, and the actual process of learning in any one classroom as the classroom teacher knows. Fortunately, Theory Y is replacing Theory X in schools. School boards are liberating the capabilities of principals through "site-based management." Principals are loosening the bureaucratic restraints on teachers through "teacher empowerment." And teachers are learning that Theory Y brings out the best in students, just as it brings out the best in themselves. Change is not uniform, of course, and not spontaneous. Long-established conventions continue in schools until someone *makes* a change. Some educational leaders still think that merit pay is the best way to motivate teachers. Some school boards still specify the hour and minute when teachers must enter and leave the building. In general, however, education is shifting from Theory X to Theory Y.

Meanwhile, Theory Z has come along. William Ouchi (1981) studied managerial practice in Japan and the United States and found some very basic differences that he characterized as follows:

Japanese Organizations	vs.	*American Organizations*
Lifetime Employment		Short-term Employment
Slow Evaluation and Promotion		Rapid Evaluation and Promotion
Non-specialized Career Paths		Specialized Career Paths
Collective Decision Making		Individual Decision Making
Collective Responsibility		Individual Responsibility
Holistic Concern		Segmented Concern

While studying companies in America, Ouchi realized that very successful corporations like Hewlett-Packard, Procter and Gamble, and Eastman Kodak had values and structures very similar to those he had found in Japan. Then he had a realization: The characteristics he thought were Japanese were actually features of effective modern management. Ouchi describes the steps a company would have to take to transform itself from Type A (typical American) to Type Z (excellent American/typical Japanese). We are struck by the potential for Type Z management in schools. Type Z seems perfect for schools. So much is there already! Schools already have a tradition of "lifetime employment," although critics of education often condemn the tenure tradition. They argue that tenure protects incompetent teachers and that schools would improve if all the incompetents were fired. But long-term employment is an opportunity to build loyalty, identity, morale, and a sound investment in professional development. Schools, in contrast to companies that emphasize short-term, bottom-line performance, offer "slow evaluation and promotion." Without question, this is dispiriting for teachers whose college classmates enjoy the prestige of an office and secretary. The answer is not to promote teachers out of the classroom, of course. Instead, we must reward teachers for every year they spend in the classroom. Although strict and sometimes bureaucratic certification procedures prevent teachers from taking full advantage of "nonspecialized career paths," there are opportunities to teach different subjects, teach at different grade levels, write and edit school publications, develop curriculum, and advise clubs. Schools are relatively small institutions with departmental organization, offering unlimited opportunities for "collective decision making." By the same token, each department has ample opportunity to assess student achievement and take "collective responsibility" for student performance. Finally, the concern that schools have for development of the "whole child" is easily extended to a concern for the "whole teacher."

Public schools have the potential to be Type Z organizations. Many independent schools have been Type Z organizations for years, exemplars as worthy as IBM, Rockwell, Dayton-Hudson, or any of the corporations described by Ouchi. In such schools, teachers enjoy a lifetime of job security and develop strong institutional loyalties. One finds three generations of alumni in some schools: one teacher who taught another teacher who taught another teacher. In a climate of high institutional standards virtually free of bureaucratic requirements, it is not unusual to find a teacher who has taught two or more subjects, worked as a college counselor, edited the alumni journal, and served for a time as assistant head of the school. Or one who teaches physics, coaches soccer, chairs the Curriculum Committee, and directs the summer school. This great range of experience enables an independent school faculty, in a very real way, to function as a team. The English teacher who has taught Spanish knows how to help the second language teachers by teaching English grammar. The math teacher who has taught science can help students use math in physics and chemistry. The sixth-grade teacher who has taught seventh-grade history can ease the transition into middle school. An academic dean who has done many of these things over a long career in the same school is a mentor and *pater familias* for the whole faculty. Academic departments enjoy a high degree of autonomy in independent schools. Many meet weekly and make decisions about curriculum, student placement, deployment of resources, grading policies, departmental assessment, and grading criteria. Whole faculties meet in the spring to discuss the progress of every single student in the school. Serious infractions of the rules bring offenders before a discipline committee, usually with student representation. Programs for faculty evaluation are worked out by teachers and school heads. Teachers are evaluated by students and peers as well as administrators. Academic deans have budgets for faculty development—including tuition for summer study at any college or university a teacher chooses. Some schools have funds for travel, research projects, and sabbaticals.

Egalitarian proponents of public schools are easily sickened by tales about "rich private schools." Nevertheless, we believe that public schools in the future will look more and more like independent schools and not because the buildings will have pillars or the students will wear uniforms. Organization and management will be similar. The trends toward site-based management, teacher empowerment, family involvement, and higher prestige for teachers are all leading public schools toward Type Z management. We know that many public schools are desperately short of funds, especially in a time of recession. We also know that many independent schools are not as rich and not as costly as educators in public schools might think. (Independent schools do like to keep up appearances.) The National Association of Independent Schools reports that in 1991–92 the average tuition for day students in member schools was $6,928. St. Johnsbury Academy in St. Johnsbury, Vermont, is a case in point. This is an independent boarding school in a rural town. It looks like a small college: a conglomeration of cupolas, verandas, pillars, brick, clapboard, plate glass, green lawns, and towering trees. It is also the public school for the town of St. Johnsbury. The town pays the tuition for local day students. The cost to taxpayers is $5,698 per student per year, about average for public schools in Vermont. The national average expenditure per student in 1990 was $4,622.

MANAGEMENT AND LEADERSHIP

X,Y, and Z are theories of management, not leadership. Rost (1991) makes a clear distinction between the two. Leadership, he says, is a relationship based on influence. Management is a relationship based on authority. When Stan Leaman gives a teacher information about Bloom's taxonomy of educational objectives and urges her to ask more questions at the higher levels, he is exercising his authority in a very direct way. When Evelyn Anders advises a teacher to develop differentiated reading groups, she is exercising her authority in an equally

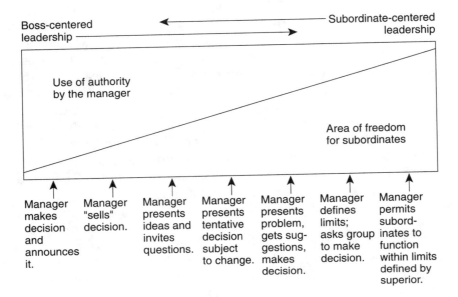

Boss-centered leadership ← → Subordinate-centered leadership

Use of authority by the manager

Area of freedom for subordinates

| Manager makes decision and announces it. | Manager "sells" decision. | Manager presents ideas and invites questions. | Manager presents tentative decision subject to change. | Manager presents problem, gets suggestions, makes decision. | Manager defines limits; asks group to make decision. | Manager permits subordinates to function within limits defined by superior. |

FIGURE 9.1. Democratic–Authoritarian Continuum.

Source: Reprinted by permission of *Harvard Business Review*. An exhibit from "How to Choose a Leadership Pattern" by R. Tannenbaum and W. H. Schmidt, May–June 1973. Copyright 1973 by the President and Fellows of Harvard College; all rights reserved.

direct way. The Deer Run teacher knows nothing about Bloom's taxonomy, has no use for it, and eventually fools Stan into thinking that she has incorporated it into her teaching. The Hillsdale teacher has a good idea of what Evelyn means by differentiated reading groups, knows the purpose of such groups, has a means for learning to use them, and most probably will incorporate them into her teaching. The effectiveness of Evelyn's intervention, however, does not make her a good leader. That much is good management.

Rost (1991) defines leadership as "an influence relationship among leaders and followers who intend real changes that reflect their mutual purposes." Relationships between leaders and followers are multidirectional and noncoercive. They are also unequal, since leaders commit more effort and resources to influencing followers than followers commit to influencing leaders. Nevertheless, the leaders-followers relationship allows for influence in both directions—actually in all directions, since followers also influence other followers. Leaders and followers intend to make *real* changes. Maintenance of the status quo, in other words, is not leadership. Leadership entails change. Change emerges from mutual purposes, and each change advances those purposes. In this way, leadership transforms institutions.

This distinction between leadership and management might help educators escape the implications of "leadership style." There is a "democratic–authoritarian" continuum in the minds of many administrators (see Fig. 9-1). At one end, as Tannenbaum and Schmidt (1973) describe it, "Manager makes decision and announces it." At the other end, "Manager permits subordinates to function within limits defined by superior." The position of a leader's behavior on this continuum is, supposedly, a dimension of leadership style. Having decided that a "democratic" style is preferable, some leaders have trouble exercising their authority in situations that require it. Rost's distinction between leadership and management allows us to see that this entire democratic–authoritarian continuum is a question of management, not leadership. Even the democratic extreme describes a relationship based on authority. Leadership is something else altogether.

Since leadership is not sacrificed by exercising the authority of one's position, a principal, a teacher, a plant manager, anyone "in charge" should feel free to be more or less authoritarian as the situation demands. The police officer who catches a thief and delivers the thief to the public prosecutor is exercising extreme authority, and just about everyone, probably even the thief, will agree that this is the proper thing to do. A principal who catches a teacher abusing a student must also act with authority, although the procedure for dealing with an abusive teacher is different from the procedure for dealing with a thief. The procedure for helping a social studies committee revise the social studies curriculum is different again. Should it be "democratic" or "authoritarian"? The best procedure is one that delivers the best service to the students. What procedure will result in the best curriculum, finished on time and implemented by capable teachers? A democratic style, surely. And yet, we can imagine a situation in which a principal might justifiably tell the members of a social studies committee to stop writing curriculum, attend a series of workshops on teaching students how to think, and resume writing curriculum when they are better informed. Under certain circumstances, such authoritarian action might be necessary, and, under certain circumstances, it might work.

A manager who is sometimes authoritarian can still be a leader, as a police officer can be a leader. A police officer can influence other police officers, including superior officers, to put an end to sexual harassment in the department, or to reduce the number of injuries caused by high-speed chases. A principal can leave a committee meeting in which he or she has read the riot act, walk down the hall to the faculty room, and enter a relationship of influence, not of authority, with teachers eating lunch. In this relationship of influence, the principal might not say a word. At about the same time, a teacher might take his or her lunch to the faculty room, find the principal sitting there, and tell her that elementary students are not too young to start doing community service. Evelyn Anders is a leader because she enters into a noncoercive relationship of influence with teachers, students, and parents on issues of purpose. She and the teachers plan to make real changes. Every year, a group consisting of all the teachers and Evelyn decides what changes will be made in the course of the year. These changes advance a set of common purposes manifesting the school's mission to educate every child. Identification of purpose, dedication to purpose, and transformation of the school are the results of leadership, not management.

COMMUNITIES OF INFLUENCE

A leader cannot be a leader all alone. Leaders influence followers and followers influence leaders. A network of mutual influence in a school connects people who have different roles and relationships in the management scheme: members of the Board, superintendent, principals, vice-principals, team leaders, teachers, parents, officers of the PTA, students, student leaders, office staff, maintenance staff, and so on, with endless additions and variations. Independent schools have different roles and different titles, although there are obvious similarities: a board of trustees, a head of the school, heads of divisions, dean of admissions, dean of studies, department chairs, teachers, parents, students, and so on, with just as many variations and awkwardness of gender. Some women have accepted titles like "Headmaster" and "Department Chairman," for example, although we are unaware of any man who has agreed to be called "Headmistress." So far we have concentrated on the role of principal as manager and leader, although Stan Leaman, with few changes, could be the headmaster of Deer Run Country Day School, and Evelyn Anders could be head of Hillsdale Academy Lower School. Principals and school heads are expected to be leaders, expected to exert a high degree of influence in the school community. If a teacher or a parent, on the other hand, attempted to exert as much influence, the teacher or the parent would be considered "pushy" or "interfering." Nevertheless, people at all levels can fulfil their roles in the management structure *and* enter into noncoercive, multidirectional relationships of influence.

Trustees and members of boards of education make policy decisions that superintendents, principals, and heads of schools translate into management decisions. The composition of the Board changes from year to year as terms of office end and new members are selected. The mission of the school is passed along from Board to Board, like a constitution. Because the mission is policy at the highest level, the Board is responsible for keeping it alive and relevant. Along with the mission, statements of philosophy, history, tradition, and values help shape and communicate policy throughout the school community. The Board causes these documents to be written and revised.

When proposals come before the Board, members must be satisfied that each proposal advances the school's mission. When reviewing decisions made by chief administrators, the Board must be satisfied that each decision is consistent with the school's educational philosophy. Since mission and philosophy are not merely documents, but a written summary of the aspirations, values, and beliefs that permeate the community, the Board must exert and be susceptible to relationships of influence. While chief administrators report to the Board routinely, other members of the community, at all levels of the hierarchy—students, parents, teachers, staff—should report occasionally. Opportunities for noncoercive influence should be built into the Board's modus operandi: time spent in classrooms, cafeteria, and faculty lounge; semi-social occasions when Board members and parents talk informally about the school; retreats that scramble the usual flow of information up and down the hierarchy and permit communication in all directions.

Boards hire the chief administrators of schools. This is usually done with the help of a search consultant, who manages the huge job of finding and screening candidates. Selecting the right consultant is almost as important as selecting the right candidate. Because the Board does not have time to meet with all the members of the community, the search consultant sometimes assumes a part of that responsibility. Usually a search committee serves as a conduit between the community and the Board, first to develop guidelines for the search and then to appraise the candidates who come for interviews. The Board must see that this process is conducted conscientiously and thoroughly. It is a crucial time for leadership. The new superintendent, principal, or head of school must have the values and skills to do the job and meet the expectations of the community.

A Board that has been concerned only with the finances and the politics of governance will be in a poor position to choose an academic leader. If the district does not have a leadership development program for developing leaders within the system, the Board must find leaders in other districts where there are such programs. "Nonspecialized career paths" found in Type Z organizations are watersheds for leadership. Executive search consultants in business turn repeatedly to "feeder companies" such as Hewlett-Packard, Procter and Gamble, and Eastman Kodak (Ouchi 1981). Academic leaders must have broad knowledge of the jobs that are done in schools, particularly the jobs done by teachers. They must be interested in education, the "nuts and bolts" of education rather than the power and politics. For Richard Wallace (1985), who has overseen a transformation of the Pittsburgh Public Schools, the essence of the superintendent's job is needs assessment, goal setting, and "fostering an instructional focus among school personnel." The data-based leadership recommended by Wallace demands two strains of expertise, the manager who can develop assessment and improvement programs in collaboration with subordinates, and the leader who can listen and respond in a noncoercive dialogue with people at all levels. Leaders learn by having been leaders—when they were teachers, counselors, department heads, or academic deans. Although much is learned in the certification programs in schools of education, leadership is not learned there. A Board should know what good leaders and good managers do and make sure that school administrators are both.

Teachers are experts in their classrooms. They know the subject they teach, they know how to manage students, they know principles of curriculum and instruction, and they make hundreds of daily decisions that translate their knowledge into meaningful procedures. Although students are not passive recipients in the process, their achievement depends to a great extent upon the expertise of teachers. At times of institutional stress we hear teachers say, "I just want to do my job. I just want to go to my classroom, teach my students, and then go home." If teachers become isolated because their interest in larger educational issues is discouraged, the school loses their participation in the network of leadership. Then they cannot be leaders and they cannot be follow-ers. They become managed "personnel." Teacher-leaders attend to the unmet needs of their students, make recommendations for improve-ment, and help develop new programs that generate enthusiasm among students and parents. They work within the organizational hierarchy. Heroic defiance is an alternative to withdrawal into the routine, but heroic defiance, while often justified, is not necessarily productive. Some people who are frustrated by the peaceful rate of change find greater satisfaction in battle. Battle speeds the rate of change but may impede the rate of improvement. Leadership entails mutual influence among people who have common, not conflicting, purposes.

Families are natural networks of influence. Parents exert enormous influence over their children; children exert enormous influence over their parents. These networks have a powerful impact on the school. Ideally, there is harmony between the school and the family: Parents feel good about sending their children to school and teachers feel good about sending their students home. Students are continually learning something difficult. As if growing up were not difficult enough in itself, teachers up the ante every day. Families have to support the child's schoolwork, and teachers have to support the child's growing up. Parental leadership in schools starts with communication. If a child never seems to have homework, or seems unable to finish the home-work, or seems afraid of going to school, or seems to be one person at home and another person at school, there is good reason for a confer-ence with a teacher, a counselor, or the principal. Such conferences are necessary. Children need them. If parents do not ask for them, schools should ask for them. Parents must enter the network of influence in the school.

There are other opportunities for parental leadership, and if there are not, parents can help create them. Parents can be very helpful in classrooms and on field trips when chaperones are needed. The PTA needs volunteers to organize meetings and provide refreshments. Schools need volunteers. Not many of these opportunities might seem at first glance like "leadership." But leadership requires a network of influence, and networks take time to grow. Getting to know the other people in the network is essential. In schools where nothing is expected of parents but cookies and transportation, a group of parents with a better idea is more likely to have an effect than one parent. On the other hand, if parent-school advisory groups already exist, parents who have volunteered elsewhere are likely to be the parents selected to meet with school administrators.

Parental representation on a committee, of course, does not mean that parents have any say in educational decisions. All sorts of people, not just school administrators, have ingenious strategies for getting the feedback they want to hear. If parents have felt left out, they will welcome a forum in which their opinions are valued. They do not have to wait until the school provides this forum. Quite independently they can organize a "third-grade" discussion group, a "minority concerns" discussion group, a "basic skills" discussion group—parents can meet to discuss anything they want, anywhere they want. It should always be clear to teachers and administrators that these meetings are intended to be constructive and helpful. If possible, school personnel should attend. Leadership, after all, brings people together to make real changes that reflect mutual purposes. Leadership tends to unify, not to divide.

SUMMARY

Research shows that effective academic leaders have a clear vision of what their schools will become (Rutherford 1985). The leader translates this vision into goals and expectations for teachers, students, and administrators. Professional development and curriculum development are based on these goals. The leader monitors progress continuously and intervenes as necessary. The entire school program is focused on student achievement, and the school climate is supportive and encouraging.

Theory Y (McGregor 1960) and Theory Z (Ouchi 1981) are useful models for management in schools. Theory Y is based on assumptions that people will exercise self-direction and self-control in the service of objectives to which they are committed. Effort to achieve these objectives is motivated by their achievement and not solely by external rewards and the threat of punishment. Theory Z is based on managerial practice in Japan and very successful companies in America. These Japanese and American companies have certain characteristics, including opportunities for lifetime employment, slow evaluation and promotion, nonspecialized career paths, collective decision making, collective responsibility, and a holistic concern for the welfare of employees. Schools already have some of these characteristics, and successful independent schools have them to a high degree.

Rost (1991) makes a distinction between leadership and management. Managers have a relationship of authority with their employees. Leaders and followers enjoy a multidirectional, noncoercive relationship of influence. Leaders influence followers, and followers influence leaders as well as other followers. Both leaders and followers are intent on making changes that reflect common purposes. Hence, leadership transforms institutions and draws people together. A network of people in a noncoercive relationship of influence will include all levels in the management hierarchy. In a school, this includes the Board, administrators, teachers, students, and parents. All are able to influence others for the common purpose of making a better school.

REFERENCES

McGregor, D. (1960). *The Human Side of Enterprise.* New York: McGraw-Hill.

Ouchi, W. (1981). *Theory Z: How American Business Can Meet the Japanese Challenge.* Reading, Mass.: Addison-Wesley.

Rost, J. C. (1991). *Leadership for the Twenty-First Century.* New York: Praeger.

Rutherford, W. L. (1985). "School Principals as Effective Leaders." *Phi Delta Kappan* 67:1, 31–34.

Tannenbaum, R., and W. H. Schmidt. "How to Choose a Leadership Pattern." *Harvard Business Review* 51:3, 162–171.

Wallace, R. C. (1985). *The Superintendent of Education: Data Based Instructional Leadership.* (ERIC Document ED256060).

Index